the
turkish
lover

the
turkish
lover

ESMERALDA SANTIAGO

A Merloyd Lawrence Book
Da Capo Press
A Member of the Perseus Books Group

Designed by Reginald Thompson
Set in 12-point ACaslon Regular by the Perseus Books Group

Library of Congress Cataloging-in-Publication Data

Santiago, Esmeralda.
    The Turkish lover / Esmeralda Santiago.
        p.   cm.
    Continues: Almost a woman.
    "A Merloyd Lawrence book."
    ISBN 0-7382-0820-5 (hardcover : alk. paper)
    1. Santiago, Esmeralda—Childhood and youth.   2. Santiago, Esmeralda—
Relations with men.   3. Puerto Rican women—New York (State)—New
York—Biography.   4. Puerto Ricans—New York (State)—New York—
Biography.   5. Brooklyn (New York, N.Y.)—Biography.   6. New York
(N.Y.)—Biography.   7. Boston (Mass.)—Biography.   I. Santiago, Esmeralda.
Almost a woman.   II. Title.
F128.9.P85S269 2004
974.7'043'092—dc22

                                                                                2004012688

Published by Da Capo Press
A Member of the Perseus Books Group
www.dacapopress.com

Da Capo Press books are available at special discounts for bulk purchases in the
U.S. by corporations, institutions, and other organizations. For more information, please contact the Special Markets Department at the Perseus Books
Group, 11 Cambridge Center, Cambridge, MA 02142, or call (800) 255-1514 or
(617) 252-5298, or e-mail special.markets@perseusbooks.com.

1 2 3 4 5 6 7 8 9—08 07 06 05 04

For Frank

Contents

El hombre que yo amo/*The man I love*   *1*

"That is not good, Chiquita."   *3*

A nena puertorriqueña decente   *7*

"Come, Chiquita, this is your job."   *21*

"I want you here, with me."   *29*

"What are you doing here?"   *35*

"Do not concern yourself, Chiquita."   *43*

"Is there something you want to tell me?"   *55*

"This I do not like."   *61*

"You think your life so bad?"   *75*

I want you together, like the fingers on my hands.   *87*

"Do you believe in reincarnation?"   *97*

"You Puerto Ricans are so romantic."   *111*

Another train will come.   *127*

"I wanted you here, with me."   *139*

"Were you a gasser biter?"   *147*

"Don't worry, you still have me."   *161*

"You are very important to me."   *171*

"I'm not neurotic!"   *183*

"Today is the first day of the rest of your life."   *195*

"I belong here!"   *205*

"My name is Esmeralda."   *215*

"Is there anything you would like to know about him?"   *233*

"Tell me about yourself."   *245*

Alterity   *255*

"You are the last person I expected to see in Boston."   *263*

"You used to be prettier."   *273*

"We have to talk."   *289*

Reify   *297*

Nisus   *305*

"Leave me out of your plans."   *319*

"You have many men friends, Chiquita."   *323*

"A pen makes a lovely graduation gift."   *329*

"It takes a long time to get over a breakup."   *333*

"Alábate pollo . . ."   *337*

Acknowledgments   *339*

About the Author   *342*

the
turkish
lover

El hombre que yo amo/
The man I love

The night before I left my mother, I wrote a letter. "*Querida* Mami*,*" it began. *Querida,* beloved, Mami, I wrote, on the same page as *el hombre que yo amo,* the man I love. I struggled with those words, because I wasn't certain they were true. Mami understood love, so I used the word and hoped I meant it. *El hombre que yo amo. Amo,* which in Spanish also means master. I didn't notice the irony.

I sealed the envelope, addressed it formally to Señora Ramona Santiago and, on my way out early the next morning, dropped it in the incoming delivery box by the front door. It was a Tuesday, Mami would check for mail in the early afternoon and by then, I'd be in Florida with my lover, *el hombre que yo . . . amo.*

I carried little. A battered leather bag once used for dance costumes now held a couple of changes of clothes, a bikini, a toothbrush, comb and hairpins, a pair of shoes and sandals, underwear. I left my tights and leotards, makeup, the showy jewelry that added spice and color to the characters I created on stage.

When I stepped onto the sidewalk, I resisted the urge to look back, to run back into the rooms where my mother, my grandmother, my ten sisters and brothers, my aunt and cousins slept. The stairs to the train station, a long block from our front door, were under my feet sooner than I would have wanted. Once I took the first step into the subway out of Brooklyn, my life changed irrevocably. Had I turned around and run back into my mother's house, into the safe, still-warm space next to my sister Delsa, it would have been too late. When I wrote the words, *el hombre que yo amo*, it was already too late. I had made a choice—a man over my family. Even if I didn't follow him to Florida, I'd taken the first step, a week after my twenty-first birthday, into the rest of my life.

"That is not good, Chiquita."

I knew little about him. He was Turkish, lived alone in a luxury apartment building a block from Bloomingdale's, wore expensive suits in muted colors with finely detailed pleats and seams. He'd traveled extensively and boasted friends all over the world. In addition to his first language, he spoke fluent German and French, but his English was heavily accented and hesitant. He had won the Golden Bear at the 1964 Berlin International Film Festival for *Susuz Yaz*, a black-and-white film made in Turkey, which he was desperate to distribute in the United States.

His name, Ulvi Dogan, sounded so foreign from my tongue, that it was sometimes difficult to pronounce it. That initial vowel made it awkward—not the rounded Puerto Rican "u" nor the puckered, sharp English "u," but a sound halfway in between, a strangled diphthong.

"Hi," I'd say when I called him on the phone, "it's me." I never said my name, because he'd christened me Chiquita, little girl. I'd grown up with a familial nickname, Negi, and was an official Esmeralda everywhere else, so his pet name felt as foreign as his name on my lips. When I tried to give him a nickname, he refused. "Ulvi," he said. "Just Ulvi." He would not let me call him darling, either, or dear, or honey, or sweetheart. Not even any of the lovely Spanish words that express affection—*querido, mi amor, mi cielo*—would convince him. Just Ulvi, he insisted. Ulvi.

With this man I barely knew, whose name reshaped my face every time I spoke it, I left my mother. On the airplane taking us to Florida, I sat next to Ulvi, my forehead pressed to the window. I swore I could see Mami's house, way down there in Brooklyn. There was the tiny square of cement that was our backyard, the larger playground directly across the street, which we were forbidden to play in because there was always the danger that a fight would break out over the outcome of a basketball game. In the distance, Manhattan's spires pierced the sky, while Brooklyn's rectangular roofs seemed to push against it, defying the clouds.

Eight years earlier, on a morning as bright as this one, I had lain on a grassy hummock behind our house in Puerto Rico seeking against the turquoise sky shapes and forms that might foretell what the United States would be like. It was the middle of hurricane season, and gloomy clouds scudded across the blue, in a hurry, like Mami, to be somewhere else. Later that afternoon aboard the propeller-driven Pan American flight to New York, I stared from above at the languid, cottony puffs that reminded me of the stuffing inside a mattress. A child could jump on them, and bounce high into an azure heaven.

I crossed the Atlantic that day in a confused haze intensified by the wonder of what was happening, but nothing could prepare me for the United States, not even the stories about the colorful *estadounidenses* profiled in the *Selecciones del Reader's Digest* that my father gave me to take on the plane.

Mami, my sister Edna, my brother Raymond and I had left San Juan in the middle of a sunny afternoon, but when we landed, it was a rain-slicked night in Brooklyn. As we drove from the airport to our new home in Williamsburg, headlights from the opposing traffic illuminated the drops that slid down the taxi's windows, making them blink and shimmer. Mami's mother, Tata, and Tata's boyfriend, Don Julio, joked about my amazed eyes as I tried to see just how high were the buildings lining the broad avenues. Even dazed and sleepy, I felt the dimensional shift from Puerto Rico's undulating horizons to the solid, vertical angles of New York City.

"We came here," Mami said some days later, "so that you can get an education and find good jobs when you grow up."

We had come, I thought, because Raymond needed medical attention for an injury to his foot that resisted the best efforts of Puerto Rican doctors. I was certain that, as soon as Raymond's foot healed, Papi would appear at the door of our apartment in Brooklyn to lure Mami back home, just as he had done countless times in Puerto Rico. That was the pattern; bitter arguments followed by separations during which Papi wooed Mami back, and a few months later, a new baby would be born so that by the time I was eight I had four sisters and two brothers. I had no reason to imagine that things would be different just because we flew across the ocean instead of taking a *público* across the island. But Papi never came. Mami sent for the rest of my sisters and brothers still in Puerto Rico to join us in New York. By the time Raymond could walk without a limp and his doctor said he didn't need to wear a special shoe anymore, Papi had married a widow none of us had ever heard of and the vision of him appearing at our door to return us to Puerto Rico vanished.

I now turned to Ulvi, who leaned over me to look at the city we had left behind. "This is only the second time I'm ever on an airplane," I said.

"Really?" He fiddled with the controls on the armrest, pushed his seat back and closed his eyes. The air around me grew cold. I rubbed the goose bumps from my arms, turned again to the tiny rectangular window as the plane droned through cotton candy.

Days earlier, when I'd told him Mami would never give me permission to go with him to Florida, Ulvi had said: "You must take the bull by the horns." I'd never heard that phrase, had no idea what it meant. He spoke less English than I did. Where did he learn it? He didn't want me to run away with him. "Talk to her woman to woman," he said, "explain the situation."

I thought of it, but couldn't look Mami in the eyes and admit that in spite of my other successes—the high school diploma, the proficient English, the clerical jobs, the college courses—I had failed as a *nena puertorriqueña decente*, a decent Puerto Rican girl. I had lost myself to Ulvi without benefit of *velo y cola*, the trailing veil Mami imagined for each one of her daughters before a Catholic altar.

"When was the first time?" Ulvi's voice was so soft, I thought at first that it came from inside my head. I turned to him. Still leaning back, his heavy-lidded eyes looked at me as if he had just met me, a stranger on the seat beside him on a plane to an exotic destination.

"Eight years ago, when we first came from Puerto Rico."

"Hmm," he closed his eyes again, turned his face toward the aisle. His black hair had picked up static from the seat, and fine strands fluttered up languidly, like soft antennae. I pressed my spine against the seat cushion and tried not to think, not to imagine Mami's reaction, the disappointment at my first rebellious act.

"What did your mother say when you told her?" Ulvi asked, and heat rose to my cheeks.

"I didn't." I closed my eyes, afraid to see the anger in his. He thought it was wrong that I hadn't told her about us, but he also refused to meet her. She will understand, he had assured me. But he didn't know Mami.

"That is not good, Chiquita. It is not good."

I would not open my eyes, did not answer. I heard him turn away from me again, and imagined the tiny hairs drifting toward the plane's low ceiling. Below us New York was becoming a memory, but the words I'd struggled with, *Querida Mami* and *el hombre que yo amo*, floated around my head, every dot over the i's, every downstroke, every loop, fine threads that twisted in and out between who I was and who I had become.

A *nena* puertorriqueña decente

Once Mami settled in Brooklyn, she refused to go back to Puerto Rico until every one of her children spoke English and had graduated from high school. She was thirty, I was thirteen, Delsa was eleven, Norma was ten, Héctor was nine, Alicia was seven, Edna was six, and Raymond, the youngest, was five. I was about to start eighth grade. For me, a high school diploma was at least five years away, for Raymond, who was starting kindergarten, twelve long years stretched ahead before Mami would consider returning to the island.

"What if," I asked, "when we graduate, you send us to Puerto Rico as a reward?"

"You're not going anywhere alone," she snapped.

Mami expected me, as the eldest, to set an example for my sisters and brothers. My task, as I understood it, was to get good grades in a new school in a foreign city, in a foreign culture, in a foreign climate, in a foreign language.

"And don't think that because we're in the United States you have permission to behave like those *americanas*," Mami warned.

"Those *americanas*" were any females my age who were not *nenas puertorriqueñas decentes*. Decent Puerto Rican girls did not wear short skirts, did not wear pants unless they were riding a horse, did not wear makeup, did not tease their hair, did not talk to boys not their brothers, did not go anywhere unchaperoned, did not argue with their mothers, did not challenge adults even when they were wrong, did not look adults in the eyes, especially if they were men, did not disrespect their alcoholic relatives.

A *nena decente* listened to her mother, learned to cook and keep a neat house, left the room when a man visiting her grandmother looked too much in her direction, sat with her legs together even when she was alone minding her own business and reading a book. The person a *nena decente* had to avoid the most was *el hombre que le hizo el daño*—the man who took the virginity of a friend, neighbor, or relative without first marrying her. *El daño*—the damage—spoiled it for the rightful "owner" of her virginity, a legitimate husband in a monogamous relationship.

A *nena puertorriqueña decente* did not give the neighbors cause to gossip. This meant she was conscious at all times of *lo que dirá la gente*, what people would say, and take that into account when weighing her actions, otherwise *¿qué dirán?*

A *nena puertorriqueña decente* was a virgin until she married in a church with her sisters as bridesmaids and her brothers as grooms. Then she became a *mujer puertorriqueña decente*. A decent Puerto Rican woman could wear makeup and dress in a way that pleased her husband but not so sexy as to provoke other men's lust. She could go out accompanied by her husband, children, or female relative *porque si no ¿qué dirán?* She honored her mother and mother-in-law, managed her home efficiently but deferred major decisions to her husband, who was to wear the pants, literally and figuratively, *porque si no ¿qué dirán?* He was served hot, home-cooked Puerto Rican food at every meal. His clothes would be clean and pressed, his shoes shined. He was not to be challenged, corrected, or laughed at, especially in public, for any reason whatsoever, even if he were misinformed, wrong, or a buffoon, *porque si no ¿qué dirán?*

Americanas had too much freedom to do as they pleased, which they abused by being sexually available to any *pendejo* who looked their way. *Americanas* were also disrespectful of their elders, contemptuous of family, lazy housekeepers dependent on prepared foods, and, in spite of their sexual freedom, did not know how to please a man. They also seemed not to care what anyone thought about their behavior, as if *el que dirán* did not exist in English.

I noticed some contradictions.

Mami, a *mujer decente*, had never married Papi and I had never seen her in church. *¿Qué dirán?* Mami dressed to accentuate an hourglass figure crowned by luxurious black hair that, in New York, she cut and learned to dye in shades of brown, blonde, and even red. *¿Qué dirán?* She curled, teased, and sprayed her hair if she had to leave our apartment. She girdled her abdomen to look as if she had not birthed seven children. When she walked down the street in her high heels, her hips swung voluptuously, *¿qué dirán?*, which elicited whistles, stares, and promises from men who seemed to stand on corners just to watch women pass by.

Six months after we came to New York, Mami fell in love with Francisco, and by our first summer in Brooklyn, he was living with us in defiance of Tata, who did not think it was appropriate for Mami to "bring a strange man into a house with teenage girls." *¿Qué dirán?* Don Julio, Tata's boyfriend, was exempt from this rule.

Mami did not invent *el que dirán* or the differences between a *nena decente* and an *americana*. Her friends and relatives spouted the same rules to their daughters and we were supposed to listen humbly and without arguments. When our mothers were elsewhere, however, we tried to make sense of what they said as opposed to what they did.

"Maybe," guessed Cousin Alma, "when they say that stuff they're talking about an ideal, not a practical reality."

Alma was a year older than me, which she insisted meant she was more mature. She was born in Puerto Rico, but Titi Ana had brought her and her sister, Corazón, to the United States when they were babies. The sisters spoke English to one another, and, when Titi Ana spoke Spanish to them, they answered her in English. When they spoke Spanish, they had accents and stumbled over words.

Alma and her sister were *nenas puertorriqueñas decentes*, but they were also Americanized, which was almost as bad as being an *americana*. This meant that their references were not to Puerto Rican culture, but to that of the United States. They liked pizza, hamburgers, and French fries more than *arroz con gandules*, *piononos*, and *bacalaítos fritos*. They listened to rock and roll, not the Spanish radio stations. They read Archie comic books, novels by Harold Robbins, and *Seventeen* Magazine, not Corín Tellado romances and *Vanidades*.

Because they were family, Mami let me walk the half block to their building by myself. Both sisters were smart, especially Corazón, who read thick science books because she wanted to be a biologist when she grew up. I liked her dark sense of humor but she was younger, so we didn't spend as much time together as I did with Alma.

Titi Ana was stricter than Mami. The girls could not leave their apartment except to go to and from school, not even to visit us. They spent their afternoons doing homework and reading until Titi Ana returned from the factory. While she made dinner, Alma and Corazón watched game shows. When I went to see them, I felt like an emissary from the outside world, even though I was only slightly more independent than they were. I had sisters and brothers to talk to, play and fight with, where Alma and Corazón only had each other. They eagerly listened to the dramas unfolding in my crazy household of seven children, a pregnant Mami, Francisco, Tata and Don Julio. I tried to make the stories entertaining while sidestepping the bleaker realities.

Mami was counting on her needle skills to get her steady work in New York's garment center. Tata's two sisters and nieces toiled in factories and assured Mami that there were more of them scattered throughout the city. By the time we arrived in Brooklyn, however, the garment industry was moving to other parts of the country or overseas, and every year there were fewer jobs.

It was harder than she expected, but Mami worked her way up from thread cutter at bra factories to sewing machine operator. When she was laid off or the factories closed, Mami collected unemployment, and when that wasn't enough, we applied for welfare. She hated being dependent on public assistance, and each time we returned from interviews at the welfare office, or after a surprise home visit by a social worker, Mami gave us a lecture.

"This is why you have to learn English, graduate from high school, and find work in offices, not factories," she said in a voice unsteady with controlled anger. "So many humiliations, all because I didn't get an education."

Tata lived with us, cooked our meals, and watched us when Mami worked. She could not sew anymore because the cold had entered her bones and caused painful arthritis. To dull the pain, Tata drank. Every evening after work, Don Julio brought six-packs of Rheingold or a jug of red Gallo wine, which they drank together sitting at the kitchen table as they smoked one cigarette after another. They could be violent if provoked, so we stayed out of their way once we had supper. Mami closed the curtain that divided our end of the apartment from theirs and we kept to our side watching Ed Sullivan, Red Skelton, or the *Million Dollar Movie*. Sometimes Tata's brother, Tío Chico, joined them, and the three talked, drank, and argued behind the flowered curtain late into the night.

Franky was born the spring I was accepted into Performing Arts High School. A couple of months later his father died.

Francisco had been a kind, quiet man from an even more rural part of Puerto Rico than Macún. He adored Mami, and didn't mind that she had seven children who required constant supervision and guidance to keep us safe in Brooklyn's treacherous streets. He played endless games of cards or dominoes with us, sang love ballads as he strummed a guitar, was respectful to the point of courtliness with me and my sisters, budding teenagers at whom other men leered. He was not a replacement for Papi, but he was as close to a loving, warm-hearted, protective father as we could have wished. His death from stomach cancer was the second big loss in our lives. We mourned him, tiptoeing around Mami, whose grief was like a dark, impenetrable bubble. She didn't smile for months. One day Raymond said something silly and Mami giggled before she could stop herself. She immediately covered her mouth, and blinked away tears, as if she had done wrong by indulging in such fleeting happiness.

I thought that, after Francisco's death, Mami would return to Puerto Rico, but she became more determined to stay in New York.

"I'm not going back there with my tail between my legs after so many sacrifices," she vowed. We knew that, once she set her mind, she didn't budge, and we all had to adjust.

There was no bilingual education in our neighborhood schools when we first arrived, which meant that my sisters and brothers and I had to learn English quickly, by immersion, or keep repeating grades until we could pass our classes. The humiliation of staying back was enough motivation to make us practice the language at home with one another until we sounded like Alma and Corazón, answering in English when Mami or Tata spoke to us in Spanish. Within two years, we were able to carry on conversations in English and it became our language with one another.

"*No me hablen esa jeringonza, que me da dolor de cabeza,*" Tata complained, covering her ears against the gibberish that gave her a headache. The only time she didn't complain about English was when she watched *Guiding Light* and *As the World Turns*. She turned the sound down and followed the vicissitudes of her favorite characters through the actors' facial expressions and body language. I once watched the soap operas with her, with the sound up, and was impressed by how much she understood of what the actors were actually saying.

Cleaning our apartments, washing endless loads of laundry, and cooking for eight children and three adults required organization. On paydays, at least one of us accompanied Mami on her weekly trek to *la marketa* for *la compra*, two carts full of groceries and ne-cessities that we dragged home then carried up three flights of stairs to our apartment. One *compra* a week was not enough, how-ever. Héctor or Raymond was sent to the bodega at least once a day for more milk, eggs, bread, dishwashing soap, toilet paper, Brillo pads.

Tata and Mami prepared our meals, the older girls washed dishes, swept, mopped, and laundered bedclothes and towels. The boys scrubbed bathrooms, shined shoes, and took the garbage to the cans on the sidewalk. Don Julio did minor repairs, installed washing machines, put hooks on the walls so we could string clotheslines across the rooms because we didn't have a dryer.

As soon as we were old enough, we learned to do our own laun-dry and iron our clothes, even the boys. Mornings before school we took turns at the ironing board for last minute touch-ups on collars or cuffs. Mami and Tata were always mending pants, hemming dresses, attaching buttons, fixing zippers, sewing curtains. When we couldn't afford the disposable kind, cotton diapers had to be scrubbed, bleached, and hung up to dry on the indoor clothesline, where they shone square and white, like a line of surrender flags.

Mami complained about my inability to perform the most rudi-mentary domestic tasks. If she asked me to start the beans before she came home from work, I would either forget to do it, or forget I had done it and burn them. If I had to change Franky's diaper, I was bound to prick him with the pins. If Mami told me to wash dishes, I'd break her favorite cup. If she asked me to iron a shirt, it might end up with the triangular shape of the iron on its back. In our cramped apartments in New York, neatness was essential, but my corner was always the messiest, my bed the one unmade, my clothes stuffed helter-skelter into our overfull closets and dressers, my shoes the ones that Héctor had to remind me needed polishing.

It wasn't that I didn't care. I was the first to grumble when the apartment was untidy or when I couldn't find a clean glass because the dishes hadn't been washed, or when the linoleum in the kitchen felt sticky because it hadn't been mopped. My sisters reminded me that it was my turn and that, "as usual," I had shirked my duties.

"You expect us to learn English and get good grades," I argued when Mami accused me of being lazy and not doing my part. "I have too much studying to do. Performing Arts will kick me out if I don't make good grades in every class."

"Do you think you're the only one with too much to do around here? I slave eight hours over a sewing machine and still come home to cook for you and the others. And look at your sisters and brothers," she reproached. "Delsa gets A's in school and works part-time, too."

It was true. Delsa, Norma, and Héctor found jobs after school and on weekends even before they were old enough to qualify for work permits. My sisters clerked in neighborhood stores and Héctor served in a pizzeria. Raymond shined shoes on the sidewalk near the check-cashing office after school and on Saturdays. I dusted and stocked shelves at a drugstore for a few weeks. With the money I made, I paid my sisters and brothers to do my chores so that I could have more time to read and study. In spite of my diligence, I failed the Regents and had to repeat geometry in summer school. When Mami saw how hard I was trying, she excused me from the hated chores, to the dismay of my siblings and cries of "It's not fair," and "You favor Negi because she's the oldest."

Performing Arts demanded high academic achievement as well as progress in our art. I entered the school two years after we arrived in Brooklyn, while still struggling with language. Homework required a dictionary and several rereadings of the same passage before it made sense. I often stayed up long after everyone had fallen asleep, working on French vocabulary, lab notes, or a book report.

I was in the drama department, but actors were required to study dance. For the first weeks at the school, my body ached constantly because I'd never had a dance class and my muscles rebelled against the pointed toes and leaps that Mr. McGraw made us perform. At the beginning of my junior year, Matteo, the ethnic-dance teacher, saw me in the hall and suggested that I should become an Indian classical dancer because, he said, I looked Indian. I became his student, and, to the consternation of my family, practiced the deep pliés and lunges of Bharata Natyam around our already lively apartment, wearing a sari and bells around my ankles.

In the winter of my junior year, Mami fell in love again. Don Carlos was a gangly, nutmeg-brown man with a quiet manner and a mysterious air due to the green-lensed glasses he wore day and night. Tata repeated the same objections against bringing a man into a house where there were teenage girls, once more excepting Don Julio. Mami argued that at thirty-four years old she could make her own decisions about whether or not to have a relationship with a man who was serious, hard working, and not fazed by the fact that she was raising eight children on her own. She was the best judge of what was and was not good for her children.

Don Carlos came to live with us. We didn't welcome him as warmly as we had Francisco, mostly because Don Carlos was not there half the time. He worked in Manhattan, and had a small business in the Bronx, helping people with their tax returns. He came for long weekends or short weeks, depending on his schedule. When he was with us, he was as patient and willing to play dominoes and cards as Francisco had been, and left discipline up to

Mami, even when we tried to get him to take our side in an argument with her. When Mami became pregnant, he was thrilled, and named the baby after himself before we knew it was a boy. He was equally delighted when, a year after Charlie, Cibi was born, and a year after that, Ciro.

My sisters and I were not allowed to date like *americanas*, who could go to a movie or for ice cream with boys they liked. In a traditional Puerto Rican courtship, the boy came to the girl's house, and asked permission to visit her at home. If granted, he came at specified times and sat with her under the eye of a parent, grandparent, or older sibling. After months of this, they might be allowed to go out, chaperoned, for a walk, to a dance, or to other public places.

Delsa and Norma had boyfriends who came to our apartment on Sunday afternoons to sit in front of the television set or to play board games with the younger kids. Had any boy been interested in doing that with me, he would have been welcome. But because I went to school in Manhattan, I didn't know any of the neighborhood boys I might have met at the local school. My only date during my teenage years was with Larry, a mournful Performing Arts classmate from the music department. I didn't tell Mami about it, didn't ask permission as was expected because I knew what she'd say. There was no way I was going to tell Larry that, if he wanted to take me out, he first had to come to East New York, Brooklyn, to meet my mother.

One afternoon when school was dismissed early for teachers' conferences, Larry and I went for a walk in Central Park. I kept expecting Mami to appear from behind a tree to remind me that *nenas decentes* didn't walk unchaperoned in the park with boys their mothers didn't know.

The Performing Arts Drama Department taught The Method, which stressed a rigorous, scholarly approach to acting. We were to study the character we portrayed, to discover aspects of his or her personality that the playwright might not have written, but had suggested through speech and action. We were encouraged to develop physical and psychological nuances of the character as if she were real. The goal was to bring the character to life, to inhabit the role, to become that person.

"Acting is believing," my favorite drama teacher, Mrs. Provet, told us, and, in addition to practicing voice and diction for Dr. Dycke's speech class, French vocabulary for Mme Gregg, modern dance for Mr. McGraw, and mudras for Matteo, I practiced believing.

I believe, I told myself, that I am carefree and happy, like the girls in Alma's *Seventeen* Magazine even though I'm also a *nena puertorriqueña decente*. I believe that when the words Puerto Rican appear in a newspaper only when preceded by "alleged" and followed by "prostitute," "drug dealer," "junkie," "gang member," or "victim of violent crime," it is possible to be a Puerto Rican who is none of those things. I believe that Don Carlos did not mean to deceive Mami when he didn't tell her he was married and already had three children. I believe he loves Mami, is telling the truth when he says he's been separated from his wife for years, and means to divorce her.

I believe that when a classmate asks me to repeat what I've just said, it's not to make fun of my pronunciation. I believe that the woman who chased me down the street screaming at me to get out of her neighborhood was crazy. I believe that the man who exposed himself on the subway did not pick me because I would just sit there, embarrassed, not knowing how to respond.

I wanted to believe that I could wake up each morning looking forward to the rest of the day, instead of dreading what new calamity might befall our family. Would Mami have a job? Would Raymond be robbed and his shoeshine kit scattered on the sidewalk? Would Cibi have another fever convulsion and need to be rushed to the emergency room? Would the landlord discover that there were twelve people, not five, as Mami had said when she rented the four-room apartment? Would we have to move in the dead of winter because, while there were radiators in the apartment, they sent up no steam?

I read Dr. Norman Vincent Peale's *The Power of Positive Thinking*, which also encouraged believing as a way of becoming. I believe that in the United States I can do whatever I set my mind to, as Mami and Dr. Peale claim.

Papi's mother, Abuela, had taught me the Lord's Prayer, and how to make the sign of the cross. Every night, I pulled the covers over my head so that Delsa, with whom I shared a bed, would not see me cross myself and beg God and the Virgin to help me through another day of believing.

Praying every night did not make me an optimist, just as three years of dramatic training could not make me a good actress. Mrs. Provet was demanding, constantly challenging us to reach deeper inside ourselves for the emotions that would enrich and make real the characters we portrayed on stage. I refused to do that, afraid of doing it too well.

I could have played alienation. Surrounded by a raucous, loving family that preferred spending time together over anything else, I watched my sisters and brothers slapping dominoes on the kitchen table or cowering before a horror movie on TV and wondered why that wasn't enough for me. I loved them desperately, but every chance I had, I found an excuse to go to the library, or a museum, or anywhere I could be alone.

I could easily cull up fear by reliving walks home from the subway station in the premature darkness of winter afternoons. Hunched inside a too-thin coat, I was alert to cars careening around corners, muttering figures lurking in doorways, a pack of boys with the same color bandana around their foreheads, a group of girls with too much makeup and hostile eyes.

Loss was familiar. An absent father, a dead stepfather, an alcoholic grandmother, who when sober was sweet and funny, but when drunk could become violent and vulgar. Loss was a Puerto Rican afternoon humming with bees, the proud cackle of a hen with chicks, the sudden, loud thunder and pounding rain of a tropical squall. Loss was not feeling safe, even in our own apartments.

Pain was a beating by neighborhood girls who said I thought I was better than them. Pain was the cavities in my mouth because, until I was seventeen, I hadn't been to a dentist. Pain cramped my frozen fingers because I lost my gloves in the subway and there was no money for another pair.

I could play the other kind of pain, too. The pain of hearing Mami's groans as she came up the stairs of the apartment building after a full day bent over a sewing machine in a sweatshop. The pain of hearing my sisters and brothers whimpering in the cold of unheated tenements. The pain of knowing that Mami, who constantly told us men only want one thing, had not believed it when she fell in love with Don Carlos.

There was so much feeling in me that if I explored it, as Mrs. Provet asked us to do, I would drown in my own emotions. I graduated from Performing Arts High School with a degree in drama, but no one knew that the reason I had no depth as an actress was that, in spite of having grown up on an island, I could not swim.

"Come, Chiquita, this is your job."

Ulvi leaned over me to watch as our plane floated over the Atlantic Ocean toward the airport in Fort Lauderdale.

"Palm trees!" I cried as the shore came into view. The sight brought a lump to my throat.

"They are beautiful," Ulvi kissed my cheek.

We took a taxi to the Gateway Arms. Ulvi had keys to an apartment on the second floor. It was huge—a bedroom, a living–dining room, a bright kitchen with dishwasher and electric stove. It was completely furnished, down to matched towels on the racks, extra linens in the closets and seascapes on the walls. There was a telephone on the table next to the king-size bed. Ulvi picked it up and smiled when he heard a dial tone. Another telephone with an extra-long cord was tacked to the wall in the kitchen. Thick, mustard-colored shag covered every room but the kitchen and bath, which were vinyl tiled. A glass slider off the dining room led to a narrow balcony overlooking a weedy lot and the fenced-in backyards of several one-story houses surrounded by lush gardens.

Ulvi's partners were letting us use the apartment while Ulvi had a hernia operation at Fort Lauderdale's Holy Cross Hospital. According to Ulvi, his partners were also paying his medical bills and had bought our airplane tickets. I found their generosity impressive, but Ulvi dismissed it. The reason they were being so nice to him, he argued, was to protect their investment. They had put money into the American version of *Susuz Yaz* with the idea that, once it found a distributor, they would share in the profits that were sure to come. Unlike him, they were not artists, and therefore, not generous and softhearted. They were businessmen who had financed one movie starring Gina Lollobrigida and were planning to make more with award-winning film artists like him. To them, he was a commodity, nothing more.

"You must not believe people too nice, Chiquita," he said. "Usually they want something else."

"You don't really believe that, do you?" I asked. He smiled, wrapped me in his arms, kissed my hair.

"Ah, Chiquita, you are innocent. The world is not so good like you imagine." In his arms, the world was a wonderful place, soft, warm, clean scented. He lifted my face, sought my eyes. "Is not always what it looks."

"I know that . . . "

"Shush, shush, do not argue. I will teach you everything. But you must listen what I say. Okay?" He waited for me to nod. "Okay."

We unpacked our belongings into the dressers, one for each, the drawers lined with scented floral paper. He pointed to my side of the walk-in closet, and I hung up my two dresses, placed the sandals side by side on the floor, across from his leather shoes, toes facing toes across the mustard shag.

We were on our way out for lunch when there was a knock at the door. Ulvi answered it, and a lanky blonde woman accompanied by a squat, ruddy man stood in the glare, their arms laden with groceries.

Ulvi greeted him with a handshake and her with a kiss on each cheek, then turned and introduced them as Leo and Iris, no last names. Iris went into the kitchen and started putting groceries away. A look and a nod from Ulvi let me know that I should follow her while he led Leo to the sofa.

"You didn't have to do this, it's so kind of you . . ." I burbled.

"Oh, I know, we didn't have to, but we wanted to. I wish we could have come sooner." She moved around the kitchen with confidence. "I'm sorry if it looks like I'm taking over," she smiled. "We've had many guests, and I'm familiar with where everything goes."

Her lips puckered into coquettish smiles whenever she looked toward the men in the living area. From time to time, she flicked back her shoulder-length platinum hair, combed straight to frame a narrow face with wide blue-green eyes, a long nose, and thin lips frosted pink. Like Leo, Iris wore too much gold jewelry: bracelets, rings, neck chains. They both smelled newly showered and perfumed. His thick black hair was matted wetly to his skull.

We returned to the living area. Iris sat, crossed her tanned legs, and in one movement, flipped her hair to one side, caressed it over her breast and leaned against Leo, who shifted toward the armrest. To me, Iris' sinuous movements were for Ulvi, not Leo, and a possessive knot formed in my stomach.

Ulvi held his hand toward me and drew me onto his lap. The tension inside me eased as I leaned against him, conscious of Iris's eyes. I could see her question "Whatever do you see in her?" I was nothing, Ulvi had told me many times. "You are poor and naïve. But I like you are young and innocent. I can teach you everything." Iris, in spite of her perky appearance, was closer in age to Ulvi and even to my inexperienced eyes looked like a woman who had learned as much as she was ever going to know.

Leo told us about Jim, who lived in the building and was another associate. "Different business from the movies," he chortled, but didn't explain. He pushed Iris away and stood up abruptly. "Well, we have to get going. We'll pick you up around six." He led the way to the front door, opened it and guided Iris through before she had a chance to trade more cheek-to-cheek kisses with Ulvi. He waved, and closed the door behind them.

I tried to exchange a look of surprise with Ulvi, but he was already moving toward the kitchen. Their visit and the promise of a meal in a few hours had eased his hunger. "Let's just have tea," he offered as he rummaged through the cabinets. "Come, Chiquita, this is your job."

"My job?"

"Make us something to eat," he grinned as he pulled a teakettle from a cabinet under the electric stovetop. He set the kettle on the counter. "I have to make some calls." He went into the bedroom and closed the door.

I had never been in a kitchen with someone depending on me for food. At home, Mami and Tata delighted in coming up with a good meal even when the only things in the refrigerator and pantry were bits of this and scraps of that. I now faced several cabinets filled with canned and boxed food, a refrigerator stocked with fresh fruits and vegetables, milk, butter, eggs and orange juice, luncheon meats in tight plastic bags, and didn't know how to begin preparing "something to eat."

"Mayonnaise! I'll make a sandwich." But a sandwich seemed too American as the first meal I ever prepared for Ulvi. Rice and beans, the staple in my diet, would take the better part of a day, if I started by soaking the beans, as Mami did, overnight. The image of my mother easily moving from stove to refrigerator to the sink back to the stove brought tears to the corners of my eyes. It was mid-afternoon. By now my sisters and brothers would be home from school, the mailman would have made his delivery, and Mami might be sitting at the kitchen table, reading my letter.

"Alright, Chiquita?" Ulvi emerged from the bedroom as if he'd just received a marvelous compliment. He scanned the empty counters and table. The cold teakettle was where he had left it. "Are you crying?" he asked when he saw my expression.

"I was thinking about my mother," I burst into sobs.

"Come on, Chiquita," he said, "you must be strong girl."

"I should have told her. It was cruel to just leave a letter."

"You left a letter, Chiquita?" He pronounced the double t's in "letter" forcefully, and I felt them like a slap to the cheek. "Did you mention my name?" His voice dropped, as if the violence of the word "letter" had frightened him, as if telling my mother his name were dangerous.

"I . . . no, I don't think so. Not your name." *El hombre que yo amo* seemed relieved.

⁓

The restaurant was on Route A1A, across the street from a long, sandy beach. The owner greeted Leo and Iris with vigorous handshakes and a toothy smile. We were introduced, Ulvi by his full name and relationship to Leo, who referred to him as his director. I was "Chiquita, his girlfriend."

The owner led us to a table in the center of the room where two men and another long-limbed blonde woman, younger and curvier than Iris, were already sitting. Janka was with Jim, the "associate in a different business from the movies." Eugene, Leo's partner, and the only other person in the group who seemed to know Ulvi, stood to shake hands. He was handsome in the way Charles Bronson was handsome, with narrow eyes that squinted beneath thick, arched eyebrows, and fleshy lips that covered square white teeth. The way he squeezed my hand and looked me in the eyes, the half smile, the slight nod, the way he pulled out my chair and waited until I settled between him and Ulvi before he sat down, relaxed the tension that had squeezed my shoulders toward my ears. He had a deep voice, which carried across the round table when he spoke in a near murmur to deferential silence from the rest of the party.

Ulvi reached under the table from time to time to squeeze my knee, or to get my attention so that I would watch him. He was teaching me how to eat European style, which he said was the proper way. This meant holding the knife and fork in the opposite hand from the way everyone else did in the United States. He also thought that I should slow down.

"You eat," he'd told me, "like somebody will take the food before it gets inside your mouth."

The moment between plate and lips had become the most important part of my meals, a few hesitant seconds which he controlled by insisting that I eat at his speed, to get used to the timing. I was to drink when he drank, to eat when he did, to blot my lips, "never wipe," when his were wet.

The men talked business. Gina Lollobrigida had been in New York the previous week, and Eugene and Leo had met with her and discussed another movie they wanted to produce.

"She's a beautiful woman," Eugene murmured. "Striking." He turned to Ulvi. "Do you know her?"

"We met in Cannes," Ulvi said. Eugene and Leo were satisfied.

Jim was in town for a couple of weeks, but he and Janka would go on the road soon. From the conversation, I gathered that Jim sold a line of portable steam saunas that Eugene and Leo manufactured. He'd been having trouble selling them for use in private homes because they took up a lot of space. Then he had an idea.

"It came to me on I-95," he said. "You get a big girl like Janka here, put her in a bikini, stand her next to the sauna and bingo! The unit looks smaller." The men laughed, and Leo reached behind Iris to pat Jim's back. Janka laughed too, stood up to demonstrate how tall she was, at least six feet, easily the tallest person at the table.

"You're a genius," Iris purred, rubbing Jim's thigh. Jim's face went slack and his eyes sought Leo's, who inclined his head in a gesture that said, "don't worry about it." Iris finished her drink and scanned for the waiter, who appeared the minute Eugene lifted his finger.

Ulvi sipped his wine, smiled mysteriously when he wasn't being addressed, listened attentively to whatever Eugene said while remaining deferential to Leo, who watched him carefully. A couple of times Eugene or Leo addressed a question to me, and I stuttered through an answer, aware that they were doing it to be polite, that I, like Iris and Janka, was there for decoration, not conversation. At the end of the evening, they knew no more about me than they had at the beginning.

Jim drove us back to the apartment in his burgundy Lincoln Continental. As I cuddled next to Ulvi in the back seat, it was hard to believe that fifteen hours earlier I'd left my mother's house to walk, frightened but resolute, into this life of luxury cars and roomy apartments with swimming pools, dinners at expensive restaurants, businessmen who could move an army of waiters with a raised finger, clever marketing strategies, Gina Lollobrigida at the Cannes Film Festival, and the man who now squeezed my shoulder, his fingers slowly making their way to my breast.

"I want you here, with me."

The light in Fort Lauderdale reminded me of the clear yellow of a Puerto Rican morning. New York, even at its brightest, always seemed gray and shadowy, the unreal sky a sheet of silk stretched between skyscrapers. New York felt like a deep box, the façades of buildings enormous labyrinthine walls that prevented any semblance of a natural world. Even Central Park, where Ulvi and I spent many afternoons, was an artificial environment bounded by gothic structures and the constant throb of vehicles. But here, in the piercing yellow light of Fort Lauderdale, I closed my eyes and remembered Puerto Rico.

If I kept my lids shut, I could see Macún. I couldn't pronounce the name of the barrio in Toa Baja where I'd grown up without wondering what it meant, who had thought up such a strange name for a place. It was near another barrio called Candelaria, which meant Candlemas, across from Pájaros, which meant birds, but Macún had no meaning. It was as foreign in Spanish as in English, an African word, perhaps, or a fool's utterance elevated to language. A nonsense place where my early life resided, never talked about, never forgotten.

Lying on a plastic lounge chair in Fort Lauderdale, I recalled a childhood that didn't seem so long ago. An ocean lay between me and the girl called Negi who had climbed Macún's trees, run up its hills, bathed in the first rains of May believing they brought good luck. I was now Chiquita, and the man who had renamed me didn't like to talk about my past.

The sun licked my skin. A quiet breeze rustled the rhododendrons along the walkways that led to the apartment. The swimming pool sparkled. I tried to enjoy the feeling of idleness that being poolside implied. Was this what being rich felt like—a warm body under a hot sun, a cool pool at my feet, nothing to do but relax in a plastic lounge chair? At the same time I wondered how anyone—no matter how rich and idle—could possibly just lie there. The thought made me anxious, but I had left my book upstairs and was afraid of the water.

Ulvi slid in to do laps, his arms stretching along the surface, grabbing, pushing, propelling himself toward then away from me. His brown body shimmered like that of a sleek sea creature, and when he turned his head to breathe, his mouth twisted to the side of his face, distorting it. It was mid-morning. In an hour, he would be going to the hospital. The surgery would be early the next day.

"No, you do not come," he'd already warned. I protested that it was my duty to be there, waiting the outcome of the surgery, but he contended that there was nothing I could do. "The doctors are in charge. You come after the operation." I gave up trying to convince him.

Watching him glide across the clear blue water, I tried to imagine what would happen if Ulvi died during surgery. I would probably have to return to the grayness of New York. But maybe I could stay beneath the warm Fort Lauderdale sun and find a job in one of the office buildings we had passed last night on the way to the restaurant. I could pay my own rent, perhaps maybe even here at the Gateway Arms.

"Let's go." Ulvi stood at the foot of my chair, glistening, his black hair plastered to his forehead. He looked healthy and vibrant and not like someone about to undergo an operation. For the first time since he'd told me about it, I believed that it would be minor surgery, not life threatening. He would go to the hospital and in a few days be back and we'd continue our life together. But I couldn't picture what that life would be like. We had known each other ten months but last night was the first we'd spent under the same roof. "A honeymoon," he'd teased, and I'd been happy because the word sounded like a promise.

"Make us some breakfast, Chiquita," he said as we entered the apartment, and again I felt the panic of the previous day. This time, however, I brushed nostalgia aside and concentrated on boiling water for tea, on toasting slices of white bread. I found jam and cheese in the refrigerator and silently thanked Iris for the groceries.

"Would you like an egg?" I called to Ulvi, in the bedroom. It was a relief when he said no, just something light. He came out dressed and ready, smiled his approval at the set table, the crisp toast cut in triangles, the pot of tea, the jam spilled into a small bowl with a spoon inside.

"Very good, Chiquita." He kissed my cheek. We sat opposite one another, he fully dressed, me in my bikini. "While I am gone," he sipped his tea, "do not answer the telephone."

"Why not?"

"In case it is business. You will not know what to tell."

"I was a secretary . . . "

"It is how I want it, Chiquita. Do not answer it." He stared me down until I dropped my gaze and mumbled okay.

"Can I call out?" I tried not to sound defiant.

"Who do you know here?"

"I might call home."

"Yes, of course you can call your mother." He spread strawberry jam from one end of his bread to the other. "You are with me of your own will, Chiquita," he said after a while. "You can go home any time."

The world caved beneath me. "I don't want to go home."

"That's good," he murmured standing, pulling me up from my chair and embracing me. "Because I want you here, with me."

I melted into the smell of him, into the soft black hair on his chest. He held me for a few minutes, caressed the panic that had made me sound hysterical and childlike. "You be good girl while I'm away," he hummed into my ear, and I broke down. He thought I cried for him, but those tears were for me.

He left in a taxi, and the minute it pulled away from the Gateway Arms, I felt lighter. Guilt made me look in the direction the taxi went, as if Ulvi could have read my mind, could have felt my relief. I could not have explained the change. Minutes earlier I'd worried that he'd die on the operating table. Now that he was gone, I was happy not to have his gaze upon me, his constant attention to every little thing I did. I needed a chance to think without having to explain what I was doing.

I planned to call Mami and tell her where I was, to apologize for causing her pain and worry. But when I returned to the apartment and faced the phone, I stared at it, imagining her on the other side, hysterical, or angry, or so hurt that my own heart would crack just to hear her voice. I paced from the kitchen to the bedroom and back, feeling the space. At home, our rooms were rarely empty. One of my sisters or brothers was always there, Tata, Don Julio, an aunt or uncle or cousin. I established a rhythm, back and forth from one room to the other until a sharp ringing stopped my pacing.

I watched the bedside phone, its black face banded with white circles upon which shiny, blacker numbers and letters appeared stark and businesslike. I counted four, five, six rings. The face showed every number in its proper order, the letters like eyebrows over them. But the combination necessary to make this particular phone ring was missing from the yellowish moon in the center of the dial. Eleven rings. I itched to pick up the receiver, to know who could be so sure someone was there that they would let the phone ring so many times. It stopped and I did pick it up, as if the ringing were insufficient proof that the phone worked. The minute I set it down, it started again. Fifteen this time. I imagined it was Ulvi, testing if I would answer. But maybe it was one of his business associates. Or it could be Mami, who had somehow discovered where I was. But how could she? Even I didn't know exactly where I was or the phone number of the apartment. Another pause. Then six rings. And finally silence. The austere circle in the center of the dial now looked like an eye watching my reaction. I threw a pillow over it.

I was certain the caller knew I was there and was daring me to pick up the phone. But maybe it was burglars checking to see if anyone was home, and they would be, that minute, making their way to what they thought was an empty apartment. I dressed quickly, found the keys and left the building with no particular idea of where to go. I just wanted to get away. My life was more important than whatever burglars might find inside. But I knew that the real reason was to avoid hearing the phone ring while I stood by, forbidden to answer it.

It was midday. The sun was high overhead, the air heavy with moisture that pressed into my clothes. I remembered the mall we had passed the night before just a few blocks down the avenue and headed for it, hoping to find an air-conditioned store where I could linger.

The stores displayed pastel-colored tops and dresses or showy jewelry like what Iris and Leo wore. In New York, I'd called fashion like this "white people clothes," because they seemed designed for pale skin and hair. If I wore those colors, my *café con leche* complexion turned ashen, and I felt conspicuous, as if the soft shades made me stand out more than the vivid colors I favored. The one time I dared enter one of the stores, the saleswoman hovered behind me as if afraid I would run off with the merchandise. Her wariness camouflaged behind an obsequious smile, she jiggled hangers from front to back of this rack or that, trailing my every move with pointless activity. I was offended by her attention, but didn't have the nerve to tell her and walked out, humiliated by her suspicions but not knowing how to challenge them.

That night I slept alone in the enormous bed in the vast apartment, conscious that the world outside the locked front door was huge, unknown and mysterious. I felt so inconsequential that Chiquita seemed like the perfect name for me. I slept fitfully, waking several times to reach out for Delsa, Norma, or any of my always-nearby siblings, only to remember I was alone. I promised myself that I would call Mami the next morning and let her know I was all right. By then, I imagined, she would have cried enough and might accept that, at twenty-one, I was old enough to make my own choices and lead my own life. I tried to picture what that life would be like, but came up against murky, incomplete images of Ulvi gracefully sliding across a shimmering pool while I stood on the edge, paralyzed by my fear of drowning.

"What are you doing here?"

Never having had to find a taxi anywhere but in New York City, I set out the next day along the Sunrise Highway expecting that at any moment a yellow Checker cab would go by. For over a half hour I was the only person walking along the road. Everyone else was in a car or pickup truck, and some drivers looked curiously in my direction, scanning the area for a reason I was on foot. A couple of men pulled over to offer me rides, and I waved them away with a thank you and a few steps in the opposite direction. Finally, a police cruiser stopped and the officer asked if everything was okay. When I explained that I was waiting for a taxi, he told me that in Fort Lauderdale one had to call ahead, and pointed to a glass-walled phone booth a few yards away where a thick, dog-eared directory dangled from a chain. He drove by a couple of times after I made my call, and each time waved at me as if he were making sure I was okay. But I was a dark-skinned Puerto Rican from the outer boroughs of New York City, and his attention was not welcome. I was certain that he, like the salesclerk the day before, was watching me so that I would not steal something.

When the taxi finally came—not a yellow Checker cab, but a plain white sedan with bold red letters on the doors—I was feeling as if I had done something wrong, when my only crime had been to be on foot on the Sunrise Highway. Unlike New York's loquacious cabbies, this driver was sullen and preoccupied, so I didn't try to make conversation, but watched the flat, low landscape speed by in a flutter of pink, green, and turquoise. Again I was reminded of Puerto Rico, but these streets, unlike those of my childhood, were richer, the homes surrounded by neat hedges and thick, well-tended lawns. The streets were deserted, except for the occasional deliveryman or bouffant-headed woman walking a dog.

The hospital was set back from the road and looked new. Inside, the floors and walls were shiny, the halls patrolled by women in white habits. The nun at the reception desk directed me to one of the upper floors. The squeaky tiles, the gleaming walls, the flowing, white nurses' uniforms, gave an impression of cleanliness and virtue. Ulvi's room was the last door before a tall narrow window that shed bright light on the long hallway. As I walked, it felt as if I were floating on a shaft of light toward the sun, and I had to squint as I came nearer his door. It took me a few seconds to focus my eyes once I entered his dim, cool room. To the right was Ulvi's high hospital bed, and Ulvi wrapped in white sheets, his mournful eyes staring at my mother, who sat on the only chair in the room, her hands clasped over her purse.

"What are you doing here?" I screeched.

"I came to bring you home," Mami stood up. Her cheeks were flushed, her eyes bloated from lack of sleep or tears or both. She bristled with anger, and I was afraid she would lift her hand and slap me in front of my lover.

"I'm not going back with you," I screamed. A nun appeared at the door and Ulvi lifted his arms weakly from under the white sheets and made a gesture as if to shoo us out of the room. He was still drugged from the surgery, his features slack, which made him look older than thirty-eight. Even through the haze, he managed to slur, "You should have told her, Chiquita."

The nun glowered at Mami and me. We stood side by side now, facing Ulvi's bed, for the moment, unable to face each other.

"Mr. Dogan needs his rest," the nun scolded. "Please leave." She settled the sheets around him and I walked out, followed by Mami, carrying a suitcase.

I couldn't speak, couldn't cry, couldn't see where I was going but yet managed to retrace my steps down the sunlit corridor. A nun passed us, and I felt dirty and sinful. Mami's anger was like a weight that dragged on me, even as my own anger and humiliation propelled me forward. I felt dizzy, and wished I could faint so that Mami's worry over me would replace her rage, which was as solid and transparent as the hospital's gleaming glass doors. I kept seeing Ulvi's face, drawn and dark over the stark white sheets, the displeasure on his drug-slackened lips, his gesture shooing us out of the room. The nun's long fingers had pulled the covers up around his shoulders and trapped his arms inside, while her translucent face scowled at Mami and me. The nun in her virginal robes and Ulvi wrapped in white sheets stood in stark contrast to Mami and me, both of us practically glowing with fury, disappointment, and humiliation. We climbed into a taxi that was, through some miracle, waiting at the curb, and I gave the driver the address. In silence, Mami and I were driven to the Gateway Arms, each looking out a different window, our backs to one another, waiting for the privacy of a locked door.

No sooner had we entered the apartment, than I began to yell at Mami. Didn't even give her time to settle her things or to look around. Didn't try to speak calmly, "woman to woman," didn't try to "take the bull by the horns." Or maybe that's what the phrase meant. I was a toreador and she was a bull and I goaded her, made her angrier than she was by being disrespectful, offensive, and insolent. How could she do this to me, I began, to show up unannounced, to sit scowling in front of a man who had just undergone an operation? What made her think I would return with her? What would I be returning to? A crowded house in a ghetto, no privacy, no room to breathe?

Mami was stunned. Her face fixed into a frown, her eyes narrowed, she stared at me as if seeing me for the first time. I was out of control and felt it. I had never spoken to her this way. Since we arrived in the United States, I'd been so conscious of how hard she worked to make sure that I and my ten sisters and brothers had what we needed, that I hadn't dared complain about how the move affected me. I now told her that silence had not meant acceptance, that every humiliation I'd suffered in the United States was her fault. That leaving Puerto Rico had been her idea. That we hadn't progressed much beyond who we were in Macún. That I would much rather have stayed with my father in that remote primitive barrio than endure the daily degradations of being a Puerto Rican in New York City. I screamed that getting an education was not worth the price of losing myself in the process. That our lives had not improved, as she had promised, but had gotten worse.

How much resentment had I stored over the previous eight years? Enough to wound Mami so that she could not answer my tirade with anything more than a hurt look and trembling hands. When I took a breath, she opened her mouth, hesitated then yelled back.

"*¡Malagradecida!* After all I've sacrificed for you, this is how you repay me."

"Ungrateful? What do I have to be grateful for?" I screeched. "I have nothing. I am nothing. I'm lucky a man like Ulvi is interested in me. Just look around here," I said, "look at where I am. A huge apartment with a swimming pool in front! This is better than anything you ever gave me! Just look! Have we ever lived anywhere like this?"

Mami did stop to look around the roomy apartment, at the picture window leading to the narrow balcony, at the shiny new
kitchen with dishwasher and garbage disposal.

"For this," her voice was tight, "you gave yourself to him?"

I couldn't answer, didn't know if what she said was true or not. "I
love him," I finally whimpered.

"He's taking advantage of you."

I responded that if so, it was fine with me. What else had I to
give him but myself? The hurt look returned to her face, but she
wasn't about to be silenced by me.

"What kind of man will take you from your family and not
marry you?" she asked and I answered that marriage hadn't seemed
so important for her with the three men she'd lived with. She
slapped me and I fell on my buttocks and covered my head with my
hands. She stood over me. "Don't you ever speak to me like that. I
don't care how old you are, even when you're a grandmother you are
not to talk to me like that. Now pack your things and let's go!"

"I'm not leaving! You can't make me!" I yelled, "I'll kill myself." I
ran to the kitchen and pulled out a knife, a small knife with a ser-
rated edge, but a knife nevertheless. Had I tried to cut my wrists, as
I threatened to do, I would have merely scratched the skin. But
Mami fought me for it as if it were a machete, and took it from my
hands.

"You would kill yourself over him?" she asked with a mixture of
wonder and disdain. The minute she spoke those words, I stopped
fighting. I leaned against the wall, my hands over my face. I had not
only disappointed Mami by choosing Ulvi over her, I was choosing
him above life. In that instant, I knew that was the greater shame.

"Go away!" I screeched. "Go away!" Mami picked up her bag and
purse, opened the door, and slammed it behind her. My heart grew
so large that it threatened to explode through my chest. I sobbed
with my whole body, had to sit on the floor and hold myself so that
I would not break into pieces. Crumpled on the shag rug, I felt how

completely alone I was now that Mami had left. Had Ulvi walked in that instant, his presence would not have compensated for her absence. Had she walked in the door, the world would not have felt as big and frightening. I sat on the floor for what seemed like a long time, crying until my eyes were so swollen, I couldn't see.

There was a knock, followed by Mami's voice, soft and not angry. "*Negi, por favor, ábreme la puerta.*" I stood at the door, hands on the knob, uncertain whether I should open it.

"I'm not going back," I said, and even as I did, I hoped she'd make me.

"It's alright," she said, "you don't have to go back. I understand."

I opened the door and fell into her arms, and shed tears I didn't think were left in me. She led me to the sofa, both of us weeping. I wanted to comfort her, but didn't know how, which saddened me even more. There was no way to take back what I'd said, no way to return home after what I had said. My invective had changed both of us, had distanced me from Mami more than I ever expected. Until that afternoon there had always been a layer of respect between us, mutual, silent admiration for what the other achieved against terrible odds. But my words had torn through that layer, had diminished her achievements. I hadn't chosen Ulvi over Mami, I had rejected her. He just happened to be there when I did. She understood the difference much sooner than I did. It would be years before I realized that by not fighting me any more, she was seeing something I was blind to. Ulvi was not the reason I had left my family. I'd been leaving for a long time. He just provided the opportunity.

Mami helped me lie down on the sofa and went to the kitchen. Cabinet doors opened and shut, the refrigerator door hissed, pots clanged against the counter, water ran. Within minutes, she was cooking something that, even through my clogged nose, I recognized as the fragrance of love.

We went for a walk after dinner, to the same mall near the apartment. We were swollen-eyed and tense, our conversation sparse, each of us determined to avoid mentioning the reason we were in Fort Lauderdale. We ambled up and down the corridors, looking into store windows, never going inside, disdainful of the clothes and costume jewelry. As it was getting dark, we headed back, swatting mosquitoes that buzzed in thick clouds near the waterway. Back at the apartment, we showered and prepared for bed. I offered her Ulvi's side, closest to the bathroom. As I drifted into sleep, I heard what might have been crying or might have been chortling.

"What is it?" I asked. "What's wrong?"

"Don't they have taxis in this town?" she chuckled.

"They don't just show up," I answered. "You have to call them."

"I felt like a fool out on that road waiting for one." She turned over and was soon asleep. I listened to my mother's breath fill the room and fell asleep to the sound of it, to the deep, slow draughts of air that made her body rise and fall like a wave in a still ocean. I wondered how she'd found us, how she'd managed to find Ulvi, whose name she didn't even know. She'd gone to great expense and effort to bring me, her eldest child, back home. It would be as humiliating for her to return without me as for me to return with her.

The next morning, while the air was still damp and the light from street lamps battled the encroaching daylight, I stood in front of the Gateway Arms and helped Mami put her bag into the back seat of a cab. I dreaded the moment when she'd ask me again to come home, but she didn't say anything but goodbye. We hugged long and hard, and when we separated, we were both crying. She looked out the back window of the cab at me standing among the lush greenery, her eyes so sad I felt once more as if I would break into pieces. When the cab took the corner, I returned to the apartment and crawled back into the still-warm bed she had just left. I was weighed with a sorrow so immense that I couldn't move. My limbs curled up to my belly, my hands against my face, I lay there for hours, unable to cry, choked beyond speech, thoughtless yet filled with images that confused me and sent me deeper under the covers, as if the cotton blankets could protect me from my past, as if they were armor against the rest of my life.

"Do not concern yourself, Chiquita."

Leo and Iris brought Ulvi home the following day. He kissed my lips, but didn't look directly at me as Leo supported him into the bedroom. Iris followed them. She put his overnight case inside the closet after quickly assessing its contents.

"He needs to rest," Leo led a reluctant Iris from the bedroom, gently closing the door behind them. "We'll stop by tomorrow." She waved as they left, leaving me in the middle of the living room.

"Chiquita," Ulvi croaked from the other side of the door, and I ran to him. "Come to me," he said, patting the bed. I lay my head on his chest, and listened to his breathing. "How was it with your mother?"

"Everything's okay now," I finger-combed his hair.

"It was shock to wake up from operation to see her."

"I'm sorry."

"You did very bad, Chiquita, not to tell."

"I didn't know how to do it," I whimpered.

He stroked my hair, wiped the tears from my face with the edge of the blanket. "We do best we can," he said, as if continuing a different conversation. Before I could ask what he meant, he was asleep, and I was trapped in his embrace, worried that if I moved I'd wake him. I lay in his arms until his even breathing lulled me into a sleep from which I would not wake for seven years.

I found out what he meant the next day, when he was less groggy. He worried that I expected him to support me now that we were living together.

"You know I have not much money," he said, "and many expenses."

"I brought my savings, and I can get a job," I answered tersely.

"If I could, I would take care of you. You know that, Chiquita."

"I can take care of myself."

He kissed my hair, the back of my neck. "I like that about you, Chiquita," he murmured. "You are not afraid to work hard."

His caresses, the sound of his voice close to my ear, were intoxicating. I felt like a woman when his hands were on me. I reveled in the power of my body to tempt, excite, and satisfy a man who had seen more than I could imagine, who had been places I could only dream of, who had chosen me to love and be loved by. Under his fingers I was Chiquita, but it was Esmeralda who responded to his kisses, his warm breath. It was Esmeralda who lay next to him and looked at our bodies side by side and marveled that they were so nearly the same shade that it was practically impossible to tell where he began and I ended.

Ulvi's financial situation had been precarious since before we met. He lived in New York's Upper East Side, wore elegant clothes, and socialized with famous people, but he constantly complained about his lack of money. He had no other job but the promotion of *Susuz Yaz*, which so far seemed merely a drain of his resources. Distributors had told him that the only way his award-winning film would interest American moviegoers was if it had more sex. In response, he filmed explicit sex scenes with an actress who looked like the original star, now half a world away in Istanbul. He spent months and thousands of dollars reediting the film, creating better subtitles, and commissioning and recording a new musical score. By the time the screening print was delivered, he worried that even more money would be needed for the film's promotion.

Money, the lack of it, the yearning for it, the fantasizing about it, had been as much a part of my life as of Ulvi's. He grew up poor in Turkey, I in Puerto Rico and Brooklyn. But there was a difference between us when it came to our relationship to money. When I needed it, I thought of getting jobs. When he needed it, there was always a scheme that involved so many people that it amazed me the problem was ever solved.

The current situation with his partners was typical. He wasn't their employee, didn't get a salary from them, but they paid for whatever he needed. Whenever I tried to understand this arrangement he told me it was "business" and that I, so innocent and inexperienced, simply could not understand its complexities. According to Ulvi, business was different from jobs. It required a subtlety and finesse unnecessary for someone like me, who had only worked for hourly wages.

"Business is not about what you get now," he told me, "it is about the future, the potential."

"Like gambling," I suggested.

"You are smart girl, Chiquita."

I didn't feel secure in the world of business. I wanted to know that at the end of the week, I could count on a fixed amount of money for an agreed-upon amount of work. How could I plan otherwise? How could I guarantee that the rent or phone bill would be paid, or the electricity, gas, and heat still be connected at the end of the month? Yes, of course, Ulvi agreed, you have to take care of your responsibilities. You must save. But I couldn't figure out where the money to be saved from "business" came from if there was no job.

⟶

Ulvi spent the days after his surgery on the lounge chairs around the pool, shifting from one to the other with the movement of the sun. I read near him and from time to time went into the kitchen to stir Lipton tea powder into a pitcher of cold water and ice. Sometimes, Jim and Janka joined us poolside. I didn't have much in common with Janka, who seemed equally uninterested in me. Jim appeared terrified of looking at any other female in his immediate vicinity. His eyes wandered to a point behind and above me when he had to speak to me.

Mid-afternoons we returned inside the apartment and Ulvi closed the door to the bedroom. He spoke on the phone for about an hour, while I sat in the living room wondering who could be so entertaining that from time to time I heard him laughing out loud. He always came out of the room in a good mood, eyes twinkling.

"Who do you talk to?" I asked once, and he said it was friends from Europe.

"Do not concern yourself, Chiquita," he said, and I understood I should be jealous when I was simply curious.

After our first day at the Gateway Arms, Ulvi realized I was not a cook, and began making our breakfast and lunch. He liked tea in the morning, and apparently had told Iris, because that's what she brought in her bags of groceries. Not wanting to make a fuss, I gave up my lifelong habit of two cups of black coffee on an empty stomach for breakfast.

Ulvi ate lightly, mostly steamed vegetables, bread, and cheese. We had dinner out a few times a week, courtesy of the partners. We always went to the same restaurant, sat around the same table, and the conversation swirled around the movie business, the international film festivals Ulvi had attended, the people he'd met there, and plans for the films he was to make for the partners. Ulvi answered their questions with tantalizing details of famous people, elegant restaurants, and exotic locales. He told them that he had driven across the United States in a white Rolls Royce and was amazed at how big a country it was.

Once he arrived in Los Angeles, he spent several weeks in the guest house of the film producer Sidney Solow.

"And what happened to the Rolls?" Eugene wanted to know.

"I sold it," Ulvi grinned and they laughed with him in a way that sounded like a joke I didn't get. He had spent time in Acapulco, where he partied with Kim Novak and Angie Dickinson. Kim, he said, loved animals and cried at the sight of an abandoned cat or homeless dog. Angie was sweet and a hard worker. At Cannes, he had been a guest on Aristotle Onassis's yacht. The partners asked if he had pictures, and he waved his hand and said "Of course!" but he had left them in Europe.

One night, when Eugene steered the conversation toward me, I mentioned that I needed a job.

"What you mean, Chiquita, is you would like to work," Ulvi corrected me, and grinned at the partners. "She's bored sitting around the pool all day," he said, stroking my hair. "She can't swim."

"But aren't you from the islands?" Janka asked.

"I didn't live near the water," I said.

"Not even a river?" Iris wondered.

"We were poor . . ."

"Her parents were farmers," Ulvi interrupted. "Too much work. No time to relax."

"Maybe we can use her in the office," Eugene suggested to Leo.

"Yeah, sure. Do you have clerical experience?"

"I was the assistant to the fabric buyer at Lady Manhattan," I said, not mentioning that I couldn't type and that she had kept me employed because she felt sorry for me.

"That's pretty good," Leo said, "come to the office on Monday. We always have work." He pushed a business card in my direction, and I was so thrilled and grateful, that everyone at the table smiled. Ulvi took the card and slipped it into his breast pocket.

"Never tell people you're poor," Ulvi said as he undressed back in the apartment. "They don't want to know."

"But I am . . ."

"Listen to me, Chiquita. It is not good idea."

"But I . . ."

"If you want to be with me," he said, inches from my face, "you must do what I tell." His nostrils flared, his eyes were hard behind his long black lashes, his brow stern. I thought for a moment he would hit me, and when his hand moved toward me, I flinched. But he gently reached for my chin and his features softened. "You have much to learn, Chiquita. I will teach you. But only if you listen."

I would listen. I would pay attention. I would be what I had always been—a good girl who rewarded her elders with loyalty and gratitude.

That night, as I lay next to him, I asked myself why it was that, since I'd come to Fort Lauderdale, my days always ended with tears.

Because I'd brought so little with me, I had to shop for "work clothes" and Ulvi offered to come with me to the mall. Expecting him to sit and wait among the potted plants, I was surprised when he followed me to the racks.

"Not that one, Chiquita," he said about a linen dress I liked, "it wrinkles too much." I put it back. "That one is not good color for you," he complained as I held a green top against my chest. I returned it. "Look how poor is made this one," he fingered the hem of another dress I'd just pulled from a rack. Sure enough, it was unraveling. I was annoyed.

"I've been choosing my own clothes since I was old enough to pay for them," I muttered.

"You do not want my help, Chiquita?" Ulvi asked, his voice soft, but with the intensity of a scream. "I wait for you." He headed toward the exit.

"Wait, I didn't mean that!" I cried before he could walk more than a few steps. Just seeing him turn his back was terrifying, as if that act alone would put an end to me in relation to him.

"What did you mean, Chiquita?" His voice was icy.

"I meant . . . I'm used to shopping alone . . . I . . . "

"Okay, do not worry," he said, touching my hair, a tender smile softening his features. "You look and try. I wait outside." He kissed my nose and walked away.

I watched him stride down the aisle, never looking back, stopping every once in a while to finger a display of scarves or a stack of cotton sweaters. He had a long torso over a narrow waist and hips, wide shoulders from which hung long arms with small, agile hands. His legs were short in proportion to the rest of him, but well formed and muscular. His large head and well-defined features were not handsome when examined individually, but on him they created the effect of exotic and mysterious beauty. Heavy-lidded dark-brown eyes protruded slightly on either side of a nose that formed an almost perfect triangle. His face was broad, with chiseled cheekbones, the taut skin darker along the shave line, which gave the lower part of his face a bluish tint. His lips seemed drawn on, with an inverted

V on the top, while the lower was the exact same size and shade, a slightly pinker brown than the rest of his skin. I loved his lips; loved how soft they felt on mine, how he moved them when he spoke his foreign language, or when he struggled with unfamiliar English vowels. Behind those delicious lips were small, white, even teeth which he brushed after every meal.

As he walked away, I had the feeling that he knew I watched him, and that every time he stopped to admire a mannequin or to examine a seam on a skirt, he was doing it so that I would call him back.

Shopping was a painful experience, as I had silk tastes but an acetate budget, unable to afford what I liked, unwilling to like what I could afford. Added to that, every time I picked up a garment, I now envisioned Ulvi's hands on it, finding a flaw, or heard his voice inside my head criticizing the color or the cut. I tried on and discarded enough outfits to irritate the once cheerful dressing room attendant, whose eyes flashed fire when I returned them to her neatly tended rack.

I couldn't find Ulvi at the front of the store. I looked inside nearby shops, returned to the one I'd just left, peered over the heads of shoppers for a glimpse of his shiny black hair. Perhaps, I thought, he went home because I took so long. I walked in that direction, wondering what to say when he noticed I had no packages. How would he respond if I said, "I don't know what I like anymore"?

Leo's business was in the tallest building on the Sunrise Highway, across from the mall, walking distance from the Gateway Arms. The receptionist led me through a warren of desks to Pearl Anne's fluorescent domain, six desks set up so that three faced the other three across an aisle in a windowless room. Pearl Anne was a large woman with a luxurious, shiny Afro and the no-nonsense attitude of someone who knew that she was good at her job. The receptionist introduced me as Amarella, and left me standing by the empty desk closest to Pearl Anne.

"We're a collection agency," Pearl Anne informed me. "Our job is to get the money people owe for things they've bought but haven't paid for."

Without introducing me to the other young women who cowered behind stacks of paper as she passed by, Pearl Anne showed me my desk. "Your purse goes there," she pulled open a locked drawer on the typewriter el and handed me the key. "Don't lose it," she warned.

My job was to open envelopes and compare the names inside with the return addresses. Each envelope was supposed to contain a check and the top half of a letter demanding payment at the risk of "further legal action." Some people sent the entire letter with scribbled comments in the margins or on the back page in which they gave a reason for not having paid sooner or for sending less than the demand.

"Don't bother reading that," Pearl Anne instructed. "It don't make no difference what flimsy excuse they come up with."

Other customers cursed whoever sent the threatening letter, which was signed Sunrise Collection Agency, calling us cowards because we didn't have the decency to sign our own names.

I was to double-check that the senders had entered the correct amount of the payment on the box for that purpose.

"Sometimes," Pearl Anne said, "they write a number that has nothing to do with reality." In most cases, people overstated the amount of the payment. "They hope we won't notice," she said. "Fat chance!"

Mine was not an exciting job, but I was paid twenty cents over minimum wage per hour and was allowed a morning and afternoon break plus a half hour for lunch. In the break room, one machine dispensed strong, boiling hot coffee, and another vended snack cakes, chips, and candy bars. The caffeine deprivation headache I'd treated with aspirin disappeared with my first cup of the brew.

Ulvi walked me to and from work every day. At noon, he brought lunch, and we sat on the lawn overlooking the busy Sunrise Highway. There was a coffee shop on the first floor, and its patrons watched us from their booths, laughing at the folly of leaving an air-conditioned building to sit in the midday heat. But Ulvi did not want me to spend money on lunch when he could bring one from the apartment.

"You must save, Chiquita," he said.

I owed him money. Over the weekend, we had returned to the mall and, this time, Ulvi had selected my clothes.

"I know about these things," he insisted. "I have a degree in textile engineering."

Just as he wasn't interested in my past, Ulvi had shared little about his. I had dragged out of him that he was seventeen years my senior, that he was born in Istanbul, where his father still lived, that he lived in Germany for many years and that he had never married. "It does not matter my life before," he said with a scowl whenever my questions annoyed him.

Now, as he chose my clothes, he laughed. "You are surprised, Chiquita."

"How do you go from being a textile engineer to film director?"

"Is long story," he laughed.

A couple of weeks later I would learn just how long a story it was.

I didn't know what Ulvi did while I was at the Sunrise Collection Agency. He never asked about my job and I didn't ask about his day. When I received my first paycheck, he said he would cash it for me. I signed it over and the next day he handed me a few dollars and kept the rest.

"You like to spend, Chiquita," he said. "I save for you. Is better, so you will not be tempted. But if you need something, ask."

It was true that money didn't last in my hands. The anxiety that gripped me when I shopped for clothes disappeared at book and stationery stores, where fine papers and fountain pens beckoned. I bought thick books written by people who had been dead for centuries. I owned several translations of my favorite books, the *Iliad* and the *Odyssey*, and had worn through three paperback copies of Edith Hamilton's *Mythology*. I loved leather-bound agendas and journals, but could only afford wide-ruled composition notebooks that I filled with doggerel, minutiae, longings, and complaints. I bought stacks of paper and matching envelopes in which I wrote chatty letters to anyone who had ever given me his or her address for that purpose. I sketched poorly, but that didn't stop me from buying an assortment of sketchpads and charcoals. I painted badly, but in Brooklyn I had left behind an easel and oils, a palette, blank canvases, and books on perspective.

Money vanished from my wallet if there were a dance studio in which to take a class, a movie theater showing a western or a musical, or a restaurant where they refilled my cup without asking if I wanted more coffee. When Ulvi said I liked to spend, I couldn't argue.

"I need personal things," I said, "lady things." He promised we would go to the drugstore. There, he glared when I lingered over the magazines. When I picked up a composition notebook, he said I didn't need it.

"But I left my writing stuff at home," I whined.

"Very well then," he said, and I bought the notebook and a Bic pen. I had filled dozens of notebooks like it with musings. Every time we moved, I dumped them rather than lug them to the next apartment, which, no matter how hard Mami tried, never had enough room for three adults and eleven children. What was in the notebooks became unimportant. What I treasured was the act of recording, of letting the page absorb the secrets of my until-recently virginal existence, as well as the tedious moments of my day.

Back at the Gateway Arms, I started to write my impressions of life with Ulvi, but it was impossible. Words fled the minute I tried to express my feelings, mostly because I wasn't sure what they were. When I wondered whether I loved him or whether he simply represented a way out of Brooklyn, I felt disloyal and could not bear to ask myself the question in writing. I worried that he would read the entries while I was at work. Carrying the notebook everywhere seemed ridiculous. It remained blank except for the date and, in fancier lettering below it, "Fort Lauderdale, Florida."

"Is there something you want to tell me?"

One night, just as we had returned from a walk on the beach and I was preparing tea, Eugene and Leo showed up at our door. Unsmiling, their faces tight, they entered and sat side by side on the sofa before Ulvi asked them to. Eugene pointed to the chair across the coffee table and Ulvi took it. I stood on the other side of the kitchen island, feeling the tension, wishing there were some way to cross unseen and disappear into the bedroom. Their serious faces, the contained anger with which they moved and spoke convinced me that, whatever Eugene and Leo came to discuss with Ulvi, I did not want to hear it.

"Is there something you want to tell me," Eugene growled.

"*We* have something to tell *you*," Leo snarled before Ulvi had a chance to answer, and Eugene raised a finger to silence him.

Ulvi crossed his leg so that his left ankle was on his right knee, settled his right elbow on the armrest, leaned his head toward his hand, and wrapped his thumb and index finger around his chin. His left arm was relaxed, the fingers seeming boneless. Dressed in a white polo shirt, navy shorts, and sandals, his forehead clear, his eyes defiant, his fingers around his chin, the posture burned into my memory and remained suspended in time. If he moved, if he changed the position of his hands or feet or head or eyes while Eugene and Leo talked to him, I never noticed.

"You did not think," Eugene said, "that we wouldn't investigate?"

"I have nothing to hide," Ulvi said softly.

"Is it true that you can't travel to Turkey?"

Ulvi shook his head. "I took my film. The government would not let me show it outside Turkey. I did it anyway. Politics," he added.

"Didn't you also take money?" Leo asked.

"I had a few coins in my pockets. It is against the law to take money out of Turkey. They look for any reason to accuse me. It was just a few coins. My film," Ulvi continued when the other men didn't speak, "is about peasant people. The government wants only to show modern Turkey. I knew the film had a chance in Europe and in America. I was right. It won the Golden Bear in Berlin. Also in Cartagena and Acapulco . . ."

Leo and Eugene stared at Ulvi for a few moments, as if considering whether his artistic integrity had caused his problems with customs in Istanbul. Slowly, without taking his eyes off Ulvi, Eugene reached inside his jacket. I had seen enough films with moments like this for panic to grip my belly. There was no gun, as I expected. Eugene pulled out a sheaf of folded papers from an inside pocket. He laid them on the coffee table, pressed them flat, and pushed them toward Ulvi. From my spot behind the kitchen island, I saw photocopies of newspaper clippings.

"You used a German diplomat to bypass Customs . . ." Leo said.

"You told us you directed the film. It says here that the director is Ismail Metin," Eugene added.

"You not only took his film out of Turkey, you took his credit," Leo growled.

I was so intent on Eugene and Leo that I hadn't looked at Ulvi. When I turned to him, tears were sliding down his cheeks. "It is my film," he said, choked up. "I produced it. Without me, it would never be so successful."

Eugene and Leo seemed embarrassed by Ulvi's reaction. They stood up.

"You understand," Eugene said, "that we are no longer in business together." He led the way out, nodding in my direction before he left, followed by Leo, who slammed the door.

I was paralyzed, not sure what to do once the men left. I was angry at them, at their humiliation of Ulvi, made worse because it took place in front of me. He did not move from where he sat, tears streaming from his eyes, the copies spread out on the coffee table as neatly as Eugene had left them. I felt sorry for him, and swallowed my own tears because this was a time to be strong. I walked over and put my arms around him. Over his head, I could see the headlines, in what I assumed to be German and Turkish. Ulvi wiped his face with the hem of his shirt, stood up, kissed me on the cheek. "Thank you, Chiquita," he said. He scooped up the pages then locked himself in the bedroom. Within seconds, he was on the phone, the cadences of German wafting through the closed door like a judgment on my inability to comfort *el hombre que yo amo*.

He didn't speak about it that night. He didn't speak about it the next day, or the day after that, or ever. Maybe he didn't think I understood everything Eugene and Leo said. My English, however, was better than his, and I heard everything. Maybe he thought I should have left him then. Maybe he knew that the image he had so carefully cultivated was now tarnished, at least before Eugene and Leo—and me. He seemed shorter when he stood up to lock himself in the bedroom. As I sat on the sofa listening to his muted voice, I wondered what would happen next.

This was surely one of the lowest moments of Ulvi's life. Just before Eugene and Leo walked in, he had been optimistic about his career and their promise of financing for more movies. The partners were Italian, and they wanted to make films with Italian-American themes. Ulvi had envisioned frequent travel to Europe, dinners with movie stars, glamorous parties. I had noticed that his plans never included me, but I didn't ask, hoping I was implicit in them.

Once I stopped worrying about what Eugene and Leo's accusations meant for Ulvi, I began to wonder about myself. If what they said was true, was Ulvi a wanted man? Was I, then, an unwitting accomplice? Because the situation involved the Turkish government, I imagined the international police handled it. International intrigue was something I had only seen in James Bond movies, and I was fully aware that the girl (me in this case), after having a torrid affair with the dashing hero (Ulvi?), often ended up dead.

It wouldn't be the first time I flirted with Interpol. A year earlier, I had been involved with Jürgen, a dashing young German who, on our first date, took me to test-drive a Porsche. He had fallen in love with me, he said, at first sight. He was so charming and persuasive that he convinced me to marry him three hours after we met.

One afternoon he took me to Central Park and rented a boat. While I gripped the sides, afraid to fall into the water, Jürgen rowed and answered questions he encouraged me to ask, such as whether he was married and had children. Then we walked in the shade along the lake and he confessed that he made his living stealing airplanes then selling them. I didn't believe him at first, but he was earnest, and assured me that I had changed him and he was giving up his criminal activities to settle down. We would live in Egypt, where he had an offer to pilot for a sheik, and we would travel to Europe frequently, to visit his parents in Hamburg and to the United States, to see my family.

It felt good to be adored by a handsome man who looked deep into my eyes and asked, "What are you thinking about?" in the lulls between conversations. But I didn't buy Jürgen's "You've changed my life" assurances. It was also difficult, after a while, to imagine marrying a man whose features I forgot the minute he left, a man who was counting on me to keep him out of mischief. While he was away on a business trip, which he swore did not involve stealing aircraft, I broke the engagement. Weeks later I met Ulvi.

Legs crossed under me, I now sat on the sofa recently vacated by Eugene and Leo and tried to imagine if I was in more trouble than if I had married Jürgen and moved to Egypt. As far as I knew, Jürgen had been honest with me about his past. Ulvi refused to talk about his except in the most general terms. Jürgen's honesty gave me the option to refuse a life that could have endangered mine. Ulvi had not given me that choice. I had to accept him and ask no questions. "I would never hurt you, Chiquita," Ulvi had said many times. "Trust me," he begged when I was full of doubts, and I did because I understood that for Ulvi loving me meant protecting me from truths that could get me in trouble.

After at least an hour on the phone, Ulvi opened the door and stood on the threshold, smiling as if nothing had happened. "Come to bed, Chiquita. It is late."

That night he held on to me as if we were lying on the edge of a cliff. He slept fitfully and woke often, yelling in Turkish or German, unable to recognize where he was. I calmed him as best I could and spent a sleepless night thrashing in my own predicament.

Surely I no longer had a job at the Sunrise Collection Agency and almost certainly we would have to leave the Gateway Arms. Beyond that, I didn't know what might, could, would, or should happen. I was afraid, but I also tingled with excitement. Dramatic scenarios from movie scenes and best-sellers swirled around my brain as Ulvi muttered and groaned on his side of the bed. Once I had exhausted the possibilities of feverish chases, gun battles, beaded evening gowns, glamorous locales, and witty dialogue, I was left with the same question that had plagued my life before I met Ulvi: what would happen next?

It was in the moist, early hours, as the sun began to break through the humid Florida morning that I made a decision. A few weeks earlier, I had walked out of my mother's life and into what I had imagined was my own. Now here I was, lying next to a man who was more and less than he pretended to be. He controlled the money I made, how I ate, what I wore, what I said, when I said it. Was this my life? Yes, it was. Had I made a mistake? Yes, I had. What was I going to do about it? I wasn't sure. All I knew was that no matter what came after last night, there was no way I was going back to Brooklyn.

"This I do not like."

The day after Eugene and Leo's visit, the phone service was cut off, so Ulvi had to use the booth on the Sunrise Highway. The phone rang every afternoon at precisely 3:00 p.m. Ulvi slid the glass door closed and pressed the receiver to his ear to compensate for the roar of traffic not ten feet away.

I sat on the grass nearby, pretending to read while straining to hear his side of the conversation in German. So far, I'd only been able to make out that he was speaking to someone named Irmchen. I asked him who Irmchen was.

"A good friend," he said.

"Have you known her long?"

"Yes," he answered, confirming my suspicion that Irmchen was a woman. "Many years. Do not concern yourself, Chiquita."

In contrast to the late-afternoon calls of the previous weeks, Ulvi was not happy when he hung up. During the conversations, he took notes on scraps of paper that he stuffed in his pockets. Back home, he consulted them, scribbled along their margins, computed figures on their backs, then tore them into bits and flushed them down the toilet.

I expected that, at any moment, Leo would evict us from the apartment, but Ulvi seemed unconcerned. He swam laps, or lounged on the plastic chairs with his eyes closed, face twitching, lips moving in silent conversations. A few times over the next couple of weeks, we walked to a bank down the street, where Ulvi received wired money. He had two follow-up appointments after his surgery, and after the second, the doctor told him that he could resume normal activities. That afternoon the conversation with Irmchen was longer than usual, more animated. He laughed frequently, and muttered conspiratorially into the phone, shook his head, murmured her name, Irmchen.

That night, as we ate our simple meal of vegetables and tea, he spoke the words I didn't want to hear.

"I am returning to Europe."

If my voice didn't quaver, if the words came out as an offer, not a demand, there was a chance he would say yes. "I can come with you."

Ulvi seemed to be considering my suggestion, as if it hadn't occurred to him that I would follow him to Europe as willingly as I had followed him to Fort Lauderdale.

"No, Chiquita, you can not," he said with finality, dismissing me from his life, confirming Mami's warning that he only wanted to take advantage of me. It infuriated me that I had believed otherwise.

"Why not?" I asked.

"Is better you wait for me," he said after a moment.

"How long?"

"Maybe one month, maybe two. You should stay with your mother."

"No, I can't go back there."

"Why you cannot go there? It is your home."

I sought a reason why I would not return where I was most welcome, a reason that would make sense to Ulvi, and tried honor. "I have shamed her," I said, "when I left with you without getting married."

His face tightened and his lips set into a straight, flat line. "I can not marry you, Chiquita," he said.

Yes, Mami was right. Men only want one thing.

"I cannot take care you in everything," he said. As if I had asked.

His tone made me angry. "You don't have to worry about me. I will get a job, find an apartment."

He shook his head. "I do not want you live alone."

"Why not?"

"Because I care about you." He didn't say I love you. "You must go your family," he insisted.

"No."

"This I do not like," Ulvi shot up from his chair, as if he were about to run out of the room. Instead, he stood in front of where I sat and glared. I lowered my eyes to the orange shag rug, ready for the scolding, but unwilling to change my mind. "I do not like," he repeated, "you want to be spoiled American girl."

Spoiled, in Ulvi-speak, meant sexually available. Now that he had done me *el daño*, his fear was that I might join the "free-love movement" that titillated and terrified people his age. When he attached "spoiled" to "American girl" I winced, remembering Mami's accusations that my Puerto Rican identity was compromised because in eight years in the United States I had learned to function comfortably outside our culture. Ulvi was unaware of the guilt I felt when he spoke those three words, spoiled American girl.

I didn't reassure him that I would not take lovers if I lived alone. I wanted to argue that I had not lost my Puerto Rican self to American culture, but didn't. It was beside the point in this particular discussion, since he was as uninterested in my Puerto Ricanness as in any of my personal struggles. I bit my lips and silenced the argument and the defense of my moral character. I would prove to him that I was not a spoiled American girl. I would swallow my pride and return to Mami's house, where I would avoid her "I told you so" looks. Men who *hacen el daño* and then leave the "spoiled" girl did not come back. I had seen it happen countless times.

I would return to Brooklyn, and stay with my family until I found a job and could afford an apartment. Ulvi would live in a part of my heart marked "First love." No, not that. I was still not sure I loved him, especially since he merely "cared" for me. "First man to make love to me." Yes, that sounded much better, much more precise, much less painful than *el hombre que yo amo*.

Ulvi admired American technological innovation, especially the space program, and wanted to stay in Florida until after the moon landing, but word came from Leo via Jim that we should leave by the end of the week. Because he had given up his apartment on East Fifty-eighth Street, Ulvi arranged to stay with his friend Tarik, in Queens. I was not welcome there, Ulvi said. Tarik's wife thought that I would be a bad example for their children because I was "living in sin."

"Why am I living in sin and you're not?" I asked Ulvi.

"I am a man, it is different for a man," he said. I knew better than to argue.

I had avoided calling Mami to let her know that I was coming back, hoping that Ulvi would change his mind about taking me to Europe, or that Tarik's wife would change her mind about my sinful ways, or that I would come up with a better plan than to return to Fulton Street. None of those things happened, and I was relieved when my sister Alicia answered the phone and I didn't have to speak to Mami directly, but left a message about when I'd be arriving.

On an oppressively hot July evening, Tarik picked us up at the air-port in New York. I had met him before, and he had always been kind and friendly. This time, he didn't look at me directly, and seemed annoyed that he would have to drop me off in Bedford Stuyvesant, a neighborhood where people from Queens didn't ven-ture. I sat in the back of his spotless car and directed him from the airport to our door in the only route I knew, which he complained was more circuitous than necessary. He and Ulvi peered out the windows as if they were visiting a foreign land with astonishing sights. They shook their heads and clicked their tongues at the burned-out buildings, at the teenagers congregating on street cor-ners, at the prostitutes under the elevated train tracks, at the broken streetlights that left our block in gloomy, menacing shadows.

"Yes, gentlemen," I said against their stifling silence, "this is the ghetto."

Ulvi turned and glared at me. "Do not make joke about that, Chiquita."

While it looked neglected, our neighborhood was better than some of the places we'd lived in when we first arrived in the United States. After years of cramped apartments and unheated tene-ments, Mami had managed to buy a three-story house on Fulton Street. The mortgage was paid for with the income from her busi-ness doing piecework for garment manufacturers. In a room to the side of the house she had set up sewing machines for herself and two employees. Titi Ana worked for her and also rented the top floor. The rest was ours, with enough space for living and dining rooms, a bedroom for the girls to share and a separate one for the boys, a small room off the kitchen for Tata, and another one for Mami and Don Carlos.

When we reached the house, Ulvi got out of the car and kissed me goodbye as Tarik retrieved my bag from the trunk. I noticed the curtains flickering, and in a moment, Mami appeared at the door, dressed in her best.

"Goodbye, Chiquita," Ulvi said hurriedly. "I will call you tomorrow."

"*¿No van a entrar?*" Mami scowled.

"They're dropping me off. He's staying in Queens."

"You come," she said to Ulvi. "Have coffee with my family." While I knew that her use of the imperative was due to her poor English, it still sounded like a command to me, and, so it seemed to Ulvi and to Tarik. They agreed wordlessly to be polite. Tarik checked that every door and the trunk of his car were locked.

Six-year-old Franky ran out of the house, gave me a hug, grabbed my bag, and disappeared inside with it. As I walked in, I heard a lot of running around and whispering upstairs, where my sisters and brothers had apparently been banished. The faces of the youngest peeked through the banisters, and Mami raised a hand and shooed them away. They disappeared.

I was leading Ulvi and Tarik to the kitchen.

"In the living room there is a surprise," Mami said in Spanish.

I stopped short at the door when I saw, for the first time in eight years, my father, sitting stiffly on the plastic-covered easy chair. His face opened into a broad smile when he saw me, and he clapped his hands as I walked in, as if I, followed by a startled Ulvi and Tarik, were making a grand, long-awaited entrance.

Don Carlos was on the chair next to Papi, and on the next, Don Julio nursed a can of beer and refused to meet my eyes. Tata leaned on the threshold to the kitchen, a Rheingold in one hand, a cigarette in the other. Behind her, my brothers, seventeen-year-old Héctor and thirteen-year-old Raymond, glowered at Ulvi and Tarik, unsure which was which. I wanted to die.

It was an ambush. Ulvi and Tarik spotted the way out of the room, just in case they had to get away quickly. But I knew that, with the possible exception of my two hormonally charged teenage brothers, everyone else in the room was incapable of violence toward a stranger. At least not inside our home, and not so long as Ulvi and Tarik were respectful. I trusted that they, from a culture where the formalities of dignity and respect were even stricter than in Puerto Rico, would know that implicitly.

Papi stood and came toward me, arms outstretched. I wanted desperately to run into that embrace and stay there, collecting years' worth of hugs and fatherly kisses. At the same time, I was aware of what had brought him to Brooklyn after years of minimal contact with his seven children. He was there to defend my honor.

Too late, I wanted to say, to scream at him. *Ya me hizo el daño.* I was so angry and resentful, I vibrated, but I refused to show it. If I didn't control the situation, the evening might end in one of the operatic scenes everyone in my family (myself included) could enact with the slightest provocation. I would do my best to keep things civil and to get Ulvi and Tarik away from there as soon as possible.

I gave Papi a quick hug, turned around and formally introduced him, Don Carlos, Don Julio, Héctor, Raymond, and Tata to Ulvi and to Tarik. Tata gave Ulvi the most openly disdainful head to toe look I had ever seen anyone give another person. She turned her back without shaking his hand and shuffled into the kitchen.

I sat between them on the sofa, in that room of dignified, angry men on plastic-covered furniture. Behind Papi's chair there were shelves laden with Mami's collection of china figurines of nineteenth-century ladies dancing, pipers piping, cardinals warbling, and winged cherubs pointing arrows at all of them. Lace doilies covered the side tables. The television was off, but above it, Jesus's eyes were perpetually turned to the thorns on his head, his right index finger pointing to his anatomically improbable heart. On the wall across from him, the handsome profiles of John F. Kennedy and Martin Luther King, Jr., faced each other on the velvet painting above our heads.

I vacillated between loyalty to my family and embarrassment before Ulvi, whose eyes scanned every surface of the room with expressions that went from interest to disbelief, to horror, to amusement. He had never wanted to know anything about me, but now he seemed fascinated by the spectacle of the men in my life trying to be both stern and well-mannered before his elegance and urbanity. Don Carlos spoke English well, but Don Julio, Papi, Mami, and Tata didn't, so I translated as the men made small talk about our flight and about the weather, made hotter in that blistering room by the tray of steaming cups of sweetened *café con leche* that Mami delivered on her best china. I had bought that service for twelve at Woolworth's and had given it to her the previous Christmas. She loved its gold trim and the delicate teacups with tiny, triangular handles that made them almost impossible to hold.

"And what are your intentions toward my daughter?" Papi asked the moment everyone had the delicate cups filled to the brim precariously balanced upon their saucers. It was as if he had rehearsed the line many times and couldn't wait to get it out. I translated, avoiding Ulvi's gaze, my scalp tingling with a blush that colored my entire body.

"I care very much about your daughter," Ulvi said vehemently. He squeezed my hand. I translated "I love your daughter very much," and everyone smiled. "But," Ulvi continued, and the smiles vanished, "my business requires I go to Europe for short time. I know you will take good care of Chiquita until I return." He kissed my knuckles. The men seemed satisfied with my unadorned translation. Tata and Mami glared daggers toward Ulvi, who on no account would look in their direction.

"Do you plan to marry her?" Don Carlos asked and Ulvi, who not three days earlier had said he couldn't do that, said "Yes, when I return." I stared at him, dumbfounded. He looked over my head at Tarik.

"I'm sorry," Tarik said, standing up. "It's late and we have a long drive." He glanced nervously toward the window, concerned about his car.

"Thank you," Ulvi said, shaking hands with Papi, with Don Carlos, Don Julio, Héctor, and Raymond. He bowed toward Mami and Tata.

I led them out. Before he left, Ulvi kissed my cheek. "Is okay, Chiquita, I call you in the morning," he murmured and ran toward Tarik's car, already idling at the curb. I leaned my forehead against the closed door, gathering my thoughts for the next part of the ordeal. When I turned around, Mami and Tata were standing in the hallway, watching me.

"*¿Qué te dijo ese hombre?*" Mami asked.

"That man," I repeated, "said he'd call me tomorrow." My younger siblings were once again on the second floor landing, peeking through the banisters. "Where will I sleep tonight?"

"With me!" Edna called.

"Okay, I'll be right there," I said, and waved goodnight in the general direction of the living room.

"Don't you think you should visit with your father a while?" Mami asked. "He's returning to Puerto Rico tomorrow."

"In the morning," I said. "I'm really tired now." I ran up the stairs into the arms of my little sisters and brothers, who only wondered one thing: "Did you bring us anything from Florida?"

"*Parece buena gente,*" Papi said loud enough for me to hear, and I scooped up two-year-old Cibi into my arms and asked Franky where he had put my bag.

I played with the kids so that I would not hear Tata disagree with Papi's assessment that Ulvi seemed like a good person. I didn't want to be in that room with people who loved me and pretend that Ulvi hadn't lied to them. I didn't want to hear them talk about how Ulvi had squinted distastefully at the best they could give, so well tended and generously offered. I didn't want to recall his amazement that anyone would think that the bleeding heart of Jesus was an appropriate decoration in a living room.

I didn't want to talk to my father, who had not been there for any other important event in my life over the past eight years, but had shown up when there was a man in my life. It didn't seem fair that my few, hard-earned successes were barely acknowledged, but the minute my virginity was in question, there he was, with a useless display of fatherly concern. Too late, too late, too late. The words rattled around my head as I played with the kids.

"It's not too late!" three-year-old Charlie argued when the words escaped from my lips. It was way past midnight and we should have been sleeping, but we ate every piece of candy I had brought. When I finally fell into a bed with Cibi in my arms, too late was the lullaby I sang to quiet her exhausted, sugar-charged whimpering.

Mami and Papi were in the kitchen when I came down the next morning, dressed and groomed for a day in Manhattan.

"Where are you going so early?" Mami frowned as she put a mug of unsweetened black coffee in front of me. The good china was back in the breakfront against the wall.

I wrapped my hands around the mug and inhaled the steam. "If I'm at the agency early enough I might get some work today."

"Good idea," Papi said. He was darker than I remembered. His wiry black hair was speckled gray. As a child, I had thought him handsome, mostly because of his big eyes, which twinkled with delight whenever he saw me. I also loved the deep, resonant music in his voice when he recited poetry, and his smile, which was generous, open, welcoming, and frequent. But now I noticed his acne-scarred skin, his broad nose, and the two missing teeth in his lower jaw. He was shorter than I remembered. When he stood up to hug me the night before, I had been surprised that he was no taller than I was.

"So the agents find you work as an actress?"

"I'm not an actress," I said. "I'm an office worker."

"A secretary? That's wonderful!"

"Not a secretary, a receptionist or clerk. Work that requires no typing."

"Oh, that's good, too!"

His enthusiasm was getting on my nerves.

"If you practice typing, you can get better jobs," Mami put a plateful of eggs and ham in front of Papi.

"What am I going to practice on?"

"Don't be disrespectful to your mother," Papi warned.

"Sorry." I stood up. "I have to go."

"Your omelet is almost ready," Mami broke two eggs into a bowl.

"I'm not hungry."

"Drink your coffee, then," she said.

I swallowed the scalding liquid in two gulps. "Thanks. See you later."

"What do I tell *el turco ese* when he calls?" Mami asked when I was already in the hallway. I stepped back into the kitchen. Papi looked from me to Mami as if trying to distinguish one from the other.

"Tell him I went to look for a job," I said. "If he leaves a number I can call him later."

Papi stood and opened his arms. "I'm returning to Puerto Rico today."

"Oh, that was a quick trip," I said innocently as I gave him a hug. "Have a good flight back."

"*Adiós, hija, que Dios te bendiga,*" he replied, holding on longer than I wanted.

"*Que la virgen te favorezca y te acompañe,*" Mami added.

The blessings, unasked for but ardently given, reminded me of what else I had lost since coming to New York. Asking for a blessing upon meeting or leaving adults had been as automatic as breathing. *La bendición,* we were told as children, protected us from dangers away from our loved ones, and was spoken in gratitude upon our safe return. *La bendición* was as essential to our well-being as a nutritious meal, and the responsibility of every adult toward every child. When had I stopped asking for blessings? When was the last time I'd received one?

I left the house overwhelmed by feelings that made my vision fuzzy and my heart gallop. My parents had blessed me, but I felt no comfort. I needed the Virgin to favor and accompany me, as Mami had prayed. I needed God to bless me, as Papi had requested. The problem was that, rather than be grateful for their good wishes, I was angry. Mami and Papi had stood next to each other, their hands over my head, blessing me. The moment, so beautiful in its simplicity and emotional power, was marred by the knowledge that he had only come to New York to scold *el hombre que le hizo el daño a Negi*, not to see me. Satisfied that Ulvi would make a decent woman of me, Papi would return to Puerto Rico and boast to his wife and friends about his visit to Nueva York and about the *buena gente* he had met there.

My parents had appealed to God and the Virgin to protect me from the dangers of the world, as they had done countless times back in Puerto Rico when I was a child, when we were a family. Then I had accepted those blessings without questions, but now, when I needed them most, I rejected them. It hurt too much to believe that their blessings would have any effect on my life. They shriveled into hard nuggets of resentment that fed the American part of me, mistrustful of the superstitious beliefs of *gente puertorriqueña decente*.

~~~

An hour later, I ascended the steps from the subway and found myself in the middle of Times Square. Midtown Manhattan, which for me meant north of Thirty-fourth and south of Fifty-seventh

Streets, river to river, was my favorite part of the city because I could walk down any street and something memorable would have happened to me there.

On the north side of Thirty-fourth Street, I had seen Garbo rummaging through a bin full of discounted shoes in the basement of Ohrbach's. On the south side of Thrity-eighth between First and Second Avenues, a woman chased me out of "her neighborhood" hurling insults and brandishing an umbrella. It was on Fiftieth Street and Fifth Avenue where I met Jürgen, the airplane thief. On Forty-ninth and Seventh, my Theory of Advertising professor suggested that a good career choice for me was to model underwear. On Forty-eighth and Eighth, I auditioned for a part in the movie *Up the Down Staircase*. Inside a phone booth on Fifty-second and Lexington, I learned that I had lost the part because I was too pretty to play a Puerto Rican girl. "But we can find work for you as an extra," the casting agent had offered.

Four blocks north and half a block east of Times Square was Performing Arts High School, where I had perfected the role of Cleopatra over three years of dramatic studies. Six blocks north and one west was the Longacre Theater, where I had made my Broadway debut as a captive Hindu princess rescued by a mango seller with the help of a talking monkey. Four blocks south were the offices of Lady Manhattan, where I had been the assistant to the fabric buyer, even though I couldn't type or muster the hyperbole necessary to invent memorable names for that season's colors. Two blocks east and two blocks south of Times Square was Woolworth's, where Ulvi had first spotted me as I sat inside a phone booth talking to my mother.

In bad weather, I could walk for several blocks through the underground passages of complexes like Rockefeller Center. I knew where every public rest room was, and every Automat. I was recognized by the staff of several hotels, who didn't bother me if I sat alone in the lobby reading a book between classes at Manhattan

Community College on Fiftieth and Sixth. I knew almost every Dottie, Sheila, Shirley, Pat, and Pam serving bottomless cups of boiling hot coffee in luncheonettes and delis on the street floor of office buildings.

What I loved most about the middle of Midtown, Forty-second Street between Third and Eighth Avenues, was its transient nature. It was a place for tourists, shoppers from other parts of Manhattan and the boroughs, office workers who crammed the subways to and from Grand Central and Times Square stations during the rush hours. It was elegant along Fifth Avenue, but the side streets became seedier as one walked west toward the A train. Peep shows, dim bars with languid dancers, XXX-rated movies, and nickelodeons stood side by side with tourist shops selling miniatures of the Empire State Building and the Statue of Liberty.

Because I had attended high school and community college in Midtown, I had spent more hours walking around it than on the streets of Brooklyn, where I lived. I strutted the same sidewalks as Broadway tappers and kickers, past the doors of theaters where the third chorus girl from the left could become the next star. I spent hours sitting in the sun on the steps of the Public Library, reading, or eating a hot dog and drinking a Yoo Hoo from the vendor on the corner of Forty-second and Fifth. I held my breath past the doorways that smelled of urine, and walked quickly beyond the lewd comments of the barkers for peep shows. I took dance classes inside decrepit buildings with creaking stairs that opened up to sunny studios lined with mirrors. I left the streets where pimps, prostitutes, and con men mingled with future movie stars, talent agents, publicists, food vendors, priests, Salvation Army trombonists, secretaries, taxi drivers, artists, and wide-eyed tourists constantly checking that their wallets were still there. I took an elevator above a deli to the end of a long, dark, marble-floored hall lined with doors looking for the one that would open into my future.

"You think your life so bad?"

Ulvi stayed with Tarik long enough to realize that Queens was not New York, and that riding the subway was not as quaint as it seemed the first time if you did it daily in fastidiously maintained European clothes. He took a room at the Lexington Hotel, a short walk from his old apartment. The room was small, furnished with a narrow bed, a dresser, and a television set with bent rabbit ears. In that hot July, though, the air conditioner fastened to its one window made it feel luxurious. He told me I could stay with him if the staff did not know he had another person in a room meant for one. We went into the hotel separately, and I waited in the hallway near the room because he had the only key. We left the hotel a few minutes apart and met down the street. I was certain that these precautions were not fooling anybody, but Ulvi insisted, and I played along because I would rather be with him in an air-conditioned room in Midtown than under the stern gaze of my mother and grandmother in Fulton Street.

"Now I know why you don't want stay there," Ulvi said about his visit to our home in Bedford Stuyvesant.

I was offended. It was one thing for me to criticize my family to myself, quite another for him to have an opinion about them. "They are good people, doing the best they can."

"Yes, Chiquita, I know," he murmured, as if he felt sorry for me. "You are good girl." He squeezed me closer as we walked down Park Avenue.

I did not feel like a good girl. Since returning to New York, I had done everything possible to avoid my family. I was ashamed at the cowardly way in which I had left and even more ashamed at the circumstances of my return. The men in my family might have believed Ulvi when he said he'd marry me upon his return from Europe, but Tata and Mami did not.

Until I left with Ulvi, our affair had been my secret. Had he slept with me then abandoned me, no one would have known. I would have felt just as betrayed, but every time Mami looked at me, her expressions would not go through so many changes, from "I told you so" to "my suffering child who has been wronged" to "I hate that man." Tata would not be so oppressively silent whenever I passed her. Don Carlos and Don Julio would not seem so superfluous had they been capable of protecting me from a man who only wanted one thing. My father would not seem so indifferent to everything in my life but the status of my virginity.

I did not blame them for what I had done. I kept our relationship from my family, did not consult them while I struggled with whether or not to follow Ulvi to Fort Lauderdale. The night before I left, I told Delsa what I was doing. We shared a bed and she had seen me pack my bag before I climbed in next to her. I did not tell her where I was going, only that the next morning I would leave New York with a man none of them knew. She tried to talk me out of it, but I refused to listen. "My mind is made up," I said. It had been my first autonomous decision as an official adult to leave with him, and I had no one to blame but myself.

When Ulvi asked me to join him at the Lexington Hotel, I could have said no. I could have redeemed myself to myself and to my family by refusing to see him again, the way I did with Jürgen, whose entreaties that he loved me and wanted to spend the rest of his life with me had sounded like a burden more than a reward. Unlike my decisiveness with Jürgen, however, whenever I heard Ulvi's voice, or felt his touch, my will evaporated. I became as pliant as a silk ribbon, transparent to his gaze, bending in the direction his fingers shaped me.

I had worked for The Grace Agency on and off since shortly after high school graduation. It offered temporary jobs with flexible hours, which allowed me to schedule dance classes and courses at Manhattan Community College while working as much as possible. The company hired only young, pretty women, whom the owner insisted should dress professionally. Before we left for our posts, we reported to the office, where Grace, the owner and only full-time employee of the company, approved our attire. If we didn't pass inspection, we didn't work that day.

"Our clients want to project a sophisticated image," Grace said as she handed me a bag full of flyers, replenished every hour from a red VW van. My job was to hand out the flyers in front of banks, jewelry stores, boutiques.

It was hard to act sophisticated as I pressed 20 percent off discount coupons into the hands of New Yorkers in a hurry. Most people accepted whatever I gave them, even if they stuffed the handout into a purse or pocket without looking at the offer. A metal trashcan at the end of the block held the crumpled remains of my labor, discarded by people too polite to refuse my "Here you go, sir" or "Special offer, ma'am."

Once, a young man in a business suit stopped in front of me and read the flyer I gave him aloud, including the fine print and exclusions on a low-interest mortgage. He then asked me for a date. I explained that we were forbidden to chat with passersby and that he was interfering with my job of handing out a flyer to everyone who passed me. I tried to move around him, but he blocked my path. I was rescued by Grace, who roamed her territory to keep an eye out for her "Flyer Girls."

"Excuse me, sir," she called in a voice heard halfway down the block. She rushed toward us as if to tackle him. The young man scurried away.

Grace was big boned and angular, imposing in her high-heeled go-go boots, her elaborately made-up face framed by a mass of blond curls that softened her masculine features. We Flyer Girls knew that Grace was a man, but she didn't seem to think it was obvious to anybody. She tried to be one of us by sharing tips on the most long-lasting mascara or extra-hold hair spray. At certain times of the month, she complained of feeling bloated. She was obsessed with the removal of body hair.

"Look at this." She rubbed her muscled calves. "I just shaved my legs this morning, and I already look like a gorilla."

Grace had been a modern dancer who had retired because of injuries caused by poor technique. "It's not like you can get the best training in Elmira, New York," she said. She appreciated my devotion to dance, and always found work for me, even when things were slow. "We dancers have to take care of each other," she said. "There's no sense in being competitive." I didn't point out that there was no competition between a black six-foot-tall modern-dancing transvestite and a five-foot-four Puerto Rican Indian temple dancer.

Grace had seen a notice in that morning's paper for a job she thought I could do. "It's as a production assistant in an advertising department. It's in Midtown, so it's near your dance classes and night school."

"I hate to answer want ads," I said. "The minute they hear my Spanish name, they tell me the job is filled."

Grace looked up from her desk, the only other piece of furniture in her one-room office other than her chair. Boxes lined two walls up to the ceiling. In the nearly two years I had worked for her, the boxes had never been moved or opened. Their content was a source of speculation for the Flyer Girls. My friend Shoshana, who had also worked for Grace between classes at Manhattan Community College, thought that the boxes were there when Grace rented the office and she had never bothered to open them.

"You're giving up before you even take a chance." Grace fluttered her false eyelashes and puckered her red lips.

"I'm not, it's just more comfortable to find work through an employment agency." The way she lowered her head and raised her eyebrows, the soft look that crossed her beautiful brown eyes let me know she didn't believe me, but wouldn't argue.

"I'll call for you," she said. "This *is* The Grace Agency, after all."

Without waiting for a response, she dialed the number on the ad. When she was connected, Grace made extravagant claims about my artistic sensibilities and capacity for work.

"She was on a job in Florida the past couple of months but she came right back to our firm. I'm sure you can appreciate that kind of loyalty." By the end of the conversation, I had an appointment with Margolis & Co.

"Just a formality," Grace said with a satisfied grin. "The job is yours."

Later that day, I spent twenty minutes in the offices of Margolis & Co. I was hired to start the following Monday, at a salary fifty cents per hour above minimum wage, with the promise of an increase and promotion within three months. I was ecstatic. An office job on Forty-second and Fifth with an advertising company was perfect. I offered Grace the fee an employment agency would charge, but she refused.

"Go on, honey. Do a good job so that I don't look bad. And don't you ever forget Grace."

⤳

Television and radio announcers bubbled with news of Ted Kennedy's accident on Chappaquiddick Island between reports of the progress of Apollo 11 on its lunar mission. Ulvi couldn't get enough of either. He sat naked on the bed surrounded by newspapers, the television turned on, the radio tuned to 1010 WINS at a low volume, the phone held against one ear as he made call after call in German, Turkish, or English. He read from the newspapers to whoever was at the other end of the line, or watched the TV screen and reported what he was seeing, or told them to hold on and turned up the radio when he heard the distinctive chimes of 1010 WINS' breaking news.

I could care less about Ted Kennedy's troubles, and was only mildly interested in the possibility that men could touch the moon.

"That is what the Kennedy family wants, Chiquita, that Americans will not pay so much attention."

"I'm not American."

Ulvi set aside the newspapers, turned down the TV and the radio, set the phone on the side table, interlaced his fingers as if he were holding something precious inside his palms. "Chiquita," he said softly and deliberately, "even if you don't like, you are American."

"I'm Puerto Rican."

"You are born American citizen. It is a good thing, Chiquita. You are very lucky. Many people in the world would like to be you."

"I doubt it."

"You think your life so bad?" he asked. "In Turkey many people so poor they cannot eat every day."

"In Brooklyn, too," I shot back.

"You have suffered hunger, Chiquita?"

"No, never," I resisted his embrace. "Food is one thing my mother made sure we always had."

"And you had clothes to wear?"

"Of course! She's a seamstress. Why are you asking this all of a sudden? You never cared before."

"I always care, Chiquita, that is why you are with me." I did not refuse his caress, folded into him as if he were a soft, warm pillow. "It does not matter if you are poor, but it is not good if you always behave like you are."

"How else am I supposed to behave?"

"Stop thinking about what you do not have and think on what you do have."

I had read the same advice in Dr. Norman Vincent Peale's books about positive thinking. It didn't work.

"You mean I should pretend to be rich?"

"Is that what you want, Chiquita, to be rich?" I burrowed deeper into his embrace. "You can be rich in your mind, even if you have nothing."

I'd read that somewhere too. "I would have never taken you for an optimist," I muttered.

"What means this?"

"An optimist is someone who always sees the bright side," I explained.

"That is not me. I only see dark days in my future," he laughed, which seemed like a strange reaction to such a depressing thought.

Margolis & Co. was at the end of a long dim hall studded with doors on the twenty-third floor of 11 West Forty-second Street, on the corner of Fifth Avenue. The company sold and scheduled the advertising for medical and scientific magazines too small to have their own ad department. They also distributed scholarly journals for scientific organizations.

I started work a few days before Neil Armstrong walked on the moon. The day after, Ulvi booked his trip to Europe. I had no intention of returning to Brooklyn, as he wished me to do, and ignored his dark looks and mutters that I was becoming "too independent."

Finding an apartment in Manhattan was impossible. I had no money for a security deposit and first month's rent, even if I could find an affordable place on my income. I refused to look in the boroughs, where I might have better luck. I visited several potential roommates, but none of them called me back. When I told Francine, Mr. Margolis's secretary, that I was having a problem finding a place to live, she suggested I check into the YWCA or the Barbizon, a residence hotel in the Upper East Side that catered to single, professional women. I could live there, she said, while I saved for my own place. It was a great solution.

Ulvi was adamant that it was a waste of money to pay for an apartment when he would be returning to the United States within a few weeks. He thought I should work, live at home, and save.

"I want you with me," he murmured in the tender moments that became more frequent as the date for his departure neared. "But I might not come back to New York. You must wait for me so that we can be together."

"I will wait," I promised, "and join you whenever and wherever you want me."

As he packed, as he pledged to return, as he swore he wanted to be with me and no one else, I began to believe in the romance of love thwarted by circumstance.

"You must wait for me, Chiquita," he repeated, "and be good girl."

"I will wait for you, don't worry."

There were no rooms available at the Barbizon, or at the YWCA, but in the Yellow Pages I found a listing for another women-only residence that was only six blocks from Margolis & Co. I thought it was a good omen that the Longacre Hotel had the same name as the theater where I had made my Broadway debut. I walked over on my lunch hour.

"This was built by the Astors around the turn of the century as a residence for nurses," Mrs. O'Dell, the manager of the Longacre, explained. "There are still a few elderly nurses living here." We entered the old-fashioned, noisy elevator. "No men are allowed above the ground floor," she said. "The front doors are locked at 11 p.m., so if you're out late, you must ring for the night guard."

We stopped at the end of a long hallway with a gleaming green-and-white vinyl tile floor, beige walls, and a high ceiling with dangling glass fixtures that cast yellow light. "This is the kitchen," Mrs. O'Dell said, opening a closet to reveal a sink and a four-burner electric stove. A fluorescent light buzzed and hissed when she turned it on. "You can cook, but we don't provide utensils. You can keep those, and your groceries, in your room." Further down the hall was the bathroom. Two deep tubs in their own enclosures and three shower stalls were pristine, and smelled of a recent scrubbing with Comet.

"The maids will make your bed, dust, and vacuum. But they will not pick up after you."

The room was on the southwestern-most corner of the seventh floor overlooking an alley, with a huge double-pane window facing west and, if I peeked around a couple of buildings, views to the Hudson River. It was furnished with a twin-size bed, a dresser, a leaf-green vinyl armchair, and a three-tier shelf. The huge walk-in closet had a mirror inside the door, and another hung above the dresser. The spinach-green carpet had been vacuumed so often, that it felt flat under my feet. While everything in it was worn and old, the room was spotless, with dust-free corners and glossy walls. It was in the back of the building, which meant relative quiet, even in the middle of the day. Its high ceilings made it feel spacious and open. The rent was twenty dollars a week, including local telephone service through a switchboard that was staffed twenty-four hours a day.

"I'll take it!"

Walking back to Margolis & Co. I was so happy that I couldn't wipe the grin from my face. Total strangers said hello or smiled, seemingly as thrilled with my new home as I was. I couldn't believe my good fortune. A job and a safe, clean place to live in Midtown were as close to perfect as I could imagine. That Ulvi would be leaving for Europe in a few days did not seem as big a deal any more. He would be returning in a couple of months, but in the meanwhile, I would be living in the middle of Manhattan.

Before returning to work, I ran into Brentano's and bought Helen Gurley Brown's *Sex and the Single Girl*. I didn't plan to be "a spoiled American girl," but it wouldn't hurt to know what that really meant.

On the Sunday he was to leave for Germany, Ulvi stepped out of a taxi and stood in front of the Longacre Hotel, unwilling to relinquish my suitcase. The weekend manager, Mr. Winslow, had just hosed down the sidewalk. He led us into the lobby, and told Ulvi that he would have to wait on a bench across from the switchboard–reception desk or in the waiting room at the back of the building. I took my suitcase and leather bag up to the shiny green-tiled hallway that led to the sunny, breezy room in the furthest corner of the seventh floor. I set my things down in the middle of the flat spinach-green carpet, bounced on the bed a few times, and raised the huge window to the muted roar of the city. To the left, fire escapes zigzagged down the walls of sand-colored brick buildings. To the right was the jagged two-dimensional sky-line and in the distance, the shimmering Hudson River.

I did not want to go down and say goodbye to Ulvi. I wanted to stay in the room and unpack my things, feel the space, lie on my bed, stare out the window at the pigeons flying in formation over the tarred roofs of Hell's Kitchen. But I could feel Ulvi seven stories below, waiting, with an opinion about the Longacre Hotel that I did not want to hear. I took my key, stood on the doorway looking in, and said to the part of me that remained inside, "I'll be back soon."

Ulvi was in the "visiting room," which was like walking into a Victorian time warp. It was ballroom size, carpeted and lushly furnished with thick-cushioned velvet-covered couches and easy chairs, side tables with fragile, curved legs, thick drapes, chandeliers. Ulvi was grinning. "Is very nice," he said, "like private club." I couldn't wait to get out of its oppressive fussiness.

"Is good place, Chiquita." Ulvi walked around, raising dust motes when he sat on the overstuffed chairs. "You did very good job to find."

We kissed, and I had the feeling that this room had seen countless scenes like the one we were enacting. Sweet caresses, promises, hugs, pledges to be true, alternated with looks deep into one another's eyes as if trying to memorize their color. For the first time since we'd met, I couldn't wait for him to be gone. I felt suspended between two worlds, one with him and one without him. I wanted desperately to see what it was like to be alone, unencumbered by family, by lover, by anything familiar except the streets outside the door.

I returned his kisses, his vows, his promises to write, to speak by phone frequently, to be together again in a couple of months. When he climbed into a taxi, I waved until the cab turned on Ninth Avenue. Instead of returning to my room, I walked east to Fifth, then north to Central Park. I felt lightheaded and unfettered. *Estoy sola*, I said aloud, I'm alone. *Sola*, alone, *sola*. I repeated the words to myself in wonder and terror, as if they were new, in English and Spanish, their syllables running into each other to form one word. Solalone. Solalone. *Sola*. Alone.

I want you together,
like the fingers on my hands.

My cousin Alma and I had been friends since soon after my arrival in the United States, but had grown apart when I began my relationship with Ulvi. Between work, dance, courses at Manhattan Community College, and Ulvi, I had little time for Alma.

"What is it like living alone?" she asked first thing when we met for dinner.

"It's the best! I'm ten minutes from my office and right in the middle of the theater district. I walk to dance classes. Do you remember my friend Allan?"

"From that children's show you did?"

"Yes." I was giddy with news and freedom. "He's in *Fiddler on the Roof.* He gets me house seats when the lead is sick and he plays the Scholar. Some nights I meet him backstage after the show and join the cast for dinner."

"Wow, that sounds like so much fun!" Alma said. "When is your husband coming back?"

The air flew out of me. "He's not my husband, he's my . . . I don't know what. We're not married."

"Are you going to marry him?"

"No. The only reason to marry him was to leave home, and I've already done that," I said, trying to sound worldly.

"That's not the only reason to get married!" she laughed.

"No, but Mami's *cantaleta* was that I could only leave home *de camino a la iglesia con velo y cola.*" Alma looked puzzled. "*Cantaleta* means her sermons, *velo y cola* means the veil and train of a wedding dress on the way to church. I never could understand that one, given that I haven't been to church in years. In any case, here I am. *No velo, no cola, no cantaletas.*"

"No husband," Alma sighed leaning back against the red plastic booth of La Crepe du Jour. I lowered my head so that she wouldn't see my eyes tear.

"Our mothers are so obsessed with us getting married," I said. "They still believe those fairy tales about princesses in rags rescued by princes on white horses. Let me tell you, those princes don't exist." I stabbed my salad.

Alma stopped picking the olives out of hers and smiled, her brown eyes dreamy. "I loved those stories. I thought they were real."

"But not now. You don't believe in them now, do you?"

"No," she said, defensively. "Do you?"

I thought a moment. Alma waited expectantly, and it felt right to tell her the truth. "Wow, this is so embarrassing!"

"Why?" she laughed.

"I just realized that I haven't entirely given up the idea that someday a prince will appear and say, 'Let me take you away from all this.'"

"But your husband . . . your boyfriend . . . whatever, did that for you." Alma seemed alarmed by my confession. "He took you to Florida, didn't he?"

"The Turk did take me away from all that." I waved in the general direction of Brooklyn. "But Florida isn't exactly fairyland. I would have preferred Paris."

We laughed and ate and enjoyed being together so much that we made a date for the following week. As I walked back to the Longacre, I wondered if Alma had the impression that I regretted leaving with Ulvi. It was true that he had freed me from my family, but I had never expected to miss them so much.

From the day we arrived in the United States, it had been easier for Mami's relatives to come to us than for us to go to them. Saturdays, we cleaned the apartment and prepared for visitors, with no idea how many would show up and how long they would stay. Sundays were filled with the sounds and smells of Tata and Mami cooking, while aunts, uncles, cousins, and friends gossiped, danced, ate, played card games and dominoes, or simply sat with us to watch horror movies or musicals on the black-and-white television set. The aunts brought shopping bags full of our cousins' outgrown clothes, or a beautiful bunch of green plantains so that Mami could fry crispy *tostones*, or a live rabbit for Tata to stew into her famous *fricasé de conejo*, or an extra six-pack so that she could make *arroz borracho*, her own recipe for yellow rice cooked with beer. The uncles and adult cousins brought samples of whatever they were making in the factories where they worked. Norma had a red leather schoolbag that I coveted, a gift from Mami's cousin Paco. His brother Jalisco gave me an Yves St. Laurent belt with a sterling silver clasp. Cousin Gury brought black satin bras that Mami thought were too racy for teenagers. I wore mine anyway.

By the time I left with Ulvi, we were eleven children living with Mami, Tata, Don Julio, and Don Carlos in the three-story house on Fulton Street. Within our walls, we were a tribe, with a chief (Mami), a *curandera* (Tata, who was constantly coming up with weird remedies to cure our illnesses), and a jester (the cheerful, passive Don Julio). Don Carlos was a visiting dignitary, treated with respect but not missed (by the villagers, at least) when not there. Seniority determined who showered first, who could stay up late, who had first turn with the iron in the morning, who didn't have to share a room or a bed if there was one to spare.

While I grumbled about the crowded rooms and Mami's over-protectiveness, now that I was not there anymore I realized that life at home had been fun. There was comfort in the number of people in each room and magic in the fact that no matter how many friends or relatives appeared at our door unannounced, there was always delicious Puerto Rican food to offer them, and strong, hot coffee. When we became old enough, Mami took us to clubs in the city, to dance to Tito Puente's timbales or Ray Baretto's congas. At home, we practiced salsa and merengue to the spinning 45s on the portable record player Don Carlos brought for us.

We were a family that touched. Mami knuckled us in painful, sharp *cocotazos*, or slapped us across the face or shoulders for a *falta de respeto* or other major infraction. More often, however, her fingers reached to tousle hair, to caress a cheek, to straighten an unbuttoned collar, to press a sweet slice of guava paste onto a salty slice of white cheese and place it inside our mouths. Her lips often tightened in anger, but they just as frequently puckered into a gentle kiss to a forehead. Tata would come up behind us and startle us with a bear hug and a sloppy kiss on the cheek. We snuggled in narrow beds and sagging couches, legs intertwined, our heads on familiar, comfortable shoulders. We sisters did each other's hair, plucked each other's eyebrows, painted one another's nails. An empty lap would soon hold a younger sibling, or the head of an older one stretched out next to us.

Besides my respect for Mami, and in spite of my desire to be independent and live my own life, it took me a long time to leave home because I felt secure there. I was temperamental and eccentric, but within my family, my behavior was accepted because "that's the way Negi is." I understood the rules, even when they made no sense. And I had in abundance what many people lacked. I was loved. I felt it in every morsel of food that went into my mouth from Tata or Mami's hand. I felt it in Don Julio's solid presence at the under-lit subway station on nights when I came home late. I heard it at least once every day of the week.

"*Ustedes se quieren mucho,*" Mami told us, defusing arguments by reminding us that we loved one another. We did love each other, took care of one another, and were loyal. We all cried at the inevitable bumps and stumbles of one, celebrated the achievements of another, sometimes in the same day. Mami, Tata, Don Julio, and even the elusive Don Carlos, constantly reminded us about the importance of family unity. As much as she struggled, Mami did not give any of us away, the Puerto Rican custom of letting friends or relatives informally adopt children whose parents were unable to provide for them.

We were close, proud of our work ethic and ambition, devoted to the concept of family and to the people in ours. As Mami dreamed of the households we would someday form on our own, she conceived of it as our husbands or wives joining our family, not of us joining theirs. My sisters' boyfriends came to our house on Sundays, sat on our couch. Héctor, who, following tradition should have been visiting his girlfriends in their homes, brought them to ours Sunday afternoons, where they did their best to impress with their domestic skills.

"*Yo los quiero a todos igual,*" Mami answered when we asked which one of us she loved the most. She loved us all the same. The second half of that often-repeated phrase was the one that kept me close to home. "*Y los quiero a todos juntos, como los dedos de mis manos.*" I want you together, like the fingers on my hands. Mami's ferocious struggles were meant to preserve her family. When I left with Ulvi, I not only disappointed her dreams of seeing me married *con velo y cola*, but I also broke from the embrace of family togetherness that she had fought so hard to maintain.

Aware of this, I made an effort to return to Fulton Street the first Sundays I lived at the Longacre, but something had changed.

No longer a member of the household, I was now a guest, and the rules of respect applied. I could not duck into a room to read a book, the way I did when I lived there, because then I wouldn't be visiting. I couldn't rummage through my sisters' wardrobe without asking. I could not accept money from Don Carlos or Don Julio, who dispensed change and singles if we did things we would have done anyway, like fetch a cold beer from the refrigerator or bring them their coat and hat from the hall closet.

I felt awkward sitting in the living room watching *lucha libre* or variety shows. I did not have much to add to the gossiping aunts and adult cousins around the kitchen table. I was embarrassed when they asked about "*tu marido,*" my husband, whom none of them had met. "He's in Europe" impressed them the first Sunday, but the longer he stayed there, the more disturbing it was that I was still in New York. I couldn't bear the pity in my relatives' eyes. My visits home dwindled to less than once a month, and even then, they were short.

Some Sundays I woke up in my room at the Longacre and cried from loneliness, remembering the gaiety of our family gatherings. My afternoons were spent along the parade route on Fifth Avenue, or at the Metropolitan Museum of Art, or wandering aimlessly around Midtown wishing I were home and that there were someone in my life to call me the familial, loving nickname, Negi.

Ulvi wrote two or three times a week. When I came in at the end of the day, Mrs. O'Dell handed me the onionskin airmail envelopes with his expansive, feminine handwriting with such joy that she might have been the recipient of his letters. Inside there was rarely more than one translucent sheet urging me to be patient, to save my money, to be a good girl, to believe in him. He always began the letters with "Dearest Chiquita," and always signed them "Love, Ulvi." I responded immediately with several pages describing my work, the wonders of New York, ending with promises to be faithful, always signed "Your Chiquita."

At Margolis & Co., I was Esmeralda, phone answerer and file cabinet arranger. When I complained to Francine that I had been hired as a production assistant, she turned over a stack of files and a procedure manual.

"If you have any questions," she said, "ask Ruth."

Ruth handled the advertising for the company's biggest clients. She was in her sixties, by far the oldest person in the office, which besides Mr. Margolis and Francine, included Mr. Charles, Vice President for Sales, his secretary, and three salesmen who spent most of their days away on calls. Mr. Margolis was in his late thirties, and Ruth often reminded him that she was "in the business" before he was born.

Ruth wore tailored skirt suits or dresses in dark colors, their necklines enhanced by a bright scarf or gold jewelry. A chestnut-colored wig combed and sprayed into immobile waves around her temples and high cheekbones had the barest suggestion of a flip just below her pearl earrings. Her face had creases in the expected places for a woman her age, but it was obvious that she had been beautiful and still had a chic, 1940s allure that I wished to duplicate. She could tell I admired her, and became my mentor before I even knew what the word meant.

"You have chutzpah, that's good, but you're too humble. That's not so good. You'll never get far if you don't know what you do well and let other people know it."

"But it sounds so conceited, to tell people you're good at this or that," I protested.

"It's not conceited if it's the truth," she said.

Ruth kept kosher, so she brought the food she would consume that day to the office inside a small picnic basket. She ate her lunch at her desk, in a corner of which she spread a white cloth and laid out color-coordinated Tupperware containers and a thermos. From a locked desk drawer she took out a pretty china plate, a matching bowl, cup and saucer, and embossed silverware. Once she laid

everything out, she bowed her head and said a prayer before starting her meal. After lunch she prayed again, then washed everything
in the ladies' room sink using a sponge she kept in a plastic bag and
dish soap from a Tupperware bottle. She dried them with the fresh
dishtowel she brought from home every day.

"It's important," she said as she packed the clean plastic containers into her basket, "to be civilized about meals. It's even more important to be grateful." She returned the china and silver to their
locked drawer. "You can tell a lot about a person by what they eat
and how they eat it."

Her elaborate rituals ensured that I would never eat in front of
Ruth. Since moving to the Longacre, my meals consisted of a slice
of pizza or Chinese takeout in my room, or I sat at the Automat
with a fork in one hand and a book in the other, so engrossed in
reading that I barely tasted the food.

Ruth's most frequent pronouncements had to do with the
relationship between men and women. She had been married to
the same man for forty years. Her eyes moistened and her voice
thickened when she talked about the late, beloved Morey.

"He was the best man who ever lived," she said, with uncharac-
teristic hyperbole. Morey had been a doctor, and according to
Ruth, had idolized her.

"I treated him like a king. I waited on him hand and foot. Even
when I worked, I had dinner on the table every night, and a pretty
gown on at bedtime." She smiled at the memory of herself in what
I imagined were Jean Harlow satins.

"I'm surprised you worked, I mean, if he was a doctor. . . . "

"He gave me whatever I wanted, but I didn't like to ask him for
money."

"I know what you mean."

"I was lucky with Morey, but I have friends stuck in terrible
marriages because they have no money of their own and no skills to
make any. There's nothing more pathetic."

"Wow, Ruth, I would never have thought you were a feminist."

"Bite your tongue! Don't believe any of this feminist stuff about men washing dishes or doing housework. A man has to be a man. Another thing," she added, "never let him see you with cold cream on your face or rollers in your hair."

Ruth and I had many talks like this in between our magazines' deadlines. We worked at adjacent desks in the rear of a room used for storing back issues. The front of the room was dark, lined with cubicles for the salesmen, but wall-to-wall windows overlooking Forty-first Street lighted our end.

One day, Ruth asked about my life, and I told her the abridged version I told everyone. "I was born in Puerto Rico, came to the United States when I was thirteen. I'm the eldest of eleven. No, my mother didn't have that many children because we're Catholic. Yes, she's heard about birth control, but doesn't believe in taking pills. No, I don't want to have lots of kids when I get married."

"Let me tell you something," Ruth offered. "Do like I did. Marry a man who loves you more than you love him. He'll always treat you right."

"How can you tell whether he loves you more than you love him?" I asked.

"Oh, you can tell," she chuckled. "Don't worry."

Next time I had dinner with Alma, I passed on Ruth's suggestion.

"I don't think you have any control over that," Alma said. "Why would he stay with you if you don't love him back?"

"I think she means you love him, but not as much as he loves you."

"That's cruel, Negi!"

"When you love somebody, you don't love him all the time," I said. "I mean, sometimes he does things that get on your nerves." I gave no examples like when he locks himself in the next room to make phone calls in a language you don't understand, or when he insists on choosing your clothes, or when he disappears to Europe for weeks on end and keeps writing to you to "be good girl." "Sometimes you wonder if you love him at all." She stared, waiting for me to say more. I squirmed. "You'll know what I mean when you fall in love."

"Who says I'm not in love now?" she asked, through tight lips.

Now it was my turn to stare. Alma's broad face was pale, like Mami's, and her hair, eyebrows, and lashes were thick and black. A constellation of tiny brown spots dotted her nose and round cheekbones. When she blushed, the freckles turned the color of wine, and her forehead and lips glowed pink.

"Who is it?" I whispered. As far as I knew, Alma had never had a boyfriend. When I was still a virgin and we discussed sex, she became uncomfortable and changed the subject. I thought she was prudish, and delighted in shocking her with pronouncements such as "If my virginity is so valuable, I should sell it to the highest bidder." Once I had sex, however, I stopped talking about it. "Who?" I pressed.

"I'll tell you some other time," Alma said. "I can't right now."

"Your boss? Are you sleeping with your boss at NBC?"

"Ugh! Why would I do that? I'd lose my job." She shuddered. "Don't even think about it!"

"Alright, alright, I was just wondering. In my office, according to Ruth, the two secretaries are sleeping with their bosses. I'm beginning to think it's a job requirement."

"Well, it's not," Alma waved at the waiter for our check.

"I'm sorry, I didn't mean to insult your profession."

She still seemed miffed, so I walked her to the subway. She dropped the token in the slot and pushed through the heavy wooden turnstile. "Did I tell you I'm moving to the Longacre?" she asked with a grin then took the steps down to the platform without waiting for my response.

"Do you believe
in reincarnation?"

Alma moved three doors from mine, into a room facing the yellow brick apartment building on Eighth Avenue. It was smaller than my room, but as sunny, with identical furniture.

"How did you ever convince Titi Ana to let you go?" I asked as I helped her drag a huge suitcase into the room.

"I talked to her," Alma said.

"It couldn't have been that easy."

"She didn't want me to leave like you did."

Heat rose from my feet to my scalp, where it lingered, as if my hair were on fire. "Is that the way it is with the family? Am I the example of how not to leave home?"

"I'm sorry, Negi. That didn't come out right. What I meant was . . . you know . . . "

"Yeah, I know," I said, ruffling my hair to let heat escape. What she meant was that we had talked incessantly about not repeating our mothers' lives, but I had prolonged the cycle of having nonmarital sex with a man who had already abandoned me.

"I'm doomed," I plopped on the green vinyl chair. "Condemned to the stereotype of the dark-skinned welfare Puerto Rican woman who sleeps around. All I need is a couple of naked babies and pink rollers in my hair."

"Geez, you're so dramatic! First of all, you're not that dark, you're not on welfare, and you're not sleeping around. Are you?" she asked to make sure.

"I wish!"

Alma blushed and turned away. "Come on, help me with this suitcase." We hefted it onto the bed and the locks unsnapped. "Good thing that didn't happen on the subway!"

The suitcase was bursting with folded skirts, Peter Pan–collared cotton blouses, and sweaters. Alma was plump (she called it big boned) and shapely, slightly taller than I was. She compared her figure to the sculpture of the Venus de Milo, with arms and fuller breasts. She didn't wear the sumptuous folds and drapes of a classical statue, however. She dressed like the mother in *The Adventures of Ozzie and Harriet,* in straight skirts, crisp blouses in pale colors, and cardigans buttoned at the waist. She thought it looked professional, I thought she looked prudish.

She sighed as if discouraged by the sight of so many skirts and blouses.

"I don't feel like unpacking now," she said. "Why don't you show me the neighborhood?"

We started in my room, where I picked up my purse. "Next door is Daisy Mae," I said. "I don't know the real name of any of the women here, so I've given them nicknames and a story," I explained. "Daisy Mae looks like an older version of the girl in *Lil' Abner,* blonde, busty, and bouncy. She wears her hair in pigtails. Next to her is Tex. She's bow legged, and has real short hair, like a man's. She wears jeans and cowboy boots. She and Daisy Mae spend all their time in one another's rooms."

"You made that up or it's real?"

"For real. They both have Southern accents and take turns cooking smelly stews that they share with other women in the building."

"Have you ever tasted any?"

"It's never been offered." When we came out of the Longacre, it was a cool and blustery October evening. "Let's go up Eighth," I said, turning in that direction. "You see those two black women with short skirts and long hair? They're Rayenne and Dayenne and they're both prostitutes."

"You've talked to them?" Alma was horrified.

"No, I made up their names," I smiled at the two women as we turned left on Eighth Avenue. Rayenne and Dayenne smiled back. "This is their corner. They live in the neighborhood I think. So do most of the other streetwalkers, but I've never seen any of them in daylight." The familiar faces of the women who walked this side of the street came in and out of the shadows of storefronts and the doorways of shabby apartment buildings. Alma couldn't believe I'd acknowledge their greetings.

"I didn't realize this was such a dangerous neighborhood," she muttered. "Aren't you worried that you will be mistaken for one of them?"

I laughed. "Alma, look at us! We look like nuns compared to them. They know we're no competition."

"But what if men approach you, thinking . . . "

"Just say you're not interested and keep walking." Alma was doubtful. "Once, this guy was bothering me," I said. "So Baby Face, that's her over there, ran over and told him to leave me alone." I smiled at Baby Face. "Last I saw them, they were heading in the opposite direction." Alma was torn between curiosity and avoiding the stares of the prostitutes. "Don't look so scared. There are undercover cops all over the place, too."

"That's not reassuring," she said, "if they're here and there are all these . . . criminals walking around."

"The cops only deal with rapes and murders," I said, "not misdemeanors." Alma looked on the verge of tears. "It's a joke!" She pretended to laugh.

We passed a storefront decorated with a beaded curtain and colored Christmas lights. "That's Cassandra's place." A gaudy sign on the door announced psychic and tarot card readings. "She's a gypsy, I think, or maybe Puerto Rican. She's not there now, but she usually sits by her door and harasses passersby to come in and hear their fortune."

"Have you ever gone in?"

"Are you kidding? The reason I call her Cassandra is that I can't imagine she'd give me anything but bad news."

"What if she has good things to say?"

"I don't want to be that well prepared. I'd rather be surprised by life."

We walked as far as the Holiday Inn on Fiftieth. I showed Alma the deli, the Chinese restaurant, the laundry, the coffee shop. We crossed the street and ended up at Michael's Pub, its wood floors sprinkled with sawdust, its walls plastered with photos of famous actors and musicians, its jukebox blaring the theme from *Hair*. "This is my favorite restaurant in the neighborhood," I said. "There are booths in the back. They make the best hamburgers and French fries." I led her to a booth in the middle of the virtually empty restaurant. "It's quiet here now. Tourists go to the flashier places down the street. But after the shows, actors and dancers come here to eat." Alma was impressed. As we sat, the jukebox song changed to Marilyn McCoo wailing about "Bill" in "Wedding Bell Blues."

Alma winced, and looked around as if someone were standing over her shoulder.

"Are you okay?" I asked.

"I'm fine. It's just . . . that song."

"Yes, the song is a little schmaltzy, but I love her voice," I said.

"I don't think it's schmaltzy," she argued.

She was upset. I thought the tour of our neighborhood had scared her. We listened to the song in silence, and her eyes misted. Then I remembered.

"Bill! His name is Bill, isn't it? The guy you're in love with . . . "

She blushed.

"Does he love you back?"

She winced. "I don't know."

Bill, Alma confided between sighs and sniffles, was a coworker at NBC. He was born in the United States of Japanese parents. They had met in the company cafeteria, had shared a couple of coffee breaks, had talked at length about art, literature, and the difficulties of juggling modern and traditional cultures.

"You have a lot in common," I said.

"We do. I don't know why he doesn't ask me out."

"Maybe you should ask him," I suggested.

Alma believed a man should take the initiative to ask her on a date, escort her to a nice restaurant, pay for the meal, and not expect a kiss at the end of the night. She had moved to the Longacre hoping that, if Bill asked her out, she could go without having to ask Titi Ana for permission.

"It's so nice to have somebody to talk to about this," Alma said, which made me feel included in her life.

The loneliness that gripped me every Sunday when I didn't visit my family was relieved with Alma's move to the Longacre. We had dinner together almost every night. On our days off, we went to museums, galleries, or the movies. After the first companionable month, however, Alma had other things to do. Sometimes a week went by and we hadn't seen each other, even when I passed her door to and from the elevator or the bathroom at least ten times daily.

It had been two months since Ulvi had left, eight weeks of letters begging me to "be good girl," be patient, trust him. "I am doing best I can," he wrote, "so we can be together again." What it was that he was doing he didn't say, and I didn't ask. My letters to him in Stuttgart were addressed care of Irmgard Bauer, the Irmchen he called every afternoon from Florida. He was living with her, I thought, his "good friend." I pictured her as older than him, stately, elegant, and rich. The wife, perhaps, of a German diplomat. I tried to feel jealous, but couldn't. If she were his mistress, there was no way I could compete with her on any level except for my youth and "innocence." "Give my regards to Irmchen," I wrote in one letter, and he wrote back the same words he had said when I asked about her. "Do not concern yourself, Chiquita," his way of telling me to mind my own business.

⤜

As soon as I could afford it, I began dancing again. I alternated between private Indian dance lessons and group classes at the International School of Dance, near Carnegie Hall. Leaving ISD one day, I noticed a woman with the turnout of a ballerina, a dance bag slung over her shoulder, walking ahead of me. A few minutes later, I was surprised to see her enter the Longacre Hotel. I caught up with her just before the elevator door closed.

"Hi," she said, "I'm Jacqueline. I've seen you at the ISD, and your tights and leotards hung out to dry in the bathroom."

She was extremely thin, pale, ghostly almost, with black hair pulled into a tight chignon. It was hard to tell how old she was. She had the huge doe eyes of a little girl, but her thin lips were those of an older woman, with fine wrinkles along the corners. She wore full makeup, including false eyelashes, as if she had just completed a performance. She invited me in for tea.

Her room was on my floor, but facing Forty-fifth Street. Every wall was covered with images of famous ballerinas captured in flight or in graceful arabesque positions. Old pointe shoes hung by frayed pink ribbons from the ceiling. On a shelf under the window, there was an electric teakettle, a set of china dishes for two, a collection of teas, International Coffees instant mixes, and cookies in a glass jar. As we entered, Jacqueline unwrapped the silk scarf she wore around her neck and draped it over the bottles of prescription drugs on the nightstand. A folding rack by the radiator held her washed dancewear.

"So, you're a ballerina," I said, sounding stupid even to myself.

"Trying to, anyway," she smiled.

"Well, you look like a ballerina to me," I said, and she stood straighter.

Jacqueline had begun ballet as soon as she could stand, she said. "My mother was a dancer," she explained, "but then she married my dad and moved to Skowhegan . . . "

"Maine?"

"Yes, do you know it?"

"I was there, or near it, on tour with a children's theater company a couple of years ago. I don't remember much about the town, but I'll never forget its name."

"It's not much of a town, I can tell you that," she laughed.

Jacqueline had been at the Longacre for over a year, on a lower floor, but had recently moved up.

"It's cheap, so I can spend my money on classes. It's been my lifelong dream," she said, "to perform Balanchine choreography on a New York stage."

Jacqueline spoke with assurance about her training, and about how much she'd learned since coming to New York. I listened but knew that, in spite of the chignon, doe eyes, and turned-out posture, she didn't look like a Balanchine ballerina. To begin with, the longer I sat with her, the older she looked, as if she were aging before my eyes. Her slight body did not have the vigor of a healthy ballerina. Her limbs lacked the soft curves and depressions of a dancer's musculature. They protruded from her square torso with the knobby straightness of branches on a bare tree. The more we talked, about good technique versus bad, Nureyev's genius, and Margot Fonteyn's longevity, the more certain I was that there was something wrong with Jacqueline.

I told Ruth about my tea with her. "It was so weird," I said, "I felt like the narrator in *Sunset Boulevard*. But Jacqueline hasn't had a career, like Norma Desmond did."

"*Meshugenah*," Ruth concluded.

"I suppose she could be crazy, but I'm fascinated by . . . I don't know . . . her passion for dance, I guess. She has devoted herself to something that will probably never happen. I wonder if she has any doubts. If it has ever occurred to her that she's too old, too short, too skinny, and too dark-haired to be the next Suzanne Farrell."

"Don't make a big deal about it. Maybe she is the next great ballerina."

"No, Ruth, there's no chance of that, believe me."

"How do you know?"

"I've seen Suzanne Farrell dance. From the balcony, granted, but still. I don't have to see Jacqueline dance to assure you that she has no chance of ever getting on the same stage."

"Should she stop thinking she can, just because it will never happen?" Ruth asked.

"It's a waste of time, isn't it? She could be . . . I don't know, painting, or . . . or writing a poem or something more productive."

"Let me tell you something, *bubuleh*," Ruth said. "Productive is overrated. Let the girl think she can be the next Anna Pavlova if she wants. What harm is it doing anybody?"

I didn't see Jacqueline again for a couple of weeks. One Saturday after dance classes, as I came out of a steamy bath, there was Jacqueline, emerging from the shower. With no makeup on, I hardly recognized her. The translucency of her skin was gone. It was yellow, like the whites of her eyes, which looked naked without false lashes. Her hair was wet, matted against her skull, but even so, I could see bald spots in the back of her head. When she saw me, a pained look crossed her face. I said hello and disappeared into my room as quickly as I could, feeling as if I had invaded her privacy by seeing her face bare of makeup.

As I dressed, an image came to mind so vivid, that I had to sit on the bed and rub my eyes for it to go away—Francisco, Mami's love, in his last days, skeletal and frail, his eyes so large and feverish that they seemed to take over his face. I sobbed so violently that the bed shook. It had been nearly six years since his death, and I had grieved then, but never alone, where no one could see me.

As I cried for Francisco, other faces materialized. Papi. Avery Lee, a Texan I had dated, who said he could only be with me if I was his mistress because marrying a "Spanish girl" would ruin his political future. Neftalí, the neighbor I'd liked, who had killed himself rather than admit to his mother that he was a heroin addict. Jürgen, the larcenous pilot. One by one, I recalled and mourned them, as if I had stored every tear I hadn't shed for every man who had been in my life and had disappeared from it. They were one, every man I had loved, however minimal the affection. Their memory echoed into my consciousness as if I had taken a drug to force remembrance.

But I didn't love Jürgen, I told myself. Yes, you did, my own voice echoed, but he scared you. I didn't love Avery Lee. Yes, you loved him, the echo repeated, but he disdained you. I don't love Ulvi, I whispered, and cried so hard that I didn't hear why I would deny it.

Jacqueline knocked on my door. She was fully made up and wore a colorful silk scarf around her head. "Would you like some tea?" she asked. I followed her to her room. She must have been certain I would join her, because everything was set as if she had been expecting me. "I knocked earlier," she said as she poured hot water over a pouch of dry chamomile flowers. "But I heard you crying . . ."

"I . . . I remembered something sad," I said.

"That happens to me too." She served me shortbread cookies on a dish decorated with purple pansies. "Sometimes I can't keep from crying. But then I remember how lucky I am to be alive, and I'm happy again."

I distrusted that kind of optimism. I never told myself it was wonderful to be alive for fear that the minute I did, something horrible would happen to change my mind.

"I would never have guessed you were superstitious," Jacqueline laughed when I told her.

"I'm not. That's what my life is like, always waiting for the other shoe to drop." As if on cue, a pair of the toe shoes dangling from the ceiling thudded to the floor, barely missing my head. We laughed so hard that I soon forgot the tears of the previous hours.

"Would you like to know why I get sad?" she asked after a pause. Her eyes fixed on the bottom of her teacup, as if the information were stored there. "I was engaged to my high school sweetheart," she said without waiting for me to say I wanted to know. "When I was diagnosed with ovarian cancer he left town without even saying goodbye. His mother came to the hospital and said she hoped I understood. He just couldn't handle watching me die."

"I'm sorry." Now I recognized her skeletal look, why she had reminded me of Francisco.

"I didn't mean to depress you again," she said. "It's just that, I feel as if we've been friends for ages. Do you believe in reincarnation?"

Uh-oh, I said to myself. "I'm not sure," I answered.

"I do," Jacqueline said vehemently. She explained that she was raised a Catholic but had been studying other forms of spirituality. "Soon after my diagnosis, a friend gave me books about Buddhism. According to my doctors, I should be dead by now. Do you know why I'm still alive?"

I shook my head.

"Because I'm still working on the lesson for this lifetime. When I realized that, I decided to come to New York and dance."

"The lesson was that you should study ballet?"

She laughed. "You don't learn the lesson until you die."

"What good does it do you then?"

"It guides you in your next incarnation."

"So in your next life you're going to be a prima ballerina."

She winced. "It's not about being something. It's about being alive every moment. What makes me feel alive is dance. That's why I do it. You must know what I'm talking about, don't you?"

"I do, yes, of course I do," I said, to stop her from saying more. Jacqueline spoke with the passion of the proselytizers who showed up at our apartments in Brooklyn on Saturday afternoons carrying *The Watchtower*, peering over our shoulders to catch a glimpse of our sinful lives. She had the wild eyes of the bald, saffron-robed Hare Krishnas, who banged drums, clanged bells, and chanted the same tune endlessly as they tried to sell wilted daisies. Her admission that she was dying was less unnerving than the possibility of being trapped in her room listening to her views on the hereafter.

"I've read a little about Buddhism, Hinduism, and Islam, because of the style of dance that I do," I said, hoping to avoid a lecture.

"Then you know that our meeting was no coincidence, that we have a lesson for each other," she said, touching my hand. Her fingers felt dry and cool.

"Uh-uh," I bit into a cookie to avoid a metaphysical argument.

Religious discussions made me uncomfortable. People always assumed that Puerto Ricans were Catholic, or at least, religious. I was neither, and teetered on the verge of atheism, but wasn't brave enough to reject God altogether. What I had to say about my religious beliefs was summed up in a Laura Nyro song made popular by Blood, Sweat, and Tears. I swore there was no heaven, but prayed there was no hell.

Later, in my room, I cried some more, for Jacqueline this time. I couldn't begin to imagine what her life must be like, knowing that every second was a gift beyond what she could have expected. It must have been a comfort to envision another life guided by the lessons of this one. But I wondered if those lessons were clear, if they came in a flash of insight, or if, like me, you stumbled through your day hoping to pick up signals and clues about greater meaning.

I admired that Jacqueline had taken what was left of her life and devoted it to art. What greater use for it could there be? My productive days, with their clerical duties and predictable salary, seemed wasteful by comparison. I didn't "feel alive" when measuring column inches for an ad in *Microbiology News*. I did when, as Jacqueline had suggested, I practiced combinations and mudras, when every muscle in my body stretched and pulsed, when I entered the trancelike concentration required to perform the intricate story-dances of Bharata Natyam.

And then there was sex. I felt completely alive then, but, unlike the dance lessons and practices, I didn't pursue it, true to the promise I had made Ulvi to wait for him and "be good girl."

That didn't mean I didn't miss it. I longed to be touched, held, kissed, and caressed. I was lonely not just for human contact, but also for male attention. But whenever a man made an overture, tried to talk to me on the street or approached me as I sat engrossed in a book at a coffee shop or at the public library, I rebuffed him as swiftly as if he smelled rotten. One of the young salesmen at work was interested in me, but I let him know that I had a boyfriend, and didn't encourage his flirting and innuendos. I didn't trust myself enough to pursue dating when what I wanted was something else.

I had an active social life, however. I went to the ballet with dancers from ISD, and to the theater with actor friends, but they could hardly be considered dates, since most of them were homosexual. Chaste kisses on the cheek, hand holding, and tight, friendly embraces, were the extent of our physical intimacy.

Alma, on the other hand, was making progress with Bill. He had finally asked her out and, after a few dates, they considered themselves a couple. They were even discussing marriage.

"That's wonderful!" I said when she told me.

"Yes," she said sadly, "but his family doesn't like me."

"Oy vey!"

Bill's parents did not want him dating, let alone marrying, Alma.

"Even before they met me they gave him a hard time," she explained, "because they thought I was black. He said if they saw me, they would change their minds. He brought me home and they were polite. But they forbid him to see me because I'm Puerto Rican." She looked up. "I can't change who I am!"

"How old is this guy?" I asked.

"He's my age, but his parents are traditional. He has to honor and respect them or they will disown him."

"Is he rich?"

"No."

"Then why should he care if they disown him? If there's nothing there, I mean."

"That's not the point, Negi!" she blew her nose. "He would never be able to see them again. He would have to choose between me and them."

Alma's situation was as romantic as a poem—true love frustrated by disapproving parents. A Japanese–Puerto Rican Romeo and Juliet.

"He will choose you," I said, reassuringly, "don't worry."

"I don't want him to choose me if it means he has to give up his family," she said. "That's not a good way to start a marriage."

I had to respect the way Alma was handling it. She was working toward a future with Bill, trying to organize her life into an orderly pattern over the course of years. She was being considerate of him and of his family. She was being unselfish. Other than moving to the Longacre Hotel, she was doing things the way a *nena puertorriqueña decente* did them, keeping foremost the wishes of parents. It made my handling of my own life seem haphazard and reactive.

When I told Ruth about Alma's dilemma, hoping she would give me advice I could pass on, she said, "If it's not meant to be, it's not meant to be."

"But what about true love overcoming difficulties?"

"That's foolishness."

"But you and Morey . . . "

"That was different," she said, but didn't elaborate.

I went home for the Christmas holidays dragging shopping bags full of presents to put under the tree. Ulvi's letters urged me to save, but I had never made as much money as I was now earning, and I loved buying toys for the younger kids, leather cases with manicure kits for the older girls, china figurines for Mami and Tata. The tables were heavy with the traditional food of the season, including the time-consuming *pasteles* made by Mami and Tata. I spent Christmas and New Year eating, drinking sweet, rum-laced *coquito*, dancing with my sisters and brothers and the aunts, uncles, and cousins who banged on the door and sang *aguinaldos* as they shimmied down the hall, their arms laden with food and presents.

We hugged, kissed, danced, made noise, and welcomed 1970 with such euphoria that I should have known things would never be the same. I was so happy in the midst of my family that I never imagined this was the last Christmas I would spend with Mami, Tata, Don Julio, Don Carlos, and my ten sisters and brothers together in one room. In the noise and laughter of our celebration, I didn't hear the other shoe drop.

"You Puerto Ricans are so romantic."

Ulvi called every other week, each time postponing his return. "It is more difficult than I thought, Chiquita," he said, "I am working hard. You must be patient."

"But it's been four months," I reminded him right after the New Year.

"It is not long time," he said. "We will be together. Don't worry."

He would not be writing for a while because he was "doing some business" in the Middle East.

"What kind of business?" I asked.

"Do not concern yourself," he said.

Four months felt like a long time to me. I did not mind being alone, solitude was something I had craved my whole life. It was the waiting that drove me nuts, the inability to make plans because Ulvi might, at any moment, ask me to join him somewhere. Every time he called, there was a new scheme, another "business" that could "make everything possible."

The first few weeks he was in Germany, there was a chance I could join him there, but then he called in a panic to say "things have changed" and it wouldn't work out after all. Then he might go to Hollywood where his friend, producer Sidney Solow, had again offered his guest house if Ulvi wanted to try to get work in films there. Once more, the plans didn't go as he wanted. He was looking into other opportunities, he said, but I stopped asking about them. Nothing ever seemed to work the way he intended.

"He's stringing you along," said Ruth. "A pretty girl like you should be dating and having fun."

"I have a lot of fun," I protested.

Ruth arched an eyebrow and resumed her work without a word.

I had only recently begun confiding in her about Ulvi. It was a mistake because Ruth was on a lifelong boycott of everything German, and disliked Ulvi the minute she learned he lived in Stuttgart. "What do you want with a man as old as your mother?" she asked. "Is that what you see in him, a substitute father?"

"Don't Freud me, Ruth," I said.

"I've been around the block a few times," she continued, "and an older man only wants one thing with a young girl like you."

"So it's not just Puerto Ricans who believe that," I answered.

"Men are the same everywhere," she said. "Nothing but *tsuris*."

"But how about Morey?" I asked.

"He was the exception," she said.

"I wonder if men talk about women the way we talk about them," I muttered after a while. "Do they think we're all trouble?"

"Probably," Ruth said.

Newspapers and magazines reported a new vision for women, a feminist ideal in which more than the men in them defined our lives, but I didn't know how to do that. Neither did Rayenne, Dayenne, Baby Face, Ruth, Alma, or Mami. The only woman I knew whose life did not seem to revolve around men was Jacqueline. After telling me that she'd been jilted by her high school sweetheart she never mentioned him again; I figured that someone with terminal cancer had bigger things to worry about.

Jacqueline disappeared for days at a time and when I asked her where she went, she said "for treatments." She didn't like to talk about her illness, she said, because she wanted to stay positive. I couldn't imagine how she could stay positive knowing that she was going to die.

"But we're all going to die," she said, which made perfect sense.

Still, I didn't like to think about it. Not enough of an optimist to think life was wonderful, I was also not such a pessimist to think death was imminent.

At the end of January, Ruth went into closed-door meetings with Mr. Margolis and emerged bristling.

"Who does he think he is?" she muttered. I wasn't sure if she was talking to me or to herself. She didn't say what the meeting was about, and I didn't press. A few days later Mr. Margolis called me into his office.

"How are you getting along with Ruth?" he asked.

"She's great," I answered. "She's taught me a lot. The clients love her, and she's fun to work with."

He seemed relieved. Francine gave me a big smile when I walked out, leading me to believe that she had heard the discussion with the boss through the closed door.

The phone on my desk was ringing when I came back. It was Mami.

"The German called," she sounded scared.

"Ulvi is Turkish," I corrected her. "He only lives in Germany."

"No, no *el turco ese*," she said. "The other one. Jergen's."

"The hand lotion?"

"Jergen's, Jergen's," she repeated, as if I were deaf. She was speaking louder, too. "The one you were going to marry."

"Jürgen?"

"*¡Ese mismo!*" she said. "He called. He's in jail! *Ay Dios mío*, Negi, what could this mean? He asked for your number, but I didn't give it to him."

"He's in jail?"

Ruth looked up from her desk. I turned around and cupped my hand over the mouthpiece. Mami was nervous, insisting that I come to Brooklyn immediately. Little by little, I dragged out of her that Jürgen had called to say he still loved me and wanted to marry me.

"He must be *loco* to call collect from jail to propose marriage."

"He called collect?"

"You'd better come here," Mami said. "*Por si llama otra vez.*"

"No, Mami," I said. "If he calls again, don't accept the charges, that's all."

"Why is he in jail?"

"I don't know! I haven't seen him in over a year."

"*¡Ay, gracias a Dios!* I thought you were with him again, now that *el turco ese* is away."

"No, Mami, I'm not with him or any other man. The Turk will be back soon," I hung up, and didn't know whether to laugh or cry.

When I turned around, Ruth was staring at me.

"What's going on?"

I was laughing, but there were tears in my eyes. "An old boyfriend called my mother collect from jail wanting to marry me."

Ruth's eyes widened. "Never a dull moment with you, is there?"

"I wasn't willing to marry him before, why would I want to marry him now?"

"You Puerto Ricans are so romantic," she chuckled. "He probably thinks you'll be impressed."

"He's not Puerto Rican," I said tersely, "he's German, might even be Jewish, for all I know," I added and returned to my work.

"Forgive me. I didn't mean it the way it sounded," Ruth said.

"It's okay." I was annoyed. What I wanted to say was "Why is it that people never mean it the way they say it? Why do they wait until they've said it before they realize they didn't mean it?"

It was Friday and Ruth left early as usual, for the Sabbath. I still had work to finish, but found it hard to concentrate. My lively imagination was a curse. It relived conversations in which I was wittier, braver, more composed than I actually was. It concocted implausible scenarios in which I played improbably heroic roles.

There was no way Jürgen could know where I now worked or lived, but I was afraid to walk out the door of 11 West Forty-second Street, envisioning him in prison stripes, holding a ball and chain, waiting in the lobby. I left by a side door barely in time to meet Alma for dinner. She was full of plans for the following Saturday's Valentine's Day. She thought Bill was ready to propose. I didn't tell her about Jürgen and the possibility that he had stolen one too many airplanes.

On Sunday, I went to Brooklyn. Mami was still rattled by Jürgen's phone call, and I once more assured her that if she didn't accept another collect call, he wouldn't bother her. She said she would change her phone number if men were calling me from jail.

"This is the only man who has ever called me from jail."

She ignored my protest. "You never know with those people. They talk to each other."

I left early, because I didn't want to get into an argument about who "those people" might be and what they might be saying about me.

Jacqueline had taped a note to my door wondering if I were free for dinner. In the months we'd known each other I had been to dance performances and recitals with her, but had never seen Jacqueline eat anything but the cookies she served with tea. It was a mild evening and we walked to the Carnegie Deli because, she said, she was craving "a real New York–style pastrami sandwich." When it was placed before her, Jacqueline inhaled deeply.

"Aaah," she sighed, "it smells so good!" In her bony fingers, the half of the sandwich she picked up looked incongruous, too big for her hands. She could barely get her teeth around it, but she took a small bite and chewed thoroughly, as if to liquefy the morsel. "Oh, this is so yummy!" she exclaimed with such enthusiasm that other diners turned around to see what she had ordered. She blushed and wiped her lips. "I haven't had one of these in so long," she said. "It's so delicious!" Her skin flush, her eyes bright, Jacqueline looked more animated than I had ever seen her. We ate mostly in silence. I wanted to plan dates for the upcoming Joffrey Ballet season, but couldn't bring myself to interrupt her extravagant enjoyment.

After the pastrami sandwich, she ordered a slice of cheesecake with cherry topping. This, too, she consumed with such delight that I ordered a slice for myself even though I was full to bursting with the mushroom and cheese omelet I had ordered. When we came out of the restaurant, the evening had cooled. A soft snow flurried from the tops of buildings, danced around the street-lights.

"It is so beautiful!" she exclaimed. She skipped ahead of me and, humming from *The Nutcracker*, danced a few steps from "The Dance of the Snowflakes." Passersby applauded, and she dipped into the full prima ballerina bow. We walked arm in arm to Times Square, letting snowflakes melt into our hair, talking about how much we loved Midtown, how energetic and lively it always was, how its seediness was part of its charm. Neither of us could understand why we didn't feel threatened in a neighborhood most people avoided. We waved at Rayenne and Dayenne as we passed them, shivering, on our corner. "Hi, girls," they called, the first time I'd heard them speak.

As we parted in front of the elevator on our floor, Jacqueline kissed my cheek. "That was so much fun," she said. "Thank you." She hugged me. "I'm so happy, I could dance all night," she said. She leaped gracefully down the hall. When she reached the end, she pirouetted and bowed. I applauded. She disappeared around the corner.

My phone was ringing.

"Jergen's called again," Mami said. "He didn't call collect this time. He wanted your number, but we told him you were married and moved away. That way he won't bother you any more."

"That was good, Mami. Thank you."

A few minutes later, the phone rang again. It was Ulvi, calling from Riyadh. We didn't talk long because the call was expensive, but he wanted to tell me things were going well and we would soon be together.

"Tomorrow I meet with a couple of princes," he said. "Some day you will come here with me, Chiquita," he added. "All the womens wear veils. It is beautiful."

After we said goodbye I imagined myself dressed like the Hollywood version of Scheherazade in sequined harem pants, wrapped in jewel-colored chiffon veils, my fingers ringed with precious stones.

At the Longacre, we had an ancient telephone system, even by 1970 standards. The desk clerk, who during weekdays was Mrs. O'Dell, directed calls in or out through a switchboard, and stayed on the line until there was a connection. When Mrs. O'Dell was on duty, I kept my conversations short because I often heard clicks and snaps that were not there at night or on weekends.

As I was leaving for work Monday morning, my phone rang. It was Mami, hysterical.

"Negi, the FBI just called here looking for you."

"What?!"

"I had to give them your number! They're probably calling about Jergen's. I knew that man would bring you problems."

"Calm down, Mami. Everything should be okay, I haven't seen him in ages. They're probably calling because he called me."

"I'm disconnecting the phone today," she said.

As soon as I hung up, the phone rang again.

"My dear," Mrs. O'Dell whispered excitedly, "there is a call for you. He says he is from the FBI. Should I put him through?"

"Yes, Mrs. O'Dell," I said, trying to sound as if this happened every day of the week.

The man identified himself as Agent Carson, and he wanted to talk "about a certain Jürgen Müller, who tried to contact you a couple of days ago."

Click, snap, click.

I suggested we meet during my lunch hour in front of the New York Public Library side entrance on Forty-second Street. When I hung up, my teeth were chattering and my fingers felt numb. When the elevator delivered me to the lobby, Mrs. O'Dell leaned over the reception desk to watch me go, her eyes behind their big glasses nearly popping out of her head.

The hours until my lunch break were excruciating. Every time I looked at the industrial clock on the wall, only five minutes had elapsed from the last time I checked. Ruth saw that I was antsy and wondered what was wrong, but I brushed her off and shuffled papers from one end of my desk to the other as if I were doing something remotely like work. I left five minutes early for the walk across the street.

It was a bright, mild day. The snow flurries of the previous night had melted and puddled in the gutters. A tall man was waiting on the steps of the library, watching me cross the street. I had to catch my breath because other than the way he dressed, he looked like Jürgen, with the same shade of blonde hair, green eyes, and chiseled features. He had a crew cut, and was dressed like one of the cops in *The Naked City*, with dark suit and tie, a starched white shirt, clunky black shoes, a dark overcoat with wide lapels. He showed me his badge and I panicked.

"Am I in trouble?" I asked.

His face did not change its neutral expression. "I just have a few questions."

I was shivering, so we went inside and sat at a corner table in the Reading Room.

"Did Jürgen Müller call you last Friday?" he asked.

"He called my mother's house. I don't live there anymore. But I guess you know that," I smiled. He didn't smile back.

"Has he tried to contact you since then?"

"He called again last night," I said. "She didn't tell him how to reach me."

"Does she know where he was calling from?"

"The first time he called collect from jail, which freaked her out." Agent Carson nodded. "The collect part didn't scare her," I amended. "We've never been called from jail before," I added so he would know we were law-abiding Puerto Ricans. "She told him I was married and had moved away. She was scared and wanted to get rid of him."

"Did you know him by any other name?"

"You mean an alias?" I asked.

Agent Carson didn't like being corrected by me. "Yes, an alias."

"No."

"You're certain you have not spoken to him the past few days?"

I glared at him, unsure why I had gone from scared to hostile.

"Jürgen Müller escaped from a federal penitentiary on Friday night," Agent Carson said after a moment, and I nearly fell off my chair.

"Oh, my God! He's been to our house. Why was he looking for me? Do I need police protection?"

"We were wondering why he was looking for you, too," he said.

"I probably know too much," I suggested, and Agent Carson's left cheek flinched. "We were engaged, but I broke it off. I haven't seen him since the summer of 1968. August," I added because I thought he needed specifics.

Agent Carson asked, and I answered truthfully, telling him everything I knew about Jürgen. He was from Hamburg, his parents still lived there. He was a pilot, and the last time we talked, he said he had a job piloting the private jet of an Egyptian sheik from Alexandria.

Agent Carson took notes in a small official-looking spiral-bound book. I waited until he stopped writing. "He told me that he stole planes and sold them in South America and the Middle East. I didn't believe him at first," I explained. "It sounded so far-fetched. Is that why he's . . . was . . . in jail?"

He ignored my question. "Did he say anything about cars?"

"On our first date we test-drove a Porsche, and then every time we went out, he had a different sports car, but it never occurred to me they could be stolen. I feel so dumb." I also felt relieved. I had never told anyone about Jürgen's criminal past.

"Where did he say he got the cars?"

"I never asked. I didn't want to know, I guess." It was embarrassing to look at stalwart Agent Carson with his crew cut and tightly knotted tie.

"When was the last time you talked to him?"

I explained that I had broken off the engagement over the phone, while Jürgen was in Los Angeles. Agent Carson prodded me, and I told him about Donny, the Irish bartender at whose apartment Jürgen stayed, about Donny's girlfriend in Long Island, about Flip, their friend who met us at Jones Beach after driving across the country in a Jaguar. "Was it stolen, too?" I asked, and Agent Carson looked away.

"Do you have any idea where he might be?" he asked.

"No."

He pulled a business card from his pocket and pushed it across the gleaming table. "Call me if he tries to contact you again, will you?"

I felt the embossed black letters on the pristine white card. On the left corner was the gold logo of the FBI. "Can I ask you something?"

"I can't give you any information that is part of our investigation."

"No, I don't expect you to do that, of course not. I just . . . want to know why he was in jail . . . and . . . and where. Should I be worried that he will come to my mother's house? He was not violent, not with me . . . I've never been in trouble with the police. She disconnected her phone . . ." I clamped my mouth shut to stop the blathering.

"He might try to get in touch with you again. Let us know if he does."

"He proposed after knowing me a few hours. I could never understand that. . . . Does this mean he really loved me? I mean, I never believed . . . He said he wasn't impulsive . . . "

Agent Carson straightened his tie, looked around the hushed room, put his hands on the table and examined them. "You're a charming girl," he said, "he probably fell in love at first sight." He spoke as if each word cost him money.

"You didn't have to say that." Now it was my turn to examine my hands. "I wasn't looking for a compliment."

"He called you because he wanted you with him. If he contacts you again, call me."

I didn't answer, dizzy with the thought that there were two men, on opposite sides of the law, vying for my attention.

"Is there anything else?" Agent Carson broke my reverie.

I had many questions, but didn't trust him to tell me the truth. We shook hands and I waited until he walked out the broad doors. I felt watched, as if every dusty scholar in the Reading Room, every myopic researcher, every librarian were an FBI agent studying my every move.

I made my way to the periodicals and looked for that weekend's *New York Times*. The jailbreak was not front-page news. Buried in the Sunday paper was the story of nine men who had escaped from the Federal House of Detention on Friday evening, hours after Jürgen's first call. According to the paper, Jürgen was Austrian, not German, so the story of him being from Hamburg was humbug. Jürgen was one of his aliases. He was in jail for illegal entry into the United States, and was being held pending a hearing.

I read the story several times, but it always yielded the same sketchy information. I wondered if Agent Carson knew about Jürgen's other illegal activities before I, in my panic and desire to be a good citizen, denounced him by giving more information than was required. I felt guilty for having betrayed Jürgen, whom Agent Carson himself had said loved me, and hoped that he wouldn't be caught. I crumpled the FBI agent's card and threw it in the trashcan in front of 11 West Forty-second Street. If Jürgen called, the only way I could make up for my disloyalty was not to turn him in. Let them find him.

I kept an eye on the papers for the rest of the week, looking for news of Jürgen's capture. The last report about the prison break came the following Saturday, Valentine's Day. Three men, described as bank robbers, were found shivering in the back of a refrigerated truck full of beef that had been hijacked a couple of days earlier. They had shaved their heads to change their appearance. None of them was Jürgen. For weeks after I expected a phone call, a summons to testify at a trial, something. But it never came.

⟿

When I returned from dance class later that Saturday afternoon, I had received a postcard from Ulvi, who was in Ceylon. "It is beautiful country," he wrote. "Some day we will see it together. I wanted you here with me. Love, Ulvi." The card was postmarked weeks earlier, when I thought he was in the Middle East.

Upstairs, I found a bouquet of pale pink roses at my door with a card attached. "Happy Valentine's Day," it said. "I didn't want to say goodbye, because I know we'll meet again. Love, Jacqueline." I ran to her room and knocked. No answer. I called the reception desk.

"I'm sorry," Mr. Winslow, the weekend desk clerk's voice cracked. "Jacqueline left us."

"She died?"

"She's gone back to her family." There was a long silence. "She was quite sick, you know."

"Yes, Mr. Winslow, I know. Do you have an address for her?"

"I'm sorry, I can't give you that information."

"If I write a letter, can you address it to her?"

"I suppose I can do that," he said doubtfully.

"Thank you," I hung up before he changed his mind.

I wrote Jacqueline a long, sappy letter about how much I would miss her and gave her Mami's address, in case Ulvi returned and I would have to move out of the Longacre Hotel.

"Do you have special plans for Valentine's Day?" Mr. Winslow asked as he looked up Jacqueline's address in the logbook.

"I wish," I said.

He started to say something, but I waved goodbye and left the building, planning to pick up dinner at the grocery store around the corner. I didn't feel like sitting alone in a restaurant crowded with adoring couples looking into one another's eyes. Rayenne and Dayenne were on the corner, shivering in their white-and-red costumes.

"Happy Valentine's Day," I said, and they laughed.

The grocery store's fluorescent glow was depressing. I walked up and down the aisles with no idea of what to eat. None of the prepared food looked fresh, so I decided to cook. My only kitchen utensils at the Longacre were a nonstick frying pan, a spatula, a spoon, a mug, and an electric teapot, bought as my cooking skills progressed to where I could now scramble eggs and boil water for instant coffee. I picked up half a dozen eggs and a stick of butter and headed for the cashier.

"Excuse me," a voice said behind me. The handsomest man I had ever seen stood grinning before me, an empty grocery basket on his left hand, and in his right, a boxed frozen dinner. "Do you know how to make this?" He spoke with a heavy accent. I picked up the box and read the instructions aloud.

"Place in pot of rapidly boiling water for three to five minutes. Drain and serve with sautéed onions or sour cream."

"Have dinner with me?" he asked.

I put the box in his grocery basket. "I do not like pierogies," I said, and walked away.

As I paid, I resisted the urge to see if he was still trying to pick up a more likely candidate for his frozen dinner. I had not walked more than a few steps onto the busy sidewalk when I heard his voice again.

"You like eggs more?" he asked.

Rayenne and Dayenne had turned their attention from the cars cruising down Eighth Avenue to my exchange with Gorgeous George.

"I am not interested," I said, and kept walking. Rayenne and Dayenne moved to stand between us.

"You do not eat eggs tonight," he grabbed my shopping bag and playfully threw it in the trashcan on the corner. I wanted to be annoyed, but instead, I laughed. Rayenne and Dayenne backed off.

"*¿Habla español?*" He had as heavy an accent in Spanish as in English. "*¿Fala portugues?*" he tried again, and his expression was so hopeful, and it was so cold outside, that I agreed to have dinner with him.

We walked through the crowd gawking at the lights on Broadway. He told me that his name was Oscar, that he was Brazilian, that he lived in Rio, and that he had followed me into the grocery store.

He had warm olive skin, hazel eyes, brown hair, a mellifluous voice that rose and dipped with soft vowels and unexpected consonants. He understood Spanish but had a hard time speaking it. I could not speak Portuguese but understood it better than his English. Somehow, we managed to communicate, he in Portuguese and me in Spanish. We sat at a dim table in the back of a narrow restaurant just off Fifth Avenue filled with couples whispering and touching hands, while champagne bottles cooled on metal stands next to their tables.

"Why," he wondered, "are you alone on the Day of Hearts?"

"My boyfriend is a bank robber who escaped from prison earlier this week so that we could marry, but he was captured last night."

Oscar whistled.

"And you?"

"I am in New York on business."

I didn't ask.

We ate and drank champagne. We understood half of what the other said, maybe less. After dinner, he wanted to go dancing, so we walked to the Coco Lounge on Fifty-third Street, which was packed. Oscar, however, knew how to tip before he received service. We were seated so far from the dance floor that, in the crowded club, it was better to stay there dancing than to return to our table after each number. He was a great dancer, loose limbed and musical. It had been months since I'd been in a heterosexual man's arms, and Oscar's felt solid and strong. He smelled good, a combination of spice and sweat that was intoxicating. We danced until dawn, and emerged into the lightening sky of a frigid morning. As the cold air hit me, the spell broke. I wanted to return to the Longacre and collapse in my narrow bed. To my surprise, Oscar didn't argue. We walked hand in hand, laughing and talking our polyglot. When we reached the corner of Forty-fifth and Eighth Avenue, he pretended to look in the trashcan for the eggs and butter he had thrown away the night before. We agreed to rest and meet later, for dinner.

I slept through Sunday. As I dressed for the evening, I told myself I wasn't being unfaithful to Ulvi if all I did was eat and dance with Oscar the Brazilian. Unfortunately, that's not all we did.

Monday, I went straight to work from the St. Regis, where I had spent the night with a man whose last name I never asked. I left Oscar fast asleep in the enormous bed in the brocaded room and walked into a bright, cold Fifth Avenue morning. I felt unburdened, but didn't want to think about what had weighed me down. I sat at the counter of a Chock Full O'Nuts and ordered a cup of coffee. The mirror behind the counter reflected a face I didn't recognize—me, happy. I avoided looking into my eyes. They reproached the person behind them. Having sullied my reputation as a *nena puertorriqueña decente* when I ran away with Ulvi, I had gleefully released my tenuous hold on being a *mujer decente* with Oscar the Brazilian. But I had no regrets, and didn't feel any less a "good girl" than on the day before Ulvi *me hizo el daño*.

Another train will come.

Ruth noticed there was something different about me, so did Francine. Sunday night's clothes, too dressy for Monday morning, smelled of cigarettes and other people's sweat, of a night dancing, of kisses during boleros. On my lunch hour, I went home to change. When I returned to the office, Francine told me that Ruth and Mr. Margolis had argued. Ruth had stormed out and was presumably on her way home to New Jersey. Francine was desperately trying to reach her because the magazines Ruth handled were supposed to close at the end of business that day and the production materials had to be sent via messenger to the printer in Long Island.

Ruth's job was more complex than mine, her clients more important to the company. She kept meticulous records, and her files were organized. I took one look at her desk, which, even in an angry huff Ruth had left tidy, and told Francine that no, I couldn't do Ruth's job.

"I'm disappointed that you won't help us in this crisis," Francine said.

I was adamant. I would not do Ruth's job because if I did, even to help management out of a jam, I would be undermining her, and I had betrayed enough people already.

Francine sat at Ruth's desk and tried to figure out what to do. She kept asking me about a layout that hadn't been approved, or whether an ad in the to-be-proofread bin was ready to go. I answered her questions without making her task easier. She missed the deadline. I returned to the Longacre, to an early bedtime and the resolution to look for another job.

When I woke up the next morning, I remembered something that had happened a few years earlier. I had left home for school later than usual, and ran to catch the train. It was rattling in as I reached the bottom step of the elevated station. I pushed through the crowd running up the stairs, but the doors clanged shut just as I reached the platform. I was furious with myself for having left the house late, for not having run fast enough, for missing the train seconds before it pulled away. Cursing under my breath, I imagined this as the beginning of a terrible day of missed connections and frustrations. I stalked to the end of the station, annoyed, looking back every few seconds, willing the next train to rumble down the tracks so that I could climb on and get to school on time. As I reached the end of the platform, the headlamps of a train emerging from the tunnel shone from the opposite direction. Another train will come. I heard the words as if someone had said them aloud, and realized I had said them. Another train will come. Why rush? Why worry? Why go crazy? Another train will come. And sure enough, another train going my way was pulling into the station. My bad mood evaporated. I entered the car smiling, certain that there would be more missed trains in my life, more closed doors in my face, but there would always be another train rumbling down the tracks in my direction.

Ruth returned after Mr. Margolis sent flowers to let her know that, as she often reminded him, she was indispensable. A few days later, a friend told me about a position as assistant to the recently named Executive Director of the Museum of Modern Art. He insisted that the job was perfect for me because they were looking to fill it with a black or Puerto Rican woman. It was the first time in my employment history where being Puerto Rican was an advantage, so I called for an appointment.

Alma helped me develop a resume that highlighted my work at Lady Manhattan and the clerical aspects of the job at Margolis. She thought I needed a conservative outfit for the interview, my style being more bohemian than she thought appropriate for an executive office. I reminded her that this was a museum, filled with artistic types who probably wore more outlandish costumes every day than what I created for dance performances.

"What happens if The Turk calls and wants you to join him in Germany?" Alma asked.

"He wants to live in New York, so it's perfect," I answered. That was his latest plan.

I rarely discussed Ulvi with Alma or other people because no one could understand my loyalty to him. He had asked me to wait for him, I had promised to do it, and while six months had elapsed with no clear idea of when or whether he would return, I waited. A part of me believed that he would never return, that he would fade into my past like Jürgen did, like Jacqueline, who had never answered my letter.

Ulvi wrote two or three times a week, called every month or so, still swore he wanted us to be together. I answered as he expected, with promises, vows, and assurances that I was still "your Chiquita," still being "a good girl." I did make some adjustments, however. My weekend with Oscar the Brazilian had shown me that I was open to romance, if not love, were it to come along.

I dated a disc jockey, the brother of a dancer at ISD. I dated one of the salesmen at Margolis until Ruth revealed he was married. I dated a man I had exchanged pleasantries with in the elevator at 11 West Forty-second for months before he had the nerve to ask me out. The dates usually ended with a decorous kiss in the lobby of the Longacre Hotel, and longing looks as the elevator door closed and I rose to my room on the eighth floor. Lacking the charm and magnetism of Oscar the Brazilian, the attraction these men held was that they didn't make too many demands. I enjoyed their company, they seemed to enjoy mine, and after a while, they became friends, our dates free of sexual tension, just as with the homosexual boys who accompanied me to the theater and the ballet. In time, I became a confidante for their more fruitful romances.

Elaine, who worked for the incoming director of the Museum of Modern Art, called me in for an interview. She was a creamy-skinned, petite woman with a tender heart hidden behind a no-nonsense attitude. She was looking for someone to be her assistant when John Hightower, her boss, began his tenure at MOMA on May first. She looked at my credentials and seemed satisfied that I could handle the work but she still had other people to talk to. A few candidates would be invited back for an interview with John, who had final say.

I didn't hear from her for a couple of weeks. In the meanwhile, things at Margolis became unbearable. The workload increased, and Ruth and I had to work longer hours in order to meet our deadlines, but because no one else could do our jobs, we couldn't take time off. The strain was wearing Ruth down. She looked like the old woman she was, at times so haggard that I worried she would collapse.

Elaine called to let me know I was one of the finalists for the job at the museum and we made an appointment for me to meet John.

Waiving Alma's suggestions, I wore a colorful dress in an Indian print and brushed my long hair until it shone. I walked into his office and John, sitting behind his enormous desk, took one look at me and, before I introduced myself, said, "You're hired."

Ruth was so happy I got the job that, for the first time since we'd known each other, she hugged me. On my last day, she handed me a card and a small velvet-covered box wrapped in tissue. Inside was a pair of pearl earrings.

"I bought them for myself with the first paycheck from my first job," she said, "long before you were born."

"Ruth, I can't accept these! They're special."

"Don't look a gift horse in the mouth," she scolded. "Let me see how they look."

I put them on and grinned.

"Gorgeous! *Gey gezunt.* Wear them in good health," Ruth said.

"Thank you so much, I will treasure them."

We hugged for the second time in our acquaintance. I kept the earrings in their velvet box, to wear on special occasions. When I looked in the mirror I always saw the girl Ruth saw, the one with chutzpah.

Days into my job as the Assistant to the Assistant of the Executive Director of the Museum of Modern Art, Elaine handed me a stack of handwritten pages clipped to the letters they answered. On my interviews, neither Elaine nor John had asked, and I had not volunteered my low skill level at a typewriter.

"Do a few a day. There's no rush," Elaine said, seeing my dismay.

Typing, daunting as it was, was not my biggest challenge at MOMA, however. I answered the phones for Elaine and John and from the beginning, almost every call to the executive director's office presented a crisis.

Mami always said that I was like Papi in the way I handled conflict. She yelled at him and, instead of yelling back, he walked away, infuriating her further. I did the same. Whenever possible, I avoided arguments and discord, at home or away from it. If I were strolling down Fifth Avenue and saw the hand-printed signs and folk-singing, fist-raising swarms of antiwar or civil rights demonstrators, I turned in a different direction. If friends at a party became vocal about Vietnam, it was time for me to go. Whenever anyone wanted to get serious about politics, religion, the upcoming elections, the failure of The Great Society, urban renewal, I shut my mouth or changed the subject to something shallow, like movies or the Top 40 hit of the week. The only things I was passionate about were my family, dance, books, and my jobs which, no matter how boring, I took seriously.

"You are not well informed, Chiquita," Ulvi often told me. "You cannot have opinions." I could have, but did not.

When I started work with John and Elaine, I didn't know that museums, and art organizations in general, were contentious institutions whose politics were more complicated than the petty dramas and sexual intrigues at Margolis & Co. I didn't know that the galleries I so lovingly explored almost every Sunday were battlegrounds, that to some people Monet's *Water Lilies* were not the tranquil refuge into beauty I had always experienced, but a symbol of white European hegemony in the art world. I didn't know what hegemony meant. I didn't know that the "art establishment," when it wasn't exploiting them, ignored "minority" artists. I had never stopped to think whether Pablo Picasso was a white man, or whether younger artists whose work was in museum collections had "sold out." I had never questioned why every name on the plaques next to great works of art belonged to men, or why most of those men were dead or older than Mami and Ulvi.

I didn't know what to make of the pushy, jeans-wearing, stragglyhaired, marijuana- and patchouli-scented men and women who insisted they deserved a place alongside Picasso, Dalí, and Giacometti. It required more intellectual sophistication than I had to understand destructivism and conceptual art, to look at a truckload of ice blocks stacked in the museum's garden in ninety-degree weather and find meaning—or not—as it melted. Why didn't the artist draw the ice blocks? Or paint them? Or even create a sculpture that would still be there the next day? I simply did not get it.

At least once a week, my phone rang and a museum security guard announced that there was a disruption. Guerilla theater groups staged performances in the galleries. Demonstrators picketed exhibits. Artists organized sit-ins in the garden. The demands were always the same: a meeting with John to air injustices that they hoped he would address.

John had headed the New York State Council of the Arts before coming to MOMA. He knew many of the protesters and was sympathetic to their points of view, but he was also honest with them. He could understand why they wanted a voice in how the museum was run, but no, he was not going to let them run it. He listened politely as they complained that the socialites who made up a large part of the board of trustees used their position to gain influence with one another rather than to promote, buy, and exhibit good art. He told them there was no possibility that the museum would sell its collection of art that was over thirty years old to make room for more contemporary artists. He understood their frustration, he said, but they had to work with him if they wanted to see changes, and they could not expect overnight results.

As the first contact between the rest of the world and the executive director's office, I was in the center of the controversies with no power to affect them. Whenever Security called to let us know there was trouble in the galleries, or on the sidewalk in front of the museum, I went down to investigate and, if I could, to defuse the situation. Usually, all it took was the promise of an appointment between John and whatever group was trying to get his attention.

At other times, Security had to call the police to remove protesters and the story would appear in the next day's *New York Times*.

One of the leaders of the demonstrations was a well-known artist whose work was in the museum's collection. Ralph Ortiz was a New York–born Puerto Rican who had written *Destructivism: A Manifesto*. His series, *Archaeological Finds*, featured broken, burned, and otherwise destroyed furniture, mostly chairs and mattresses. He was involved with the Guerilla Art Action Group, and performed a series of works under the name *Destruction Realizations*, in which he smashed more furniture and musical instruments. He also sacrificed chickens. Other than the fact that we both had Puerto Rican parents, we had nothing in common I thought. I was wrong.

Even as he disputed many of MOMA's policies, Ralph was founding El Museo del Barrio, a community-based museum that he envisioned would be devoted to the work of Puerto Rican and other Latin American artists. He had a passion for pre-Colombian art, for the rituals of the native people of the American hemisphere, for their traditions. But he was not so ethnocentric that he didn't listen to classical music, read Nietzsche, Kierkegaard, and Sartre, and discourse passionately about the role of the artist in society. He was the first Puerto Rican intellectual I had ever met. He was not as rich as Avery Lee the Texas oilman, as mysterious as Jürgen the federal fugitive, as handsome as Oscar the Brazilian, or as elegant as Ulvi, but I still fell for him.

My position between the bellicose artists and the museum administration complicated my relationship with Ralph. Where would my loyalties be? Whenever one of the groups he was involved with showed up to object to an exhibit, disrupt an opening, or upset a board of trustees meeting, I went down to handle it. In these confrontations, I represented the Establishment and he was the future of art. At least, that's the way they saw it. The irony of me as pawn of the Establishment made me laugh.

In one encounter, protesters gathered in front of the Museum after members of a guerilla theater group were ejected from the galleries following an impromptu performance involving sheep's blood. At the front of the group was Ralph, pumping his fist, yelling slogans, demanding that John come down and meet with them. I was five feet four inches and weighed barely a hundred pounds. Ralph was well over six feet and wore his hair in an Afro that he groomed with a vacuum cleaner to puff it fuller. Confronted with him and his angry friends, I was scared. Here was the man in whose arms I had lain the night before, his face contorted in fury, screaming. It felt as if he were yelling at me, not at the policies of the museum. I was nearly in tears as I asked them to please go away. John would meet with their representatives, but not then, not there.

They would not be appeased. They challenged me. How could I, a Puerto Rican, not understand where they were coming from? I had sold out, I was acting white.

They looked like me, those brown faces grimacing in my direction, yelling, calling me names. I should be standing alongside them, not on the opposite side of the argument.

"I'm the only Puerto Rican in an administrative position here," I said, for the moment putting aside their challenge to my identity. "You demand representation of Puerto Ricans and blacks in the museum staff. Well, I'm here, and you need to help me succeed at my job so that more people like me will be hired."

My logic, arrived at on the spot, made sense to them. Ralph and Tom, another of the leaders, calmed the protesters. I promised to set up a meeting with John. They went away, grudgingly, still muttering that I had betrayed my people. I pretended I didn't hear them, but every word and their hate-filled inflections were like hot needles pricking my skin.

When we were alone, Ralph tried to assure me that he and his friends had nothing against me personally, that I shouldn't interpret their actions as an attack against Esmeralda Santiago. It was arrogant, he said, to think that way, since he knew, and they knew, that I had little power to do more than make appointments. I was, in short, a token.

In less than twelve hours, I was accused of being a sellout, a traitor to my people, and a token, but the day wasn't over.

"Where were you last night?" Ulvi asked when I answered the phone at the Longacre later that night. I couldn't think fast enough to come up with a better lie, other than I was sick and spent the night in the emergency room. He asked me what was so wrong that I had to go to the hospital, and I piled one lie on top of the next, hoping he would believe them. The more details he asked for, the more creative I became with the personalities of the nurses who treated me, the doctor who could not figure out what was wrong, the specialist who was called, the tests and X-rays. Whatever had made me so sick had cleared up on its own and I was sent home, which is why he reached me at the Longacre this night and not last. I convinced myself that was what had happened, but I could hear that the same wasn't true for Ulvi. He said he knew I was lying, and hung up on me.

I had no phone number where I could call him back. Ulvi didn't usually call on weekdays. He rarely called more than once a month, and he'd already done that a few days earlier. In recent weeks, he must have noticed my coolness toward him, fewer and shorter letters, and a reluctance to write or say too much about my job. After eleven months, I had given up the idea that he would ever return, and had gone on with my life.

A couple of days later I received a special-delivery letter in which Ulvi explained how hard he had been working toward a future with me. "It is not easy, Chiquita," he wrote, and I wondered whether he thought it was easier for me, a healthy twenty-two-year-old to live in expectation of his happily-ever-after scenarios when he had said that he couldn't marry me. What kind of future was he talking about? Was I to be his "girlfriend" the rest of my life? My romances, at least, did not come with promises, and I appreciated that about them. No promises, no disappointments. It was cleaner that way.

"How can you do that?" Alma wanted to know. "Your husband is in Europe and you're seeing other men. It's not right."

"He's not my husband."

Alma's romance with Bill had survived his parents' objections. It seemed that love for Alma had conquered their opposition. They still didn't like her, but Bill didn't care. He had been drafted, and wanted to marry Alma before he was shipped off. She would wait for him to return. Chastely, I assumed.

Ulvi called a few days later. He had forgiven me, he said. He understood how hard it was for me to be alone all that time, and he had a surprise. He had an opportunity in Texas.

"I have not decided yet, Chiquita, it depends on you."

"On me? How?"

"Let us meet somewhere. I can get cheap ticket to Bahamas. A friend told me about a place, Paradise Island. It will be a honeymoon. We can discuss. I hope you have saved your money. I cannot pay for your ticket."

To this day, I don't know why I said yes.

"I wanted you here, with me."

We took flights that would land in Nassau within minutes of one another, Ulvi from Stuttgart, me from New York. I was nervous about seeing him, about being seen by him. Would he look as old as he was? Would he be able to tell that I had not sat in my room at the Longacre Hotel for a year waiting for his call?

When I came into the terminal outside customs, there he was, youthful, happy to see me, waving and smiling. My doubts vanished. I rushed into his arms and plunged into his world. In Ulvi's arms, I forgot everything and everyone. I felt safe and loved. I didn't notice the willowy blonde next to us until he introduced her.

"This is Claudine," he said. "This is Chiquita, my girlfriend."

Claudine was happy, she said, to meet me, and as soon as she kissed my cheeks, she turned and asked us to follow her to a waiting car, where Ulvi's luggage had already been stowed. In the front sat Reinhardt, a young man who had also arrived on the flight from Stuttgart and was staying at The Paradise Hotel, where we were heading. Claudine was its manager.

The hotel was a long, low building facing a magnificent white-sand crescent beach. Before we checked in, Ulvi took my hand and told me we would have a look around.

"Are we staying here?" I asked.

"Maybe," he said.

The open-air office and restaurant were in the middle of the cement-covered cinderblock building with a corrugated zinc roof. It was run-down enough to be described as casual in the brochure I picked up from the front desk. The guestrooms faced the beach. At the far end, a thatched bar squatted by a swimming pool crawling with sunburned Germans.

"We'll stay," Ulvi said after our walk through.

Claudine had changed into a bikini and a sarong, and was now officially receiving guests. She signed us in herself, and assured Ulvi that she had given us one of the best rooms. It was large and comfortable, with a ceiling fan, a window air conditioner, and a queen-size bed. As we entered, I felt nervous and resisted Ulvi's embrace.

"Why you so shy?" he asked.

"I . . . I don't know. It's been so long." He liked that response, and was gentle and considerate, luring me back into his life of caresses and secrets.

The next morning, we sat in the lobby addressing the postcards with a picture of the hotel that Claudine encouraged guests to send home. I wrote one to Mami, one to Alma, and another to Elaine and John. As we stood at the counter purchasing stamps, I caught a glimpse of a couple of the cards Ulvi was sending, one to Irmchen in Stuttgart and another to Siri, in Ceylon. I could only read the last line of Siri's card: "I wanted you here, with me. Love, Your Ulvi." He noticed that I had read over his shoulder and glared at my rude manners. I turned my eyes away, and wondered who Siri was, but didn't ask because that would have confirmed that I was prying.

Ulvi wanted to relax and have fun, so we didn't talk about his plans for the first few days. He swam in the ocean while I sat on a lounge chair, immersed in Sartre, whom Ralph had insisted I should read. We went to Nassau with Reinhardt, who had rented a car and was intent on exploring the island. Afternoons, we drove to seaside villages and waited on the shore for the fishermen to come in with their catch. We ate quivering sweet conch meat right out of the shell with a spritz of lime juice. At night we went to nightclubs and casinos, again with Reinhardt, who seemed to have endless amounts of cash and liked to spend it on us. Claudine threw herself a birthday party in her apartment at the other end of the hotel, which Ulvi and I left as soon as the guests started smoking pot. A man Ulvi met at one of the casinos flew us in his small plane to another of the Bahamian islands, where he was developing a village of condominiums along a pristine shore. Ulvi had convinced him that we might invest in one. Every time I wanted to talk to Ulvi about "our future," there was some place to go, people to meet, other things that were more important.

"Patience, Chiquita," he said, "there is time."

I had requested and been granted eight days vacation, even though I'd been at the museum less than three months. I had eight days in which to secure a future with Ulvi or say goodbye to him forever. It had seemed like a long time then. They had seemed like clear choices when I locked the door to my room behind me, when I stopped at Alma's on the way to the airport to say goodbye, when I sat on the plane reading *Being and Nothingness,* anguished by the inescapable responsibility for my own life.

After breakfast on the fifth day of our trip, Ulvi decided it was time we "discussed things," and I discovered that throughout those days of leisure followed by partying, he had been observing me.

"I do not like you drink now, Chiquita," he said, because I had ordered a Coke laced with rum and lime juice, twice that week. "Your bikini very small," he said about the swimsuit I'd worn for five days with no comments from him. "You speak very free," he said about my ability to hold a trivial conversation with Reinhardt and the condominium developer.

I apologized for drinking rum twice in one week, but he had too, and it didn't seem to be a problem at the time. My bikini was small because a year ago, when he was choosing my clothes, he had bought it for me. I spoke freely to Reinhardt and the businessman because they asked questions I thought would have been rude not to answer.

"Very well, Chiquita, do not worry," he forgave me. "This is the situation."

He had many, how you say, irons in the fire in Europe and the Middle East, many possibilities for making money and for directing films. He would need to stay in Europe another "couple months" until the possibilities became realities. "No, Chiquita, you cannot come with me, you must wait in New York."

"I have already waited one year," I protested, but he didn't think a year was a long time when we considered that if just one of his possibilities came through, we would be together. "Will we be married?" I asked.

He grimaced in irritation. "No, I cannot marry you."

"Why should I wait then, why should I be with you? What kind of future are you talking about?"

"We will be together," he said, "for long time."

"We haven't been able to manage more than a few months. Why should I believe that if I wait another week, month, or year, things will be different?"

"You must trust me, Chiquita," he said. "You cannot be with me if you do not trust me. Do you trust me, Chiquita?" His question came with caresses, hugs, and kisses, so that it was impossible to say No, I don't trust you, or No, I don't want to be with you. How could I, when he held me so tight, when he said he loved me? Yes, in the Bahamas, and in spite of the postcards to Irmchen and to Siri, he said he loved me.

"I trust you."

The moment he let me go, though, the minute I had time to think, to revisit every encounter since we had come to Paradise Island, I wasn't so sure. Before his touch had cooled on my skin, I was arguing with him again. If he loved me, it wasn't right for him to be in Germany, or traveling to far-flung cities, while I sat in my room at the Longacre Hotel, alone, waiting. I didn't confess that I had friends, that I dated, that there were men in my life. It was a question of fairness, as far as I was concerned. He owed me at least seven months, from the day he left, until the day I met Oscar the Brazilian. I was angry at him for having abandoned me, at myself for having waited, at his promises, at my lies. I hated myself, and I blamed him for it.

I cried constantly, those last three days in that run-down hotel in Paradise Island along the shore of that unspoiled beach. My tears softened him. His little Chiquita was weeping, sometimes uncontrollably, because she loved him so much, she wanted to be with him so much, she had missed him so much. That is what he said. He begged me to please stop, please control yourself, he said, let us talk about this calmly.

What Ulvi didn't know, and I only barely understood, was that half the time my tears had nothing to do with what we were discussing. I'd tune out what he was saying and get choked by the swallowed rage of old injustices, by long-repressed grief, by the indignity of insults I hadn't answered, by fears I couldn't overcome. I was too embarrassed to say, "I'm not crying for you, I'm crying for when I dropped the last dime I had and it rolled into a grate and I had to stand by the subway station begging for change so that I could get home to Brooklyn. Have you ever begged, Ulvi? Have you ever seen people's expressions when you beg? I just wanted to get home."

I was sure Ulvi was sorry he had asked me to meet him in the Bahamas, and I was sorry I had come. What was I thinking? In

New York, I had a good job, an interesting boyfriend, a cheap place to live, entertaining friends, a loving family.

"I do not need you, Ulvi Dogan," I said in the middle of one of our arguments, and he wrapped me in his arms and said, "Yes, you do, Chiquita."

⌒

The last night on Paradise Island, I pressed my ear to his chest and listened to his heart as he stroked my hair. He lifted my chin so that we could be face to face, and said that my tears had proved how difficult the past year had been for me. He didn't want to tell me before, because he didn't want to get my hopes up. He had an opportunity in Texas.

I had forgotten about the opportunity in Texas.

"You know I am not American citizen," he continued, "I cannot go in and out of the United States like you can." He had an acceptance to graduate school at Texas Tech University, in Lubbock. So long as he was a student, he could remain in the United States.

I sat up and glared. "Were you going to move to Texas without telling me?"

"No, I had not made my decision until now," he said. He didn't know if it would be possible for me to come with him because he had no idea where he would be living. He had little money. He could not support two people.

"I can work," I offered. "I can help you."

He thanked me, but said that nothing could be decided until he went to Lubbock. He wasn't sure about being a student again, he was almost forty and it had been a long time since he'd done homework. His English might not be good enough. It was the only way, however, that he could live in the United States legally. He did not want to do it the way other foreigners did, by overstaying their visas.

"Whatever I decide, I will take good care you, Chiquita, I promise."

"You're crazy to be doing this," Elaine said when I told her I was quitting as her assistant to move to Texas with a man a year older than my mother. In the three months I had worked at the museum, my relationship with Elaine had been strictly professional. We were not girlfriends, did not discuss our private lives, or gossip about others. Her vehemence surprised me. She was so certain I was making a mistake, that she took me to lunch at an expensive restaurant and invited Carol, the head of the Prints Department. Carol was older than Elaine, and I guessed she was there to provide a mature woman's perspective.

"A man seventeen years older than you only wants one thing," Carol advised.

"I thought it was only Puerto Rican and Jewish women who believe that," I muttered.

"White Episcopalians do too," she said.

"Because it's true," Elaine added.

They each told me about a decision she had faced in her life, and how she had made the wrong choice and was still regretting it.

Thanks to Sartre, I knew about the negative consequences of every choice, and had made a list of what I would be giving up but had still decided to go with Ulvi. "I've learned that there is no such thing as a good choice," I said. "There is only the choice whose consequences you can live with or the choice that kills you."

"You're willing to stake your life on this guy?" Elaine asked.

"No, but I want no regrets later. I should follow through on the decision to leave my mother so that I could be with him."

"Esmeralda, that makes no sense," Elaine said. "There is just as good a chance that you will regret having left everything to follow him."

"But at least, I've made a conscious choice," I said.

"You're taking this existentialist stuff much too seriously," Carol added.

"If I say no to him now, I'll never get another chance. If I say yes, I can always change my mind."

"But then you'll be in Lubbock, Texas," Elaine reminded me.

"Just don't get pregnant," Carol suggested.

Ulvi sent a telegram within days of his arrival in Lubbock. He didn't want me to join him because he was having trouble finding an apartment for a couple.

"I already gave notice at work," I said, when he phoned.

"That is not smart, Chiquita," he said. "I told you I was not sure I would stay."

I had forgotten that part.

He called again after a few days to say he had found a place. I booked my flight and called Mami to tell her I was moving to Texas.

"*¿Con el turco ese?*" she asked.

"Yes, Mami, with that Turk."

"*Ay, mi'ja*, I don't know why you think that after all this time . . ."

"Mami, please."

"It's your life, I know . . . "

"Yes, it's my life."

"*Que la virgen te favorezca y te acompañe,*" she said, letting me go with a blessing.

"Were you a gasser biter?"

I had heard the expression Big Sky Country, but it was still a shock to stand in the yard of our apartment and look up at the huge bowl above us. The sky in West Texas *was* bigger, the ground flat as a tortilla. The temperature outside was over 100 degrees. The Texas Panhandle was in the middle of one of the worst droughts since the Great Depression. Lawns were the color of oatmeal and crackled underfoot. The air was heavy with fine, red, bitter dust that caught in my hair and the folds on my skin and was impossible to wash out.

Our place was in a ranch house in a residential development a couple of blocks from the university. The owners lived in front. We rented the back, one furnished room with a bath and kitchenette. When the owners met me, they wanted to know if I was Mexican.

"No, I'm Puerto Rican," I said.

"Oh, good," said the wife, but the husband was not so sure.

Classes had not started so, on my first day in Lubbock, Ulvi pulled out two lounge chairs from the garage and we sat in the hundred-degree afternoon to sunbathe. As soon as I relaxed, Ulvi wanted to talk.

"Where were you the night I called and you said you were in the hospital?"

For the next couple of hours he grilled me about every aspect of the story I had told him. He remembered the details better than I did, and pointed out the inconsistencies.

"You are telling me lies," he said.

"How can you ask me to trust you," I asked, "when you don't trust me?"

"Because I do not lie to you, Chiquita. I only tell the truth."

"Me too," I argued. "Why can't you accept that?"

"If you admit you lie to me, I will accept it," he said.

"I'm not lying," I insisted.

"Very well, Chiquita, I will not mention it again." He never did.

Two weeks after we moved in, our landlords told us we had to find another place to live. The neighbors had complained.

"You have to understand," the husband said, "there are no other coloreds in this neighborhood."

"It might be uncomfortable for you," the wife suggested.

"Why did you rent to us in the first place?" I asked, and Ulvi glared at me.

"We will find another place," he said to them.

"We'll return your security deposit," the husband offered.

"It's the neighbors," the wife said, dropping her head to one side and peeking coyly from beneath her lashes, as if she were Scarlett O'Hara.

"Thank you," said Ulvi as they left.

I threw a pillow against the door the husband and wife closed as they left.

"That doesn't help, Chiquita," Ulvi said. His equanimity was infuriating.

"Racist, prejudiced jerks. Doesn't it make you mad?"

"It is no good to get excited," Ulvi tried to calm me down. "It will not change anything."

"Aren't you angry?"

"This is not first time it happens. In Germany is the same. People prejudiced against *Gastarbeiter*."

"Against who?"

"Guest workers is what they call the Turkish and other peoples who come to work. The Germans don't like them because they bring their customs and their language from the old country. They are different from the Germans."

"Were you a gasser biter?"

"*Gastarbeiter*. No, I came to Germany as a student." He pulled me up from the sofa. "Let's go, Chiquita, we have to find apartment."

While Ulvi visited Texas Tech housing, I went to the employment office. The longest jobs I'd held were five months as a clerk with Fisher Scientific Company, five months as a secretary at Lady Manhattan, and eight months at Margolis & Co. But the three months at the Museum of Modern Art impressed the agent most. She sent me to the library, to be interviewed by Mrs. Crisp, a small, thin woman with puckered lips and eyes crinkled with crow's feet. She asked if I could start the next day.

Ulvi had some leads to apartments, but it was hard to get around in Lubbock without a car. "Did you bring your money, Chiquita?" he asked.

I had about $300 after the trip to the Bahamas and the airfare to Texas. I gave it to him, and he promised to return it whenever I asked.

"It will make down payment for car," he said. A couple of days later, he picked me up at the library in a brand-new turquoise-blue Camaro.

We found an apartment on the other end of campus, near the football stadium and tennis courts. A couple of blocks away, railroad tracks divided the Mexican community from the rest of the town. The previous May, a tornado had devastated the neighborhood, killing 26 people and injuring 500. I had yet to meet a single

Mexican, or anyone with coloring remotely like Ulvi's and mine. Texas Tech University and Lubbock were the whitest places I'd ever been in.

"I thought there were lots of black people in the South," I said to Mrs. Crisp.

"This is not the South," she said, "this is Texas."

The circulation desk faced an atrium with a fountain, around which students congregated to chat and study. My first turns checking out books and answering students' questions were stressful because I had to get used to the West Texas accent.

"My I heive appease uh piper?" a young woman asked, and had to repeat it at least three times before I understood she was asking if she could have a piece of paper. I felt like an idiot.

I also had to get used to Texas style. In New York, straight long hair parted in the middle, a natural look for lips and eyes, Indian paisleys, and colorful "psychedelic" prints were stylish for women. To the horror of my bra-making mother, it was chic to go braless even if you were busty enough to bounce with every step. In Texas, heavy eye makeup, solidly sprayed teased hair, pert, immobile breasts, and crisp clothes in pastel colors were fashionable. Boys rolled up the hems of their jeans Elvis-style, or wore pleated chinos with plaid shirts open at the neck. My miniskirts were scandalous at the library, even though by New York standards they were barely mini. My coworkers made frequent suggestions for how I might change my natural look to something more West Texan. I was willing, but Ulvi wouldn't hear of it.

"You will look like cheap girl," he said.

The library was always busy, and, while the work didn't require more than minimal concentration, it was never boring. My favorite part was shelving, when I wandered around the library returning books to their place and making sure nothing was out of order. Occasionally I discovered amorous couples in remote corners. They jumped apart and tugged at their clothes the minute they saw me, while I pretended to straighten books in stacks that had not been disturbed for weeks.

Ulvi was in the Master of Science program in industrial engineering. Between classes, he sat in the library atrium working out formulae with his slide rule. Different cliques had staked out territory and I came to recognize who were the cheerleaders, who the athletes, who the science majors.

One of the cheerleaders, Doreen, was a titled beauty queen. She had teased, long honey-colored hair, immaculately made-up blue eyes, frosted lipstick, and clothes that made the most of her narrow waist and long legs. She was always surrounded by other bubbly blondes, or by thick-necked tight ends and running backs.

I looked up from my desk one day and, to my surprise, saw Ulvi sitting with the cheerleaders. Doreen was perched on the arm of his chair smiling as if she'd just won Miss Congeniality. He saw me, but made no effort to at least pretend he wasn't flirting. He sat with the giggly girls for a while longer and, when he came to pick me up at the end of the day, didn't say a thing about it, and neither did I.

Asking what he was doing with Doreen practically on his lap brought memories of Mami's arguments with Papi and with Don Carlos over other women. It recalled women sobbing to their social workers that their husbands had left them for *una puta*. It reminded me of disheveled women arguing over a man right there on the sidewalk, where neighbors pointed and laughed at their foolishness.

A woman fighting over a man was pathetic, and I had decided, while still a girl, that jealousy would not be a part of my life—or at least, its public display. I refused to be baited by Ulvi's flirting. I would not give him the satisfaction of letting him know that he had hurt my feelings. I did not know it then, but the list maker in me was compiling a record, storing every little hurt and insult for one big blowup.

⌒

We made friends in Lubbock or, rather, Ulvi did and introduced me to them. There was a group of Air Force officers with such brilliant careers ahead of them, that the United States government was putting them through engineering school. They had all-American names like Don, Joe, Pete, and Jerry. Friday nights we met at Cappy's, just outside the city limits, to gorge on fried catfish, biscuits dribbled with honey, and, for the men, domestic beer.

Lubbock was a dry town, but there were private clubs you could join for the night so that you could get as drunk as you liked. Around the periphery of the city, there were wet towns with liquor stores and one bar after another. On Friday and Saturday nights, the roads leading to them were jammed with college students and revelers.

Ulvi's best friend in Lubbock was Gene Hemmle, whom he had met years earlier when Ulvi drove across the country in his white Rolls Royce and, for reasons I never knew, stopped in Lubbock.

Gene was the chairman of the music department at Texas Tech. He was a wonderful singer, and still gave concerts and recitals to appreciative friends and colleagues. He lived on the outskirts of town in a converted depot he bought and transported to a lot next to his mother's house and antique shop. His parties in The Depot gathered the most interesting and artistic people of Lubbock and the surrounding area, the top professors in the arts and humanities, and a coterie of rich, old women who doted on Gene and funded his projects.

After most of Gene's guests departed, a few of us stayed to sip cordials and admire his collections of Native American rugs, pottery, and jewelry. Gene was also a gifted raconteur, and after a couple of brandies told stories about his eccentric patrons.

"She measured her Cadillac to make sure it was longer than Trudy's, and when it wasn't, she had the fins elongated half a foot. Well, you can imagine that Trudy wasn't going to let it stop there!"

When we weren't hanging out with the Air Force or the artists, we went to dinner at the homes of Middle Eastern faculty and students. Metin was a Turkish professor who was in awe of Ulvi. He arranged for a screening of *Susuz Yaz*, and it was there that we met more Middle Eastern people than I would have guessed lived in Lubbock, Texas. The university had a reputation as an excellent school for petroleum engineering and arid agriculture. There were also Lebanese architects, Turkish mathematicians, Egyptian medical students, Syrian engineers, Jordanian geologists, Palestinian linguists.

When we were invited to their homes, the men sat in one room discussing politics, while their wives served them. After the men ate, the women retreated to the kitchen or bedroom to gossip, eat, and dance. Most of the women were also graduate students, biologists or chemists who spoke the clipped English of British boarding schools. They were servile to the men in the living room, but with one another, they were loud and raunchy, telling dirty jokes that made me blush. More than the parties at The Depot or the dinners out with the Air Force, the get-togethers with our Middle Eastern friends made me homesick. They reminded me of my family's Sunday afternoons, the vats of food, the music, the laughter, gossip, and constant touching, hugging, kissing of both cheeks, squeezed hands, and rubbed shoulders among the women.

At every gathering, the plaintive strings of the oud, the sharp tambours, and ululations of Greek, Turkish, and Lebanese music followed the elaborate meals. The men danced in circles in the living room. The women crimped their blouses under their bras, rolled their skirts below their hips, and danced in the kitchen or bedroom. No matter how serious a scientist she was, each woman could snake arms, quiver abdomens, and shimmy buttocks with grace and precision.

At one of the parties, the host heard us dancing in the kitchen and called us to perform for the men. They sat on the floor in a circle and clapped as, beginning with his wife, we each took a turn. To show their appreciation, the men threw coins at the feet of the dancers. I was among the last to dance. The music, the clapping and hooting, the joy of dancing again was exhilarating. As the women had taught me, I did figure eights with my hips, belly rolled, snake-armed, and shimmied with such abandon that the audience would not let me go.

"More!" they shouted. "Again!"

Snapping my fingers, undulating, twirling until the room was a blur, the music and voices a hum, sweat dribbling down my temples, collecting between my breasts, I danced, frenzied with pleasure. Until I caught sight of Ulvi, sulking.

Back at the apartment, he slapped my face. "You shame me," he said, "in front of my friends."

My greatest joy, dancing, was forbidden, unless I danced with him.

~~~

Because I worked at the library and knew my way around it, Ulvi asked me to help with his research. I spent hours with the *Reader's Guide to Periodical Literature*, creating a bibliography on 3x5 cards of articles that addressed the themes for his papers and potential thesis. His English was not good enough to grasp the technical language of the articles. I read and summarized them for him in simpler language, a dictionary at hand, because many of the terms were as foreign to me as to him. By the end of the semester, I knew more than I ever imagined about the topic of his industrial engineering thesis: the history and potential industrial uses of photo-electric technology.

As the holidays neared, the little hurts I'd been storing grew with the overwhelming sadness and isolation I felt in Lubbock. I had no friends of my own. I could not answer the phone ("it might be business"), could not go anywhere alone because I didn't know how to drive and anyway, where would I go in Lubbock, Texas? Ulvi's friendship with the cheerleaders irked me. The calls from

Irmchen at strange hours of the day or night (*"Ich liebe dich, ich liebe dich, ich liebe dich!"* he exclaimed during a particularly cheerful call) depressed me. The visits to the Middle Eastern households stopped, so I lost the camaraderie of women. I lived surrounded by a high fence with a gate controlled by Ulvi that grew higher every day as its walls contracted inwards, narrowing the space in which I moved.

I hid it well. Accustomed to disengaging Negi from Esmeralda in New York, I now split both from Chiquita. Esmeralda did not exist in Lubbock. No one could pronounce my name, which was truncated to Ez at work. Deferent and quiet in our apartment and with our friends, I was helpful and cheerful at the library. My coworkers liked Ez, but, with the exception of Gene, everyone else treated me as the extension of Ulvi that I was, invisible without him.

Two students taking a Spanish literature course offered to pay me if I reviewed their term papers for errors before they turned them in. I agreed, finishing the job a day before they expected. When the two young men walked into the library, I told them I was done but had left the papers at home. They offered to drive me during my lunch hour to pick them up so that they could deliver them to the typing service. They waited in the lobby of the building while I retrieved the pages. As we were leaving, Ulvi drove up and climbed out of the car as if afraid we would leave without him. He stopped short in front of us and glared at the two men, whose smiles and casual manner dissolved. I introduced them and explained why we were there. He shook their hands and told them he would drive me back to work. He didn't speak on the ride to the library, but when he picked me up that evening, he had been stewing for hours.

"Why you bring men into our home?" he asked as soon as we entered the apartment.

I explained that the whole exchange with the students had taken less than ten minutes. "It takes less than that to do it," he said, implying that I had sex not with one, but two men during the half hour allotted for lunch.

"How can you think such a thing?" I screamed. "All these months I haven't even been able to breathe without checking with you first. You know where I am at all times. How can you accuse me of being unfaithful?" He could not be convinced that neither of the boys were my lovers.

I spent a sleepless night going over the list of hurts I'd compiled in the four months we'd been in Lubbock. The next morning, instead of going to work, I called Mrs. Crisp and quit my job. I packed my belongings and called Continental Airlines. Because I turned over my salary to him each week, I had to ask Ulvi for money so that I could buy a ticket home.

Just as he couldn't believe I wasn't cheating on him, he didn't believe I would leave him. A smirk on his face, he drove me to the bank, where he withdrew three hundred dollars. He drove me to the airport in hostile silence, expecting that at any moment I would burst into tears and beg his forgiveness. As I climbed out of the Camaro in front of Departures, it became real that I was serious. He took my hand.

"Chiquita, do not do this," he said softly.

I did not look back as I entered the terminal. By lunchtime, I was in New York, in a taxi heading for Fulton Street.

"Surprise!" I said when Mami answered my knock.

In the year and a half I had lived away from home, everything had changed. Norma and Alicia had boyfriends and Héctor had a serious girlfriend. Delsa was studying X-ray technology at New York Medical Center, and had moved into the dorms there. Alma had married Bill, and they were living in Queens. Her sister, Corazón, had also moved away, and Titi Ana had left the apartment in Mami's house because it was too big without her daughters. Don Carlos and Mami had separated. Don Julio and Tata were not speaking.

Dropping unexpectedly into the turmoil of my relatives' lives, I didn't have to explain too much. They assumed I had come to be with them for the holidays, but my long face and listless attitude probably gave away my mood. I danced and ate and celebrated with the same abandon of earlier years, but every time the phone rang I started, expecting it to be Ulvi.

I went into Manhattan and filled out job applications at a couple of agencies, but the holidays were a terrible time to look for work. A recording informed me that the phone at The Grace Agency was disconnected. When I dropped in, Grace's name was no longer on the list of tenants in the lobby and the door to her office was locked. Through the pebbled glass I could see the boxes she never opened still stacked against the walls.

According to the *New York Times*, John was under siege from both the board of trustees and the staff at the Museum of Modern Art. The employees were organizing to unionize, and the board was expecting him to keep them from doing so or to resign. It didn't seem like a good time to drop in on him and Elaine. Margolis & Co. had moved from 11 West Forty-second Street. I stopped by the Longacre and Mrs. O'Dell said, "No, dear, I'm sorry, we don't have any vacancies. Didn't you like Texas?"

Everywhere I turned, New York was as hostile as always when I was lonely, confused, and didn't know what I wanted. I wished I could have lunch with Elaine and Carol again, to tell them they were right. I regretted leaving my great job, my challenging boyfriend, my sunny room at the Longacre, and my energetic family. I felt as lost as on the first day I arrived in the United States, uncertain of where I stood and scared of what would happen next.

What happened next was that Ulvi called.

~~

Mami had wondered why Ulvi hadn't phoned since I'd come to Brooklyn. "He's traveling," I said, which turned out to be true. He had spent the holidays in Santa Fe with Gene.

"I was angry with you, Chiquita," he said. "But we must discuss in person."

"I'm not going back."

He coughed, and I heard him put the phone down and blow his nose.

"I have cold," he said. He had been sick and feverish for days. He didn't want to bother me because he knew I enjoyed my family. He hoped I had a good holiday. He hoped I would consider returning.

"I'm not going back," I repeated.

"We must talk about this, Chiquita," he said. "Why did you leave so sudden?"

I should have hung up. Instead, I decided to answer his question. It was tricky to say what I needed to from the single phone Mami had, a wall unit in the kitchen, the busiest room in the house. I sat on the floor, faced the wall, wrapped the cord around me, hunched over the handset, and told Ulvi how hurt I was that he expected me to trust him but he didn't trust me.

Behind me, Tata, wrapped in a haze of cigarette smoke, shuffled out of her room to start supper. She ran water, banged pots, scraped pans and scuffed from pantry to sink to counter to stove muttering complains about Don Julio, who was not there to hear them.

I cupped the mouthpiece, and hunched further into a crouch over the phone. "You slapped me," I said to Ulvi, swallowing tears. "It hurt my feelings more than my cheek, because it was wrong for you to do that. Men shouldn't hit women."

"I am sorry, Chiquita," he said, his voice full of regret. "It will never happen again."

Raymond ran through chasing the dog, which yipped and sought refuge on my lap. I pushed it off and waved at Raymond to go away.

"You criticize every little thing I do or don't do," I muttered into the phone.

"I only mean to teach you the right way." He was as sweet as guava jelly. "You have many things to learn . . . "

Norma went by with a load of laundry asking if anyone needed to add dirty whites because she was starting the machine and, "where's the Clorox?"

"It's not my fault I'm not a good housekeeper," I said to Ulvi. "My mother didn't insist I do chores because I'm the intelligent one and had to study."

"I know you are smart girl, Chiquita."

Franky and Charlie tugged on my shirt because they wanted to play marbles. I covered the mouthpiece and screamed at them to leave me alone then returned to my conversation.

"I work all day and then I have to do your research and it's not fair to expect me to clean house and cook supper on top of that," I said once I'd returned to my conversation with Ulvi.

"I understand," he murmured.

Alicia tapped me on the shoulder and wondered when I was going to finish the phone call. "You've been talking for hours!"

"Do you want to return?" Ulvi asked hoarsely, and, when I didn't respond, said "Come back, Chiquita."

"My sister needs the phone," I said. "I can't talk anymore."

The next morning, I received a telegram. "IF YOU PREFER TO BE BACK AM EXPECTING YOU LOVE. PLEASE CALL. ULVI."

By lunchtime the next day, I was back in Lubbock.

"Don't worry,
you still have me."

I found a job as secretary to the administrator of a small private hospital only two blocks from our apartment. I was replacing Donna, a black-haired, hazel-eyed, peachy-skinned young woman with teeth the same brown color as Tata's nicotine-stained fingertips. Donna smoked, but she said her brown teeth were caused by Lubbock's water.

"You'll notice a lot of people around here have brown stains on their teeth," she said. I had noticed.

My boss, Mr. Parks, was a gangly, long-faced man with a reedy voice and a sober, humorless manner. He spent hours away from the office, which gave me an opportunity to practice typing until I could get through a whole letter and carbon copies with no mistakes.

When Mr. Parks was in, he talked on the phone, or met with the doctors who owned the hospital. The partners made the major medical or administrative decisions, and Mr. Parks carried out their plans and desires. Among these, the most important were the details around the completion of a new, state-of-the-art hospital on the outskirts of town. The project was behind schedule, and Mr.

Parks was under assault from the doctors on one side and from architects, contractors, and suppliers on the other.

One of my jobs was to field his calls, and I was soon the most popular employee in the hospital. Everyone wanted to see Mr. Parks. Suppliers brought me candy, flowers, trinkets, so that I would fit them into his appointment book. Department heads brought me coffee and cookies when I had not had a chance to take a break then asked whether Mr. Parks had reviewed the budget they had submitted for new desks and file cabinets. The contractor called me honey and asked about Mr. Parks's mood before dropping in with news of yet another unforeseen delay.

I was happier working in the hospital than at the library. It was my world, not Ulvi's. I didn't see him from the moment I left the apartment for the short walk to my office in the morning until after work in the evening. I preferred not knowing what he was up to, although I frequently came across scraps of paper with women's names and phone numbers written in their hand. Nancy, Mary Lou, Betty, Cindy, Bobbie Jo, Susie. The names were always those of whom I imagined to be "spoiled American girls," otherwise, why would they give their phone numbers to a thirty-nine-year-old foreign man with a leather jacket and a sports car?

The calls to Irmchen diminished during the hours I was home, but in his corner of the dresser we shared, stacks of her letters grew as if pollinated by absence. He never discarded them, even when every other piece of paper went to the garbage as soon as it was no longer useful. Once, at the beginning of our relationship in New York, I had gone through his belongings, but had not found anything to worry me. Now that we were living together and there were letters, scraps of paper, and mysterious envelopes from Germany and Turkey, I did not look. I didn't want to know, afraid of what that knowledge meant.

I was making good money at the hospital, especially if I put in extra hours helping Donna or the department heads as we prepared to move to the new site. Ulvi, too, had found a job, working part-time in the library bindery.

He took on the domestic chores that I so poorly executed. His gift for order soon relieved me of the anxiety that gripped me when called upon to maintain my surroundings. He kept the apartment tidy and clear of clutter, shopped for and cooked our meals when we were not invited out, and took clothes to and from the laundry. I happily traded the cleaning, cooking, and picking up for hours bent over musty volumes, doing the research for his master's thesis in industrial engineering. The promising future of photocell technology in the automation of repetitive tasks was infinitely more fascinating than the grease-cutting power of Palmolive dish detergent versus Lemon Joy, or the squeezability of Charmin toilet tissue.

Ulvi was a popular guest at dinner parties. He read several newspapers a day, subscribed to *Time* and *Newsweek*, sat engrossed before the television evening news and Sunday morning political discussions. His travels added credibility to his opinions, which he expressed with passion and authority. He hated Richard Nixon, and Henry Kissinger. He thought Jews controlled the media and big business. He discoursed extensively about the Hollywood monopoly on entertainment and placed himself alongside film artists like Visconti, Bergman, Polanski, and Antonioni, all of whom he claimed to have met and observed at work. At home, and with his foreign friends, he often stated, "Americans are so naïve." It astounded him that Americans were so ignorant about the rest of the world and so optimistic about the United States' place in it. He preferred the company of people who had traveled, especially if they had forgone the traditional European vacation for something more adventurous.

Our favorite evenings were spent at the home of Günter and Laila. He was the image of Aryan pride, tall, blonde, blue-eyed, handsome, straight-backed, with a resonant voice, a broad smile of even, white teeth, a hearty manner that disappeared if he was crossed. Günter was so spectacular a specimen of German maleness and beauty that it was hard to understand what he saw in quiet, plain, small, timid Laila, who was Swedish but had not inherited her Viking ancestors' vigor. Laila was so thin and delicate that the first time I met her I thought she was ill. As I came to know them both I saw that her strength was in her character and not in her physical appearance. She could silence Günter's raucous humor with a flutter of her lashes.

Friday nights Günter and Laila hosted slide-viewing parties. Laila was an accomplished baker of artisanal breads from recipes she found in obscure or ancient books and pamphlets in Swedish, German, or English. The guests brought wine and cheese. Günter and Laila served warm rolls or crispy domes of nutty whole-grain breads that we broke into fragrant chunks as hearty as a meal. We had to comment on the bread as Laila wrote down our impressions. She was compiling the more successful recipes for a book.

The person whose turn it was to share his or her slides narrated what we were seeing on the opalescent roll-up screen. In Günter and Laila's darkened living room, with the smells of bread, wine, and cheese around us, the world grew before my astonished eyes.

Big-bellied Biafran children stared impassively, the corners of their eyes and lips dotted with flies. "Was that child alive when you took the picture?" I asked. Yes, she was, and hungry.

Termite domes rose over the plains of Kenya, tall as a house. The giraffe women of Thailand smiled toothlessly, their elongated necks decked with brass rings that raised their heads so high above their shoulders that they didn't seem to belong to their bodies. An Indian fakir covered in ashes dangled a cinder block from his penis. Attenuated saints smiled benevolently from the faded walls of the rock cathedrals of Cappadocia.

Ulvi and I were always the darkest people in the room. Because of this, we were expected to have insights into the cultures in the slides even if they were as foreign to us as to the rest of the guests. Ulvi could discourse eloquently about politics, governments, and religions. I had no opinions, only questions.

"Why," I asked once, "does every slide we see at these gatherings show poor people? Why is poverty so fascinating?"

The question hung like an accusation. No one answered, not any of the four philosophy graduate students in the room, not the psychologist, not the Master in social work. I felt embarrassed to have challenged them, and Ulvi, who had better manners than I did, changed the subject to something our friends didn't have to defend.

From then on, I kept those kinds of questions to myself, and focused only on the information in the pictures. What did the language in the colorful signs on a crowded Japanese street sound like? What were the utensils for the daily tasks of cooking, planting, and building in a Philippine village? The photographer was surprised that I noticed a tool on the ground next to a Samoan man and wondered what it was used for. The cloth around a Nigerian woman's waist had suspiciously unnatural colors and regular patterns. Was it factory-made? "Is he wearing thongs?" I asked, and indeed, in the middle of the Masai desert, a warrior was wearing green rubber flip-flops. It became a running joke that I saw details no one else noticed because they were looking at the picture, while I focused on the minutiae.

"We see the forest," Günter laughed, "Chiquita sees the teeth in the worm chewing the leaves on the tree."

Weeknights after work, Ulvi and I had dinner, then he dropped me off at the library, where I did his research until closing time. I spent most of the weekend at the library, or in the apartment, reviewing and revising the textual parts of the papers he wrote, which were full of incomprehensible formulae I wouldn't even look at. A professional typist prepared them in the standard format before Ulvi turned them in to his professors.

When he didn't have an experiment or other pressing work at the engineering school, Ulvi liked to drive with no clear destination. He picked me up at the hospital and we headed out of town.

"Where are we going?" I asked.

"I don't know," he answered.

"Will we be back tonight?"

"No."

"I didn't bring my toothbrush."

"This is America," he said. "You can buy toothbrush anywhere."

We stopped at diners or Mexican restaurants along two-lane blacktop that disappeared into the flat horizon. I was thrilled the first time tumbleweed rolled across the landscape in front of us like in the western movies I loved. We pulled over to visit obscure monuments or historical markers that were often little more than a plaque on a metal pole commemorating a skirmish or the name of a long untraveled cattle trail. We stayed in five-dollar-a-night motels with hissing neon signs. One announced "Vaca cy," which made me giggle because I read it in Spanish, *Vaca si*, cow yes.

We were in the car for hours, but no intimacies were exchanged, no long conversations about life, politics, the future. Ulvi tuned the radio to a pop music station and we listened to Tony Orlando and Dawn's "Knock Three Times" or to Donny Osmond pleading "Go Away Little Girl." My head turned to the passenger window, I watched the miles whiz by, catching glimpses of whatever surprised me along the straight, deserted roads. A buzzard picking at a carcass. A distant tractor crawling along a cotton field followed by a cloud of dust. A line of oil derricks pumping slowly, like giant birds dipping their beaks into sand.

Sometimes I wondered what Ulvi thought about on those long drives. My own mind was busy with ideas, mostly related to his thesis or to ways to improve my job. Did he think in Turkish, German, English? Did he think at all, or was his mind blank and quiet, like his face? I began conversations that he ended with monosyllabic responses. I asked questions that elicited a terse "I don't know, Chiquita." After a few attempts to engage his attention, I let him go, and entered my own mind, thoughts racing through it in English and Spanish, unrestrained, unfocused, unchallenged, unspoken.

⟶

Once the hospital moved to the outskirts of Lubbock, I was completely dependent on Ulvi for rides to and from work. I asked him to teach me to drive, but he said that wasn't a good idea, since we only had one car, which he needed, and it was an unnecessary expense to buy another car that would be parked in a lot all day long.

The first few weeks in the new hospital were exciting. There were open houses for citizens, walk-throughs for the press and politicians, new doctors joining the partnership, training sessions for new employees. As the gatekeeper to Mr. Parks, I was at the center of these activities, answering phones, making appointments, receiving visitors.

As the only Spanish-English bilingual on the staff, doctors frequently asked me to translate for patients or their families. I finally met the Mexicans of Lubbock. They appeared at the doctors' offices or emergency room only when seriously injured or so ill that little more could be done for them than to make their last days comfortable. Their relatives sat by their bedsides, whispering endearments or taking turns praying the rosary. They kissed the doctors' hands when, through a miracle of science, the patient improved or gained consciousness enough to recognize a loved one. Their deaths were accompanied by heartbroken wailing, and injections of sedatives into the flailing arms of a distraught wife or a hysterical husband.

Some of the foreign doctors on staff spoke with thick accents. Trixie, the head of Medical Records, often called me to listen to sections of their dictations because the transcriptionist couldn't make out what the doctor was saying. Accustomed to foreigners, I had no trouble deciphering the often rushed, garbled recordings.

I preferred the direct contact with patients and doctors to the increasingly tedious routine of office administration. When I learned there was an opening in medical records, I asked Trixie to consider me for the job.

"But this would be a demotion for you," she said. "You're an executive secretary. The job I have is for another transcriptionist."

"I don't care about the title as long as I make the same amount of money."

When I switched to medical records, I came to love the work. Fingertips poised over the keys of a new IBM Selectric, earphones plugged to the recorder, I typed the reports that doctors dictated after every patient encounter. I learned the medical terminology quickly because so much of it came from Latin, and it was close enough to Spanish that I could spell words I'd never heard without having to look them up. I was astounded at the richness of medical words, at their complexity, at the beauty of the language for disease, healing and death. I shuddered at a diagnosis of metastatic astrocytic carcinoma, mourned a fatal abdominal aneurysm, rejoiced that paroxysmal atrial fibrillation of unknown etiology was not necessarily going to kill the young man who had it.

I felt intimately connected to the doctors, some of whom I never saw, but whose voices were in my head eight hours a day. I came to recognize the emotions they didn't display during examinations or surgeries but which colored the stark scientific language of their work. I could tell when a patient affected a doctor because his voice broke, or there were silences before or after a diagnosis that had nothing to do with losing his train of thought or checking notes. I wished there were some way to comfort a doctor who had just lost a patient despite his best efforts. I wondered about a doctor whose usually rote surgery notes became overly explicit as he sought phrases that would protect him from a medical malpractice suit.

Dr. Fletcher, the cardiologist, dictated elegant, grammatically complex sentences in an even, dispassionate tone. He took pains to pronounce difficult words, and sometimes even spelled them for us because he refused to sign anything that wasn't perfectly spelled. Dr. Omar, the Egyptian ear, nose, and throat specialist pronounced amygdala as if it were a sweet, juicy fruit, and paused over cochlea, drawing out the vowels. Dr. Parker, the gynecologist, lowered his voice when he said vaginal, as if the word, as well as the place, were dangerous. Dr. Mirza, the Palestinian obstetrician, delighted in announcing that "the patient was delivered of a healthy baby boy." No female physicians worked at the hospital. My head resonated with male voices speaking in familiar rhythms, their emotions so well hidden that I had to listen carefully to hear them feel.

⟿

I never called home because I knew Mami didn't approve of my life with Ulvi and I didn't want to hear the reproach in her voice. Except for me, no one in my family was much of a correspondent. Mami didn't have time to answer letters, and I didn't know what to say if I were to write one.

Delsa, who no longer lived at home, called me when Abuela died, and I wrote Papi a condolence letter with remembrances of his saintly mother. But months went by and I neither spoke to nor heard from anyone in Brooklyn. Bad news, I knew, would find me. Good news would accumulate until the next time we saw each other.

In late spring, Delsa called to say that Mami had moved to Puerto Rico.

"Why?"

Because, Delsa said, Brooklyn was becoming too dangerous and Mami was afraid for the kids. She had sold the house, had turned over her sewing business to a friend, and was taking eight of my siblings back to the island. Delsa refused to go because she wanted to finish her degree in X-ray technology. Héctor had moved in with his girlfriend and their baby.

"I have a niece?"

"Yeah, and she's so cute!"

"When did Mami and the kids leave?" I asked.

"A couple of weeks ago," Delsa said.

I was upset that no one had let me know earlier, that Mami had not called to say goodbye. It felt as if, now that I was no longer at home, I didn't count. But that's the way we were in my family. We were close but not *pegajosos*, sticky. Once away from home, we earned privacy over our lives. When I was there, they were there. When I was gone, they were gone.

"Is everything alright, Chiquita?" Ulvi asked when he noticed my long face.

"My family returned to Puerto Rico," I said as breezily as I could manage.

"All of them?" he asked.

"Just about," I said.

"Don't worry," he kissed my forehead, "you still have me."

"You are
very important to me."

At the end of his second semester, Ulvi learned that he had enough credits to pursue a Master of Arts in mass communications concurrently with the Master of Science in engineering. He could also work as a graduate assistant in photojournalism.

"You have no experience in that," I pointed out.

"My film is journalism," he said, "it is based on real life."

"But it's not news," I argued. "Journalism is about news."

He laughed. "Do not concern yourself, Chiquita."

He planned to finish his engineering thesis and six months later, submit a second one in communications.

"I need your help," he said. "I cannot do it alone."

"What do I have to do?"

"More of what you have been doing," he said, "but maybe is better if you also type the papers so there are not so many expensive mistakes like you always find."

It was frustrating, and costly, that I often returned pages to his typist because she had made spelling errors or was careless in the formatting, which had to adhere to the rules in the *Chicago Manual of Style*.

"We don't have a typewriter," I reminded him.

"I will get one for you."

Within a couple of days, he had not only secured an IBM Executive typewriter, but also a new apartment, brighter and bigger than the one by the tracks. Ours was the second door on the ground floor of a two-story building facing a garden around a swimming pool. The drought had turned the lawn the color and texture of hay, and the decorative bushes along the edges were bare of leaves. Ulvi loved the building because he could practically dive into the deep end of the pool from the walkway that led to the apartments. The typewriter belonged to the manager, a widow named Mildred who occupied the rooms closest to the washing machines and the rear entrance from the parking lot. Ulvi had charmed her into letting us borrow the machine permanently. Because the place was furnished, we didn't have to move much but our clothes, books and portable television, which Ulvi set up in the bedroom so that he could close the door and watch it while I read or worked in the front room.

The hospital covered the cost of college courses for its full-time employees, so, over the summer, I signed up for an American Literature class. In the hours when I wasn't researching the spectral sensitivity of different photocathode materials or the history of television broadcast news, I wrote a paper about religious imagery in *The Grapes of Wrath*. At the end of the summer, I told Ulvi that I was changing my work hours so that I could take more courses. He worried that I was doing too much, with a full-time job at the hospital, literature courses, and my "job" as his researcher-editor.

"It is most important that I finish my thesis," he said, and I swore that it was my first priority.

I fell into a routine that tested the discipline I had developed at Performing Arts and as a dancer. I chose two courses that met from 8:00 to 9:30 a.m. From classes I walked to the library and did Ulvi's research or studied. At noon he drove me to the hospital, where I transcribed physical exams and surgery notes until he came for me. Some of my coworkers lived near us and offered me rides home, but Ulvi would not hear of it. If he couldn't pick me up at 8 p.m., I worked until he arrived.

Back at the apartment, Ulvi had dinner waiting. He and the Air Force officers loved White Castle, and he would sometimes bring me a bagful of the tiny hamburgers and a vanilla milkshake, which I consumed in the car on the way home.

Because he only spent money on "good" or "expensive" clothes, we didn't wear them indoors when we were alone. As soon as we entered the apartment, we stripped and hung our garments to air. We lived naked and barefoot, even in winter, the heat turned up to 80 degrees, the shades drawn to thwart voyeurs.

After a short nap, I skimmed the handwritten pages Ulvi had for me to type, queried him for footnotes, and went through copies of articles that he wanted me to read and mark for him.

Because I was so busy, Ulvi had a social life without me. I was both grateful and resentful of his evenings out. I liked having the apartment to myself. I enjoyed reading the demanding scientific literature for his theses and trying to understand what he was trying to say in the painstakingly written notes he left after reading the literature and discussing his theories with his professors. But it also annoyed me that I should be in the apartment alone, doing his work, while he had a good time with his friends. I never had a night off, no friends of my own, couldn't even go for a walk without him by my side.

The one time I brought it up, he reminded me that, in the Bahamas, I had offered to help him.

"It was your decision, Chiquita," Ulvi said. "You pushed me to come to Lubbock. I had many other opportunities in Europe."

He curtailed his evenings out, however, and most of the time after that, sat on the sofa reading through the pages I'd marked as relevant to his thesis or through articles he had copied from the notes on 3x5 cards that I gave him after my stints at the library. We talked about the organization of the thesis, the topics to be covered, the formulae needed to support his theories. I quizzed him on the likely questions for his oral exam from a list he had developed with the help of his military buddies.

Our long car trips became mini vacations. To get the time off from the hospital, I traded overtime pay for consecutive days off. Ulvi and I climbed into the Camaro and drove to Denver, to the Florida Keys, to Houston, to Aspen and Vail, to Taos, to Little Rock, Arkansas. We spent many weekends in Santa Fe, where we joined Gene and, during the season, accompanied him to the magnificent opera house for glittering musical evenings.

On a cool spring day, Ulvi drove up to a lookout point high in the Santa Fe National Forest. It was late afternoon, and ours was the only car in the parking area. We stood at the edge of a peak looming over high rolling hills that fell off to the Great Plains on the East while to the West behind us rose the snowcapped crests of the Rockies. The view was spectacular and, confronted with majestic nature in high, thin air, I was euphoric. When we returned to the car, Ulvi said that he was almost out of gas.

"How did we get up here?"

"We had enough petrol to drive up," he said, "but not enough to go down."

"Maybe if we wait, somebody will give us a ride to town so we can get some?"

"No, Chiquita. It will be dark soon. We cannot stay. We will go down in neutral."

"What does that mean?"

He didn't answer. He turned the car around to face the incline, and for a moment, I thought he was teasing me about not having enough gas. As soon as he had poised the car's nose at the top of the slope, he shifted to neutral and coasted down the steep, packed dirt road snaking around the mountainside. It was like being on a roller coaster, the car careening sideways sometimes, gravel shooting from beneath the wheels and cascading down the slopes into forested chasms.

"Ulvi, stop, this is scary!"

He didn't speak. He kept his eyes on the road, his arms stretched, fingers gripping the steering wheel, which he controlled with minute turns or sudden jerks that sent me bouncing against the passenger door and the roof. I pressed my hands against the dashboard to keep from banging my teeth against it. The seat belt around my lap tugged against my hips, scraped the tops of my thighs. I screamed at him to stop but he couldn't, not as we hurtled down the packed dirt toward the main road at the bottom, stones and pebbles clattering beneath us. My biggest fear was not only that we would fall over the edge, which seemed to be his intention, but that another car would be coming up as we were going down and we would take a couple of people to their deaths with us. Ulvi steered as if in a trance, oblivious to my panic, his lips set into a hard line.

Somehow, we reached the bottom alive. He shifted, turned the car on, grinned with self-satisfaction, and drove to the nearest gas station, while, in the passenger seat, I shook and wondered why he was trying to kill us.

"I am a good driver, Chiquita," he said back at the hotel, when I had calmed down. "Nothing was going to happen."

"How do you know? A truck could be coming up as we went down . . . "

"Nothing was going to happen," he repeated. "I would never hurt you, never. You are very important to me."

"You almost killed me," I wailed.

"No, Chiquita, I was in control, I promise you." He caressed my face, kissed my eyes. "Only one other person is so important to me like you," he said.

I tensed and waited. Irmchen? Siri in Ceylon? Doreen the cheerleader?

He took a black-and-white picture from his wallet, like the ones you could get in a strip of four in booths at Woolworth's. A sad-eyed little girl with unruly black hair tried to smile but couldn't.

"Who is she?" I asked, noticing the resemblance.

He took the picture, looked at it, returned it to his wallet, and gazed into the distance. "My sister."

"How old is she?"

"About ten," he said. "She is little girl."

"Why is she so much younger than you?"

The question seemed to embarrass him. "She is from my, how you say? My father's other wife."

"Your stepmother?"

He nodded.

"Where is your mother?"

He thought a moment, reluctant to say the words. "She is died."

"I'm sorry," I hugged him. "What's her name?"

"My mother?"

"No, your sister."

"Ulviye."

"Like your name?"

"Yes, but with a ye at the end. It is how we do in Turkey."

"Why is she named after you and not after your stepmother?"

"Because," he sighed, and I could tell he was getting annoyed at my questions, "I am very famous man in Turkey and my father want to honor me."

I wanted to ask his father's name, what he did, where they lived, what Ulviye liked, but Ulvi began to rummage in the closet. "Come, Chiquita, let's get dressed for dinner." The conversation was over.

I was happy that, next to his sister, I was the most important person in Ulvi's life, even if he had just tried to kill me with the Camaro. Maybe he was planning to kill us both, and the thought of his father and sister in Istanbul made him reconsider. I shook my head to clear the morbid scenarios. Of course Ulvi had not tried to kill us. He was a good driver, had not had a single accident since I'd known him, even though he drove faster than the speed limit. If I'd had life insurance, I might have worried, but I didn't. Still, from then on, every time I climbed into the Camaro, I checked the gas gauge and fastened my seat belt.

~

Ulvi passed his oral exams and received a Master of Science degree in industrial engineering. Gene threw a party for him and made jokes about a textile engineer turned Berlin Film Festival Golden Bear Award winner turned industrial engineer studying to become a Master of mass communications.

"When are you going to figure out what you want to be when you grow up?" he asked Ulvi, and they laughed over his many incarnations and how hard it was to "make it."

"You deserve congratulations, too," Gene lifted a glass in my direction.

"What did I do?" I was embarrassed to be the center of attention in a group that usually ignored me.

"We all know," Gene said, "that this guy here," he patted Ulvi's shoulder, "could never have written that thesis on his own. His English is not good enough."

Ulvi's face grew ashen, his eyes hardened, but he kept his smile on. "Chiquita was big help," he said. "Thank you." He tipped his wine toward me.

"All I did was correct some spelling," I said. I bit my tongue so that I wouldn't continue, so that I wouldn't claim the credit I deserved for the hours at the library, the hundreds of 3x5 cards with precise notes, the abstracts of what began as incomprehensible jargon and became lucid facts as I learned to interpret the scientific language. "And I typed the final draft." I clamped my mouth shut.

"To Chiquita," Gene said, and the guests toasted my typing skills.

⁓

I declared a major in communications because that department offered early morning courses, and my business, marketing, and advertising credits from Manhattan Community College were acceptable
toward their bachelor's degree. It was a small department, and I
discovered that Doreen the cheerleader was a classmate. She wanted
to be a television news anchor when she grew up. Her boyfriend,
Roy, dreamed of being a sportscaster, and the three of us were in the
same History of Cable Television and Radio Communications
classes. I liked Roy, a bigheaded quarterback with a goofy sense of
humor and an obsession with quadraphonic sound systems.

We had to pick a project for our finals and I chose to write, produce, direct, and narrate a series of public service announcements in
Spanish for broadcast over Texas Tech radio. The spots were ten to
thirty seconds long and encouraged teenagers to stay in school.

None of my professors spoke Spanish, and they weren't sure that
any Spanish speakers listened to the college station, which was
staffed by students and focused on the rock-and-roll needs and
tastes of undergraduates. By surfing the local radio dial, I found a
low wattage station that served the Mexican community. The
owner-announcer agreed to take the PSAs if he didn't have to do
anything but play them.

Our department was planning a series of panels, lectures, seminars, and other events for Mass Communications Week, in the
middle of February. Posters went up in the hallways encouraging
female students to compete for Miss Mass Communications, who
would greet and introduce speakers and dignitaries, and be a
spokesperson to the media. She would also have the use of a new
car to get her to and from activities.

While waiting for Professor Kestrel to start class, Doreen and
Roy were talking about the car.

"It's a convertible," she purred. "With an eight-track player. I'll let you drive it."

The entitlement in her voice was infuriating. She was sure she had won the contest, even though some of our classmates had also entered. Her confidence brought out a competitive part of me I didn't know existed.

After class, I went right over to the department secretary and paid for the entry fee with my lunch money. Other than auditions, I had never entered contests of any kind, least of all a beauty contest, which is what I imagined this was, otherwise, why limit it to women? I didn't tell Ulvi about it, not until the evening of the interviews, when I had to leave work early and he had to drive me to the University Center.

"Why you do this?" he asked, annoyed.

"Because it sounds like fun," I said.

"Is not fun to be in public all the time."

"It's only for a week. I won't win anyway. Your friend Doreen has already offered the car to her boyfriend."

He tightened his lips and didn't speak another word.

A board of prominent Lubbock citizens tested our knowledge of communications and evaluated us on poise, appearance, and ability to respond quickly and appropriately to a series of general questions. Several candidates were eliminated right away, and as the evening wore on, only three of us remained, Doreen, our classmate Lynette, and me.

In that room full of the best Lubbock had to offer, I did my best to impress a city official, two housewives, the sales manager for a radio station, and the public relations supervisor for the phone company.

Doreen might have been prettier and better dressed, a veteran of beauty contests, a master of platitudes and crowd-pleasing banalities, but each time my turn with the panel came, I entered that room with purpose, defining the competition as substance over fluff.

The theme for the activities the college planned was "The Revolution in Mass Communications." I let the panel know that such a revolution could not take place without people like me, ignored by the media to the point of invisibility, but unwilling to remain silent.

I planted my feet firmly on the floor, dropped my voice, and put on my most convincing Standard American Speech. "My experience translating for my mother and others has instilled in me a vision of myself as a voice for those who, because of language or cultural issues, will not or cannot speak for themselves." If they noticed the pompous, pedantic nature of my statement, they didn't show it. They had already read it on the application as the reason why I was competing.

Three months in a classroom with Doreen had shown me that there was no possibility she would come up with a theory of her own value to society, even if prompted. Remembering Ruth's advice that I should not be humble about what I did well, I told the panel about my work translating at the hospital, about the Spanish PSAs which had been running for a few weeks, about my plans to do another series focusing on health issues.

Sometimes, in moments of stress, I separate from myself, so that a part of me is an observer as the other part enacts whatever is happening. During the interviews, the ghost me was like a cheering section, reminding me to breathe, to smile, to make eye contact, to state my point clearly, to control my emotions, to be enthusiastic but not appear desperate. At the end of the last interview, I returned to myself and relaxed, knowing I had done everything possible to at least demonstrate that Doreen might not be the best representative of "The Revolution in Mass Communications,"

The three finalists, Doreen, Lynette, and me, waited in the hall outside the conference room as the panel deliberated. Doreen chewed on what we call in Spanish *la yema de los dedos*, the soft, fleshy yolk of the fingers. The habit was probably adapted from nail biting, an activity not appropriate for beauty queens. Lynette sat with her hands under her thighs, her shoulders hunched and her head bowed so that her long brown hair shaded her upturned nose.

After the tension of the interviews, I was relaxed, and sat quietly reading a monograph about the first Telsat satellites. Years of accompanying Mami with convulsing babies to emergency rooms had taught me to resist the useless, counterproductive attacks of *los nervios* that plagued every Puerto Rican woman I knew.

When a photographer appeared out of nowhere, the panel was ready to announce their decision. We were called into the conference room and, after complimenting us on our performance, Mrs. A. C. Verner announced me as the winner. Doreen and Lynette smiled gamely, and left the room. When Ulvi came to pick me up, I was still smiling for the photographer.

Ulvi was thrilled with the white convertible with "Pollard Ford Congratulates Miss Mass Communications" on the doors. For the next two weeks, everywhere we went in Lubbock, people turned to wave. Pictures and interviews appeared in the college and local newspapers. I received a gold pendant from Payson's Jewelers, which I wore throughout Mass Communications Week, in the photographs with dignitaries, and, best of all, dangling from a gold chain in classes where Doreen was sure to see it.

As his second year at Texas Tech began, Ulvi had to figure out what to do following graduation. His visa would expire, but could be renewed if he needed more time to finish a degree. He decided to go for a Ph.D., which would gain him at least another couple of years. His graduate studies had not kept him from exploring ways to bring *Susuz Yaz* to an American audience. He thought of himself as a filmmaker, not an engineer, and he hoped that a doctorate would give him more credibility as he sought ways to stay "in the business."

He applied to every doctoral program in communications he could find, all of them in cities far from the center of commercial movie-making. He was accepted to every one, but only Syracuse University offered a teaching post.

Because he was so preoccupied with his work as a photojournalism teaching assistant, with the paperwork and the interviews for the doctoral program applications, he expected me to do more of the work on his thesis, such as write whole passages that he then reviewed and approved. It was more efficient, and I enjoyed the writing. Ulvi, however, didn't think that my colloquial style was scientific enough for the subject matter—the utilization of Super 8mm film for television news—so he began giving me handwritten notes that closely paraphrased entire pages of text from books and monographs. It was obvious that he had not written them because I had done the research, had read the material before him and knew it well.

"You can't do this without attribution," I protested.

"What means this?"

"You can't include this in your thesis as if they were your own findings. You have to quote the passage and then enter a footnote about who wrote it, where it was published, and when."

"Do whatever is correct."

Sorting his interpretations from the quoted passages was difficult, because he had not indicated where one ended and the other began. He often took one paragraph or sentence from one place, wrote in a connecting phrase, and then continued with material from a different source. As the deadline for submission neared, we fought nightly because he thought I should stop being so picky, and just type what he told me to type.

"Don't worry so much, Chiquita," he said.

"It's my work too," I insisted. "I want it to be right."

"It is not your work," he shouted. "It is my name on it, not yours."

I remembered Eugene and Leo's accusations that Ulvi had taken someone else's film and claimed the credit for it, and would have reminded Ulvi of it if I'd had the courage. Instead, I swallowed my pride and typed what he told me to type, worrying only about my part of it, accurate spelling and formatting according to the *Chicago Manual of Style*. The content was his responsibility. After all, it was his name on it, not mine.

"I'm not neurotic!"

"It's called passive-aggressive behavior, and it's not a healthy basis for a relationship," Shirley suggested.

"Yes, that's the problem. He's too aggressive and I'm too passive."

"That's not what it means," she laughed.

Shirley was a graduate student in psychology. I came to know her that spring when we kept running into each other in the stacks at the library. When she opened her mouth and spoke in a familiar Brooklyn accent, I sighed with such relief that students turned around to shush her loud laughter. Shirley volunteered at a mental health clinic three blocks from the university, where most of her patients were divorced women. She dressed in long skirts and gauze shirts, wore sandals, let her wild, curly hair do what it would, smoked marijuana as if it were Virginia Slims, and used the word "fuck" liberally. I adored her, and envied her free spirit and intelligence even as I felt intimidated by her liberal ideas and apparent carelessness over *el que dirán*. I only saw Shirley at the library or coffee shop because she was the kind of woman who repelled Ulvi. "Too free" he would have said about her, "too independent. A spoiled American girl."

Shirley was married to Lenny, who was also a graduate student in psychology and seemed dropped straight from a draft card burning at Columbia University into the middle of Texas Tech. In 1972, Lenny was one of the few activists on campus, complete with the straggly long hair and Pancho Villa mustache, the radical opinions and the dogged, ill-fated attempts to politically mobilize the white, middle-class, Baptist, football-loving, military-joining, red-meat-eating, pickup-truck-driving-with-a-loaded-rifle-in-the-rack-on-the-back-window students of Texas Tech University and its surroundings. This was the Texas Panhandle, and no longhaired Jewish New York hippie was going to tell its people what to do, but Lenny kept trying.

Some days after Ulvi told me that it was his name on the thesis and not mine, I ran into Shirley at the library and after gentle prompting, told her what was bothering me. Our conversations until then had been about New York, books, and the dissertation she was writing on the link between age at first sexual experience and the stability of subsequent intimate relationships. When I told her about my change in attitude vis-à-vis Ulvi's thesis, Shirley mentioned the passive-aggressive pattern, and when I had no idea what she was talking about, explained what it was.

"Couples form systems," she said, "to keep the relationship going. When the systems are not based on equality and mutual respect, neurosis develops."

"I'm not neurotic!" I protested. "I think he is, though."

She laughed her loud, crackling laugh. "Everyone is neurotic," she said, "it's a question of degrees."

Because of her training as a psychologist, her kindness and generosity, our visits at the library became therapy sessions. Mostly, I complained about Ulvi, and Shirley asked "what are you planning to do about that?" which was annoying, since what I wanted was for somebody to tell me what to do.

"I can't tell you what to do," she said, "I can help you see things in a different way. But, it's your life. You have to make it work."

I pressed my fists into my eye sockets. "It's so hard!"

She took my wrists, opened my hands and rubbed them between hers. "Why do you stay with him, if you're so unhappy?" she asked.

I wanted to say, other than a sister and brother I seldom talk to and haven't seen in two years, I am alone in the United States. I don't know how to drive. Ulvi controls my money and I'm embarrassed to ask him for more than he gives me because he knows I like to spend. It's my fault we're in Lubbock because I insisted he stay in the United States with me when he had many opportunities in Europe. Besides, I believe he loves me and he's the only person in the United States who does. What I said was:

"I'm tired of being in charge of my life. Ulvi takes care of me and all I have to do is the research for his thesis and typing."

"That's all?" I avoided her eyes, but felt her waiting for me to admit that I had oversimplified things. When I didn't, she sighed, exhausted by my stubbornness. "That's the deal you've made then, isn't it?" she let go of my hands.

I hung my head.

Going into details about my personal life was difficult even with Shirley's gentle probing. "The deal," as she called it, went beyond what she ever imagined or I could admit out loud. Ulvi gave me entry into a world that until he came along had been inaccessible to me. As Alma had pointed out, he had whispered in my ear and taken me "away from all this."

"All this" was the insistent awareness of my life and circumstances endorsed as future material to nourish our acting by the teachers at Performing Arts High School. The only problem was that first I had to live through the experiences. "All this" was the depressing, run-down neighborhoods in which I had lived, the desperate mothers for whom I had translated at the welfare office, the indolent men on street corners, the girls withering on tenement windowsills. "All this" was believing that I could have a better life than those women, those girls, but not quite believing I could. "All this" was the self-hatred engendered by racist remarks from total strangers, who spit out "Spick!" as I passed them on the sidewalk as if they had been waiting for just such an opportunity. "All this" was the stress of balancing what was expected by people who loved me, with avoiding what was expected by people who called me names on the street. "All this" was reading that women were taking charge of their lives while every day I relinquished more control over mine.

I would rather pretend that everything was fine, smile my way through my days to divert attention from the shame and sadness that weighed me down if I stopped to think about "all this." Shirley was breaking through the pretense. The more I talked to her, the harder it was to keep my mind blank of anything unrelated to my work at the hospital and my work for Ulvi. So long as she asked, prodded, held my hands, I couldn't get away from myself.

I stopped going to the library during the hours when I knew she was there. If I saw her coming, I turned in the opposite direction. If we passed on one of the paths around the campus, I pretended not to see her. Once when Ulvi and I were at the college bookstore, Shirley came around the corner of the psychology shelves. She started to say hello but then saw Ulvi who, as if sensing she was a friend to me, took my hand and tugged me toward the cashiers. Before I turned, our gazes met and held for a few seconds. I saw such pity in Shirley's eyes that I had to look away.

~~~

Ulvi was asked to be the best man at the wedding of Don, one of the Air Force officers. A couple of days before the wedding we argued, again because I felt guilty typing pages of text without proper attribution. I was so frustrated, and ashamed, that I ran out of the apartment with no sense of where I was going. I thought of phoning Shirley and asking her if I could stay with her for a few days, until my next paycheck and the possibility that I could buy an airplane ticket out of Lubbock, but I was embarrassed to call after avoiding her for weeks.

While I deliberated with the phone in my hand whether to call or not, Ulvi drove by and spotted me in the booth. I hung up and ran down the street, but he followed, talking through the lowered passenger side window.

"Why you do this, Chiquita?" he asked. "Why you run away? Come, let us talk. Get in the car, Chiquita, please. Do not do this. We have to talk about."

I had no place to go, no one to turn to. He pleaded with me, and I climbed into the Camaro, belted myself in, and sat in the further-most corner of the passenger seat, feeling more alone than ever.

In the apartment, Ulvi was gentle and understanding of why it was so hard for me to do what he asked. "You are good girl, Chiquita, I know." The reality was, he said, that being nearly at the end of the thesis, we didn't have time to go back to change the passages that "are incorrect." There was no time to locate all the sources, to retype tens of pages in order to put quote marks where they belonged, to rephrase elegant scientific language with my functional colloquialisms. "It has to be this way, Chiquita. We are very close to the end. Do not spoil."

I did not spoil it. Ulvi went to Don's bachelor party and I stayed in the apartment, transferring his notes onto 25 percent rag bond.

The next morning, as we were getting ready for the wedding, Ulvi asked, "Who were you calling last night from the phone booth?"

"No one," I said.

"You were talking to somebody, Chiquita, I saw you."

"I did not call anyone."

"Don't lie to me!" He slapped my face.

I ran to the living room and was about to escape the apartment again, but he reached the door before I did.

"Get ready," he said, "we can not be late."

"I'm not going!"

"You are combing your hair and you are putting on your shoes and you are coming with me."

"I'm not going to a wedding to pretend we're a happy couple."

His face went through so many different expressions, that they were impossible to interpret because I didn't know the thought process behind them.

"Very well, Chiquita," he finally said, "you do not come." He returned to the bedroom, and I heard him rustle around as he finished putting on his tuxedo.

I lay crumpled on the sofa, my back to the room, the pretty dress I had bought for the wedding wrinkling beneath me. I heard him return to the living room, stand behind me for a moment, waiting for me to move or say something. I was afraid he would pull me up and drag me to the church, where Don and the groomsmen waited, but Ulvi just turned around and left, slamming the door.

Ulvi submitted his thesis, it was accepted, and he passed the oral exams. No one checked the footnotes or bibliography. No one complained about the inconsistent language. I wondered if anyone had read it. We made plans to leave for Syracuse. I had a vague idea to go that far with him and, once in New York, take a train or bus into Manhattan and begin anew, without him.

A couple of weeks before our cross-country drive, I answered a knock at the door and found Alma, smiling sheepishly. "Hi!" she said.

Ulvi, who was in the bedroom about to settle down with Walter Cronkite, came out, expecting it to be one of his friends. After I introduced them, and he learned Alma was my cousin from New York, he excused himself and returned to the bedroom, closing the door behind him. He turned the volume up louder than usual to let me know my visitor was not welcome.

"What are you doing in Lubbock?" I asked, as soon as I'd served Alma some iced tea and we had settled across from one another on the sofa.

"My husband is stationed at Reese Air Force base," she said. Her eyes darted between the bedroom door and me. "Monday I start a job at the university."

She had been in Lubbock for two weeks already, living on base. It had taken her and Bill a while to settle in.

"I knew you were in Lubbock, but didn't have your address. Then I remembered the Turk's name," she glanced at the door, "and that he was a student here. That's how I found you."

We talked for a while about my job, about life in the Texas Panhandle. I told her about our favorite stores, about the cultural events sponsored by the university, especially in Gene's music department, which offered a rich selection of concerts and recitals.

"It's really not the end of the universe," I joked.

"I'm excited to be living where Buddy Holly was born."

"Who?"

I had been in Lubbock for almost two years and had never heard of Buddy Holly or of his wife Maria, who, Alma said, was Puerto Rican.

"I thought I was the only Puerto Rican in West Texas," I laughed. "No one told me about Buddy and Maria."

"He's dead, you know," she said.

"That's what I get for hanging out with foreigners," I sighed. "Total ignorance of American culture."

"I hear that the wife of the university president is also Puerto Rican."

"You're kidding!"

"We're everywhere," she laughed.

"It's too bad that, just as you're moving here, we're moving to Syracuse."

She lowered her head and seemed about to say something, but thought better of it. "I'm sorry I dropped in on you without warning," she said. "Your husband seemed annoyed."

"No, he's just addicted to the news, that's all. He's obsessed with this whole Watergate thing. I don't get it."

She stood up. "It was great to see you," she said. "Maybe we can get together sometime before you move."

"That sounds great." I jotted down our home number. "But it's better if you call me at the office," I said, writing that down too. "We're here for another three weeks."

As she was stepping out, Alma fixed her eyes on the closed door to the bedroom, then on me. "Is everything alright with you . . . with him?"

"Everything's fine."

She stared at the door again, fearfully I thought. "I'll call you," she said, and was gone.

I pressed my back against the wall and shut my eyes. So much had happened in the two years since we'd last seen each other. The Longacre Hotel seemed like a dream from a long time ago. Alma looked different. There was a solidity around her that was not there before, a barrier almost, between us. I thought it was because she knew that everything was not all right with me.

During one of the dinners following Ulvi's graduation, I met Carmen, the university president's wife. She was a petite, middle-aged woman with the translucent paleness and delicate appearance I remembered on Jacqueline, my ballerina friend at the Longacre Hotel.

"I saw your photograph in the paper," Carmen said, "but I was in the hospital and didn't have a chance to call and congratulate you."

Like Jacqueline, she was battling cancer, and had spent most of the past two years in Dallas. She was easily tired, so she didn't entertain or go out much. "But it's so nice to speak *la lengua madre* with someone who has the same accent," she smiled.

We exchanged reminiscences of Puerto Rico, which made us both nostalgic. She had not visited the island in years, but she longed for it. "It's like missing your mother," she said, closing her eyes as she remembered. "I just want to go back to our *finca* in Utu- ado, grab a handful of that rich soil, and rub it over my body." She opened her eyes and blushed. "Ay, *Dios mío*, listen to me, talking like that. *¿Qué dirá la gente?*"

"Nobody else heard you," I said, "I wish I could do the same."

Alma didn't call. I tried the Texas Tech directory, but she was not listed, at least not under her maiden name, and I didn't know Bill's last name. The day before Ulvi and I were to drive off on the first leg of our journey to Syracuse, the phone rang. It was a secretary in the Chemistry Department asking if I had any idea where Alma was.

"She gave your name as next of kin," she said. "She hasn't been at work in a couple of days, and we're worried about her."

"Did you call her husband?"

"We've not been able to reach him."

"That's strange," I said.

"We're worried because . . . I don't know if I should say this . . . "

"Please, she's my cousin, I should know."

"She came in the other day and she was bruised pretty bad. Her arms were black and blue, her lip was swollen and her eye . . . "

"Oh, God!"

"I'm sorry I said anything."

"No, that's okay. Thank you. You did the right thing." My fin- gers hurt from gripping the receiver against my ear.

"If she gets in touch, will you let her know we're trying to reach her?"

"I will."

I recalled Alma's anxious gaze at the door behind which Ulvi sat watching the news. She might have been worried about me, but she was more afraid about what would happen when she returned behind her own closed doors.

The phone number I had for her in Queens was disconnected. I had no other way to reach her, no idea where she could have gone. She disappeared as thoroughly as if she never existed, and it would be twenty-five years before we saw each other again.

⁓

Ulvi and I packed our belongings in a small U-Haul trailer and said goodbye to our friends in West Texas. As we pulled away from the building, Mildred, our landlady, splashed a bucketful of water behind us to ensure we would someday return to Lubbock.

We drove into the dusty, flat landscape, the Camaro's radio tuned to news stations that babbled endlessly about what it could mean that a cashier's check meant for President Nixon's reelection campaign ended up in the bank account of one of the Watergate burglars.

"Can we listen to music?" I asked.

Grudgingly, Ulvi tuned the radio to a Top 40 station. "Bye, bye, Miss American Pie," sang Don McLean. I hummed along to mask his impatience to return to the news. We listened to Michael Jackson sing "Ben" and to Sammy Davis, Jr.'s "The Candy Man." With the first strains of Helen Reddy's "I am woman, hear me roar," Ulvi decided I'd heard enough music.

"It is important, these news," he said. "You should pay attention. You will be voting for president in couple months. How will you know who to vote for?"

"That's easy, George McGovern."

"Why do you vote for him?" he asked.

"Because he looks like a nice man."

"Nice men do not make good presidents," he said. "Politics is dirty business."

He was excited, the way he became with his friends when they talked about current events. In such a discussion, I couldn't keep up.

"Your Mr. Nixon is a corrupt man," Ulvi said when I didn't respond.

"He's not my Mr. Nixon, I didn't vote for him."

"He's your president. You are affected by what he does."

"Can we listen to music now?"

"No, we listen to the news." He tuned the radio to an AM station in Oklahoma, and kept switching frequencies every time the signal weakened. I tuned out, and for the rest of the trip, stared at the changing landscape, at the horizon punctuated by silos and farmhouses, or studded with cities whose jagged skylines rose from the flatness of the Midwest like paintings on postcards. By the end of the day, my neck hurt from having it twisted away from Ulvi.

I did not feel as if I had left Texas until the first night away from Lubbock, when I showered and washed my hair and the orange dust of the Texas Panhandle whirled down the drain. Later, while Ulvi showered, I pulled the phone book from the bedside drawer and looked for names that sounded Spanish. It was a comfort when I ran across an Ortiz, a Fernandez, Rodriguez, Gonzalez, Guillen, even if none of them had the accent where it belonged.

We ate at noisy roadside diners, slept in funky motels with toilets SANITIZED FOR YOUR CONVENIENCE, and beds that vibrated if I dropped a quarter in a slot. After a leisurely two weeks on the road, the sparse lights of Syracuse winked at us as if letting us in on a joke. We entered the city in the dark of a steamy August night and registered at a Holiday Inn near the university. The next morning, Ulvi went to check in at the college while I walked the half block from our hotel to Snelling and Snelling Employment Agency. By the end of the day, Ulvi had found us an apartment, and I had a job as a bilingual secretary at Bristol Myers International. I had also learned that Syracuse was at least a six-hour drive to New York City, longer by bus. I had no idea New York was so big. Syracuse was psychologically almost as far away from Manhattan as Lubbock had been. It would take more than a long bus ride to return there.

"Today is the first day of the rest of your life."

Mr. Darling, my boss at Bristol Myers International, hunkered in his office, smoking unfiltered cigarettes, drinking coffee, and drafting letters in English or Spanish in a small, tight handwriting with precisely crossed t's, dotted i's, and narrow margins. He clipped his drafts to the outside of creased manila folders bursting with correspondence and the blurred carbon copies of his replies. In between letters, he made phone calls in English, Spanish, and German. He had a deep, rumbling voice, made throatier by hoarseness from frequent attacks of coughing that turned his face red and made his eyes water. Every piece of furniture and paper in his office had an unpleasant sticky film, the yellow air was stale, the walls as brown as flypaper. Overstuffed folders were stacked on his desk and on the credenza under the window. They were crammed into shelves along the walls, teetered on piles along the baseboard. He had been without a secretary for over a month and his outbox was full of correspondence that spilled over into a crate by his chair.

"Start with the older letters first," he instructed, "the ones going overseas have precedence because it takes longer for them to get there."

It was a good thing that I could now type with speed and accuracy. It took me over a month just to catch up with Mr. Darling's overdue correspondence.

Bristol Myers International was on the fourth floor of a six-story building near downtown Syracuse, about twenty minutes from the stacks that spewed foul-smelling vapor over the plant where the company manufactured penicillin. My desk was directly in front of Mr. Darling's door. A row of three-drawer metal file cabinets demarcated our territory from the next executive's and his secretary.

The secretarial pool was a windowless, fluorescent hall with desks in front of the bosses' doors. All the executives were men, all the secretaries female. Each woman had personalized her space with figurines, pictures of her family, plastic flowers in ceramic pots, or trailing vines of hardy philodendron. Walking from one end of the secretarial pool to the other, I could guess the personality of the woman working at that desk by reading what she had pasted on the wall behind her.

Written in calligraphy inside a frame studded with seashells and starfish was the optimistic legend: "Today is the first day of the rest of your life." A sign painted on wood hung behind a desk with photos of a dark-haired family squinting on the deck of a cabin cruiser: "Which part of NO don't you understand?" Under a picture of a terrified kitten dangling by its claws from a branch, a poster advised, "Hang in there, baby!" A garden of yellow happy faces surrounded a cheerful "Have a nice day!" Taped to another wall was a photocopy of a circle with instructions: "Bang head here."

During coffee and lunch breaks, the secretaries met in a lounge outside the women's rest room to smoke, play cards, and gossip. It was here that I learned Mr. Darling's previous secretary had quit because he had made a pass at her.

"He took her into the storage room and felt her up," said Vicky, the woman with the dangling kitty on her wall.

"Don't ever let him close the door to the office when you're in there with him," advised Pam of the happy faces.

"Don't wear clothes that might lead him on," suggested Liz with a place to bang her head.

Mr. Darling, who smelled of nicotine and onions, who sat in his office eight hours a day engulfed in smoke, whose frayed-cuffed, button-down shirts already had sweat stains in the armpits by the time he came in, was not my idea of a Lothario. But every woman in that office swore that he made a pass at virtually every female who worked for him. It was useless to insist that he had not once so much as hinted that he saw me as anything but the girl who typed his letters and answered his phone.

"Just wait," said Kelly, for whom this was the first day of the rest of her life.

Our apartment was within walking distance to the Newhouse School at the university, but too far from my job for me to get there on foot so Ulvi drove me to and from work. He had found us a one-bedroom apartment on the seventeenth floor of a new building on Harrison Street built for senior citizens and low-income residents of the city. One wall was a sliding glass door to a balcony that commanded an uninterrupted view of I-81 snaking through the rolling hills of the Onondaga valley. To our left was the Upstate Medical Center and beyond it, the Syracuse University campus. We were the first tenants within the stark white walls and vinyl-tiled floors of the apartment.

Because we had lived in furnished housing in Lubbock, we spent a week at the Holiday Inn until a bed and living room set was delivered to our new place. We also had to buy a typewriter, since we had returned Mildred's when we left Lubbock.

"I'd like to sign up for courses," I told Ulvi, but he discouraged me because the papers he would have to write and the research and writing of the doctoral dissertation would be more demanding than the work for the masters degrees.

"You promised to help me, Chiquita," he reminded me.

Within days of our arrival in the city, I was back to the routine established in Lubbock. Ulvi drove me to work in the morning and picked me up at the end of the day. He had dinner waiting. As he watched the news, I took a short nap. He then drove me to the library, where I filled stacks of 3x5 cards with references to books and articles about the past, present, and projected future of satellite communications. He picked me up at an agreed-upon time and drove me home, where I typed his papers for a couple more hours.

As in Lubbock, Ulvi forbid me to answer the phone. His side of the dresser was strewn with scraps of paper with women's names and phone numbers on them. The letters and phone calls from Irmchen came regularly. He sent money to Turkey, to help his father, he said, and for his little sister's education. Ulviye wrote frequently and a couple of times a year sent him pictures.

"It is too bad," he said once, looking at the most recent black-and-white photograph. "She is not beautiful."

"She has lovely eyes," I said. They were big, dark, intelligent.

"She looks too much like me."

It was true, as she matured, Ulviye looked like a miniature Ulvi, which would have been better if she were a boy.

Every week, I turned over my paycheck to Ulvi and he gave me an allowance. He bought my clothes because I never chose "elegant" things. Whatever he gave me came with instructions.

"This is silk, Chiquita. You must be careful not to spill on it."

Of course I spilled.

We took our clothes off as soon as we entered the apartment, its thermostat always set to a balmy 80 degrees. Because it was so high up and there were no buildings nearby anywhere as tall as ours, we didn't bother with curtains. We felt completely free with only the clouds and the distant woods and lakes to witness our nakedness.

Whether because it was so much farther north than Lubbock, or because the sky clouded and snow began to fall in mid-October and didn't let up until the spring, Syracuse seemed to have shorter days. By mid-afternoon in December, night had already dropped over the city. My windowless days at Bristol Myers International followed by drives in the dark to the blue fluorescence of the university library depressed me. I felt claustrophobic and looked forward to Saturdays and Sundays in our high apartment, where I had a view of the sky and of the feeble sun trying to burn through clouds.

Ulvi's friends at the university invited us to dinners at their homes almost every Friday and Saturday night. It was my reward for a week of hard work, he said. Unlike our friends at Texas Tech, who were mostly foreign graduate students, the people we spent time with in Syracuse were Caucasian North Americans who were either faculty or longtime residents of the city. Ulvi met them through his work as a teaching assistant at the Newhouse School and through his persistent attempts to get his movie seen.

By 1972, the black-and-white *Susuz Yaz* was eight years old, and Ulvi had begun to refer to it as a classic of Turkish cinema. He based the film, he said, on a true story about the lives and struggles of Turkish peasants. He made movies that explored cultural and political issues, he said, and in order to preserve his artistic and political vision, he had to work independent of Hollywood.

He referred to the film by its English title, *Dry Summer*, and said *Susuz Yaz* was his first film, when, as far as I knew, it was his only. He thought of the Americanized version as a second movie, because the changes were substantial from the winner of the Golden Bear in Berlin in 1964. Since then, Ulvi had added an original music score by Academy Award–winning Greek composer Manos Hadjidakis and recorded by a group of Juilliard-trained musicians who played together as the New York Rock & Roll Ensemble. A few weeks before we met, Ulvi had shot nude sex scenes with a girl from Long Island who looked like the film's original leading actress, Hulya Kocigit. After he incorporated the sex scenes into the film, he added new credits to include his American collaborators, and changed Hulya's name to Julie Kotch. The idea was that, if people in the film business, which he said was dominated by Jews, saw more Jewish names on the credits, they would be more likely to distribute the film.

When I asked, Ulvi admitted that he had not asked Hulya for permission to use a body double in scenes where her character appeared nude.

"But don't you think it's unfair," I wondered. "People will think she's doing nude scenes."

"It does not matter what she thinks," he said. "It must be done to make the movie easier to market in the United States."

"But if it's confusing to me," I argued, "it must be confusing to other people, too."

"Do not concern yourself, Chiquita."

A *mujer puertorriqueña decente* does not question or challenge her *hombre*, even when she suspects he's not telling the truth. I was as confused about who really made and owned *Susuz Yaz* as were Eugene and Leo in Fort Lauderdale.

They maintained that Ulvi starred in the movie, but had nothing more to do with its production. At different times and to different people Ulvi claimed to have produced, directed, and/or written the film in addition to acting in it. The *New York Times* article I'd read about the Berlin Film Festival Award, called him its producer and actor. In the English version, William Shelton was credited as producer, David Durston as director, and Kemal Inci as screenwriter. None of these men were on the original team that won the film its awards.

When I asked him about these inconsistencies, Ulvi refused to discuss it.

"Do not concern yourself, Chiquita."

"But people think *Susuz Yaz* and *Dry Summer* are two different movies."

"They are two different movies," he said.

"Not really. It's the same movie with sex," I argued.

"In business," he said, "sometimes you have to exaggerate."

His "exaggerations" troubled me because in the three years we had been together he seemed increasingly to believe his own hyperbole. The more he embellished his successes, however, the narrower our circle of friends grew as we came closer to the center of power. Our friends were no longer easy-to-impress foreign or graduate students of low means. We went to the homes of tenured professors and deans, business owners and local politicians. Ulvi's oft-spoken phrase, "Americans are so naïve," began to make sense.

Among these mainly white middle-class professionals in Syracuse, as in Lubbock, Ulvi impressed with his accomplishments, his European manners and wardrobe, his multilingualism, his informed opinions about American and world politics, and the fearless, authoritative way in which he expressed them. When he stumbled over a phrase, people were not impatient because his English wasn't perfect. Fingers steepled against his lips, Ulvi gazed at the ceiling as his listeners waited good-naturedly while he thought about what he wanted to say. When he finally spoke, they hung on his every word, as if his opinions were more valuable than their own, as if he were a sage preparing to enlighten them.

As an extension of Ulvi, these same people sometimes expected a word of wisdom from me. Ulvi squeezed my hand.

"Chiquita does not bother," he told them, "mostly I keep up with these matters."

I squeezed back. "People expect that, because my name is Esmeralda Santiago and I have dark skin, long hair, and an accent, I am wiser than your average white middle-class Mary Smith," I laughed, but no one else did. Later, Ulvi told me I should not make those kinds of jokes.

I remained invisible not only because Ulvi shone brighter than I did, but because I continued to hide behind him. As much as I thought and questioned other things, it took me years to accept that truth as the basis of our relationship. I might never have done so, had Mr. Darling not made a pass at me.

⌒

One day I was in the file room, looking for a folder that Mr. Darling urgently needed as he prepared for a trip to the Philippines. It was taking so long to find, that he came in to show me where he thought his previous secretary had stored it. He pulled open a cabinet, and pointed to papers poking haphazardly from a crumpled folder. When I leaned over to pull the heavy folder out, he squeezed one of my buttocks. I yelped, dropped the file, and jumped away from him, scattering pages on the floor. He stared at me as if I had done something stupid. I backed out of the room, alternating shame with anger, but not knowing what to do about either. I left him among the typed letters and carbon copies and ran to the bathroom. The other secretaries came after me, ignoring the shrill ringing of their telephones.

"What did I tell you," said Liz.

"Son of a bitch pervert," muttered Vicky.

"You take care of her and I'll answer the phones," said Pam, returning to the secretarial pool. A few minutes later, she returned with a message from Mr. Darling. "He says he doesn't know what came over you," she rolled her eyes. "He wants you to get back to work or he'll miss his flight."

"The nerve!" Kelly spit out. "What does he need to get out of here?"

"He has everything except for the file I dropped on the floor."

"I'll get it. You stay here. We'll let you know when he's gone."

Liz and Kelly made sure Mr. Darling was set for his trip. After he left, I called the Snelling and Snelling Employment Agency, explained my situation to the counselor, and learned that the perfect job had just become available less than two blocks from where I lived. By the time Mr. Darling returned from his trip two weeks later, I was the Supervisor of Coding in Crouse Irving Memorial Hospital's Medical Records Department.

"I belong here!"

Hospitals have a distinctive odor. In Lubbock, even after we moved to the new building, powerful cleaning solutions could not eliminate the scent of disease, medicines, and bodily emanations. Crouse Irving, much larger and older, greeted me with the familiar cloying smell of sickness and death masked by antiseptics and with the urgent squawking of the paging system embedded in the ceilings. The hospital complex connected through a tunnel near the cafeteria to the Upstate Medical Center, which buzzed with sleep-deprived medical students and cocky residents. Half a block away was the I-81 overpass, and across from it the parking lot of my apartment building. I was no longer dependent on Ulvi for rides to and from work.

I supervised ten women whose ages ranged from twenty-one to fifty-five years old. Three of them, Ruth, Eileen, and Mary, had each worked in the hospital for two decades or more. Ruth, a former psychiatric patient, was the youngest of the three, but had been there the longest. I was met with suspicion by these older women and with open rebellion by the younger staff, who had loved the woman I was replacing and felt that someone within the department should have been promoted when she left.

As someone who had spent most of her life avoiding conflict, I was unprepared to be the target of hostility. Two of the younger workers were particularly vicious, spreading gossip and openly defying me in front of doctors. One of them went so far as to use the word spick, not to my face, but when I was sure to hear it.

I didn't want to consult Paula, my boss, because she had hired me to handle the Coding Unit, not to cause her more problems. Instead, I went to Marie, the assistant director of personnel.

Marie had sapphire blue eyes and milky skin set off by bright red hair, eyebrows, and lashes. Freckles gave her sweet face a playful look. She was building a career in human resources, a business dominated by men who answered to upper management, most of them also men. I liked Marie from our first meeting, and was honest with her about my lack of managerial experience.

"Being a supervisor is like being the oldest sibling. Your position is one of leadership, which means you are respected as well as resented. I'm sure you've noticed that in your family."

"I've never thought of it that way . . . "

"You have to establish authority. They're expecting you to prove to them that you are the best person for the job."

"I don't know if I am . . . "

"I do," Marie said, "that's why you were hired. You can do this job. Use the tools that come with it. You have the right to promote, demote, or fire, if you can prove the work is not up to the standards of the department."

Within a couple of months, I had purged our unit of half the staff after private interviews and written evaluations. The three older women formed the backbone of the coding section because of their experience and the respect they had earned from the medical staff. The younger ones constantly interrupted me with questions designed to prove that I didn't know as much as they did about coding. I encouraged them to consult with Eileen, Ruth, and Mary. This freed me from the constant challenges and raised the older women's status, which they deserved and appreciated.

In contrast to Marie's serious, professional manner, Paula, the head of medical records, had a more casual approach to her job. She frequently came in at least an hour after everyone else, often took long lunches, and left promptly at five o'clock. Like Marie, she was a redhead, but of the Lady Clairol variety. She dressed younger than she was but it became her shapely figure and lively personality.

"The important thing for you to remember," she said, "is that the employees don't have to like you, but they do have to do their jobs to your satisfaction." It was a new concept, ignoring *el que dirán* in the interest of effectiveness.

Slowly, the new hires and the veterans became a cohesive group. I still felt the contempt of the employees I was unable to fire, but they were outnumbered. Marie encouraged me to use my authority and, like Paula, urged me to quit worrying about whether they liked me. As I gained confidence in my job, *el que dirán* began to lose its power to influence my decisions in other parts of my life. It was as big an insight as the day I realized that another train would come. If I was clear about what I had to do, if I was clear about where I stood and who I was, *el que dirán* didn't matter. It could not keep me from doing or being. All I had to do was figure out what I wanted to do and who I wanted to be.

Because my job was so demanding, I finally became what Ulvi insisted I was, his typist not his collaborator. I did his research, but no longer abstracted monographs or went through the material with the same care and involvement. I typed his papers, but didn't have the time or interest in satellite communications that I did in photocell technology. I transcribed his term papers and dissertation notes, correcting spelling and grammar but no longer judging or caring about the source material so long as my part of it, the correct formatting and error-free transfer to the page, was perfect.

At the hospital I was valued by my superiors and respected, eventually, by my staff. I couldn't wait to get to work in the morning and often stayed late without worrying about Ulvi waiting in the car in front of the building.

He argued that my job was stealing time from the reason we were in Syracuse. "You promised to help, Chiquita," he said.

"I *am* helping," I said. "The services charge for every page of text you bring them to type."

"Should I pay you, then?" he sneered.

"You should appreciate that I'm doing as much as I can."

"I do appreciate," he said, and meant it.

I felt more valued at work, however. The administration was lavish in praising Paula for how well the department functioned, and she passed the compliments along.

I looked for ways to make the Coding Unit more responsive and useful to the doctors and residents. Part of my job, as I saw it, was to collect and publish statistics that accurate coding made possible for the hospital administration to use in long- and short-term planning. The work was creative, much more so than typing Ulvi's papers, or researching the jargon-filled documents from NASA that formed the bulk of the material for his dissertation.

As the Coding Unit's efficiency improved, my meetings with Marie turned from work-related matters to my personal life. She couldn't believe that I would turn over my paycheck to Ulvi every week, that he forbid me to answer the phone, that he bought my clothes, that I had no friends independent of his, that I didn't go anywhere he didn't take me.

"You're so smart," she said. "Use that brain to change your life."

What I couldn't explain to Marie was that the smart part of my brain turned off the minute I walked into the apartment high above the hills of Syracuse. As in Brooklyn, where I had been Negi at home and an official Esmeralda to outsiders, I was Chiquita with Ulvi and his friends, but answered to the shorter, less intimidating Es or Essie at Crouse Irving Memorial Hospital. It was such a conscious shift from Esmeralda to Essie to Chiquita that I actually felt my body contract and diminish in stature on the walk from the hospital to our building on Harrison Street. Inside 1704, stripped of the "elegant" clothes that Essie wore to work, Chiquita ate the simple meal of steamed vegetables that Ulvi had prepared, nibbled on the crusty bread, sipped the strong *cha*. Chiquita took the pages Ulvi had left next to the typewriter, reviewed them, and typed them on a clean sheet.

Chiquita made love with Ulvi, who whispered he loved her in English, not the Spanish she heard in her head, not in his native Turkish, not in the German *ich liebe dich* reserved for Irmchen. I love you, Chiquita, he said, and I knew he didn't, couldn't, wouldn't love Esmeralda.

It was less painful to be Chiquita for him and Essie at work, than to expose Esmeralda to the disdainful gaze of those who would judge me. Esmeralda was the dark-skinned girl from the ends of rural Puerto Rico who had grown up in the ghettos of Brooklyn. She was the first child of a teenage mother who had never married the fathers of her eleven children. Esmeralda had waited alongside Mami for the welfare check on the third of the month and had eagerly rummaged through the used clothing bins at the secondhand stores looking for something "new" to wear. She liked loud salsa music and bright colors. She liked her big breasts and round hips, and she walked with a jiggle in her buttocks, just as her mother did, her grandmother, and sisters. The clothes she would have chosen were not elegant. They would be too tight and too low cut except that I made the conscious effort to be conservative and respectable.

I gave the world a shadow me, a me who looked like me but wasn't, a me that could function according to the rules that would get me what I wanted and needed. I reserved the real Esmeralda in a quiet, secret place no one could reach, not Marie with her feminist theories, not Ulvi with his broken English and business deals, his hopes and promises. I kept that me so hidden, that I was invisible even to myself.

～～

After the long winter, summer in northern New York State felt like a gift from the gods. As the days grew longer and the snow melted into the rivers, brooks, and lakes, Ulvi and I began our exploration of the area by Camaro. If there were no Watergate Committee Hearings or television specials about them, he picked me up at the hospital on Friday afternoons and we drove west toward the Finger Lakes, following numbered two-lane routes where they led. On warm days, we settled on the sandy beach at the northern end of Skaneateles Lake. If the sun hid behind clouds, we drove east as far as the mountains of Vermont until we found a charming town or a historic village. We loved county fairs, the fast-talking auctioneers, the prize-winning pigs and heifers of 4-H clubs, the midway rides and horse shows. At one of them, Ulvi told me he had served in the Turkish Cavalry as a young man.

"Really? What does the Turkish Cavalry do?"

"Parades," he snorted.

Getting information about his past was also a gift. I had learned to wait until he disclosed something, not to ask too many questions following a revelation. The moment I did, he clammed up, as if letting me into his life were dangerous.

In August, Ulvi asked me to take time off from work so we could have a vacation.

"We will be very busy the next two semesters, finishing the dissertation," he said. "I also have to look for a job, so I can stay in the United States."

"What kind of job?"

"With a doctor degree I can teach. The United States needs teachers, but they already have too many businessmen," he chuckled.

I had only been working at the hospital about eight months, but both Paula and Marie agreed that I deserved a few days away from the office. I left Eileen in charge of the Coding Unit, and Ulvi and I climbed into the Camaro and headed East on I-90 with Maine as our destination. He needed to be near the ocean, Ulvi said, and planned to visit friends in Bar Harbor. I didn't ask who they were or where he had met them.

We would pass nowhere near Skowhegan, which was in the interior of the state. I was sad that I wouldn't be able to look for Jacqueline. As soon as Ulvi told me we were going to Maine, it had become important to find her, or to have news of her.

At the first motel we stayed in, just outside Portland, I found the phone book by the bedside stand and looked for her last name among the listings, but it did not exist in Skowhegan. Jacqueline had probably become one of the Wilis, the jilted maidens in the ballet *Giselle* who die before their wedding night. Unable to exhaust her passion for dance in life, I imagined Jacqueline and the other Maine Wilis at midnight in a quaint cemetery, dancing around the markers, waiting for her Albrecht, who, remorseful for having abandoned her, could not bear to stay away from her grave.

I asked Ulvi to turn the television down.

"What's the matter, Chiquita?"

"I have a headache," I said, and he reached over and felt my forehead, the way Mami used to when I was sick.

"Shall I get you some aspirin?"

"No, thank you, I will be okay in a minute. It's the heat, I think."

I lay back on the bed and covered my face with the pillow. I could not tell him that the reason I'd asked him to turn the TV down was because the plaintive music of Giselle's death from a broken heart had taken over my brain, competing with highlights of the day's developments in the Watergate hearings.

The next day, we resumed our drive east as the sun was rising. We stopped at the beach in Seal Harbor to cool off. It was a brutally hot August day. Radio announcers kept quoting the temperature as it rose and stayed over 100 degrees, even as far north as Mt. Desert Island. We never found Ulvi's friends in Bar Harbor. Written on a scrap torn from a notebook, the number did not have a name attached to it. Ulvi called several times, but no one answered. We spent the blistering afternoon walking around the town, and I had the impression that Ulvi was hoping to run into his friends on the street, along the docks, inside a hotel lobby, in the drugstore. He was actively seeking someone who wasn't there, but he wouldn't admit it and I didn't push.

As evening fell, we looked for a hotel with a vacancy. We drove out of town, hoping to find a place to stay further from the lively center. In Northeast Harbor, we saw a hand-lettered "Rooms Available" sign in front of a bed and breakfast with lace curtains on the windows and a luxurious flower garden with fountains and gravel paths. When the owner opened the door to find us, exhausted and disheveled from a day wandering the streets of Bar Harbor, she recoiled.

"No vacancy," she said and locked the door in our faces.

We were too exhausted to argue, to feel angry, even. Sticky from the morning's dip in the ocean, we longed for a shower and a soft bed. After a couple of hours of driving with no success, we stopped at a diner and ate a hearty meal served by a cheerful waitress who had no suggestions for a place to stay.

"Everything's full up," she said, "what with the heat wave and all . . ."

We left the diner and drove south until Ulvi was too sleepy to continue. He turned off the main road and pulled over.

"We sleep in the car," he suggested. Too exhausted to argue, I curled up in the back. He lowered the bucket seat as far as it went and slept, half sitting, until daybreak. The next night, heading back via Boothbay Harbor, we slept in the car again, this time in a church parking lot.

Ulvi wanted to visit Boston, which we had skirted on the way up to Bar Harbor.

"I want to go home," I groaned, "to my own bed."

"Come on, Chiquita, it will be fun. We will look for a hotel as soon as we get there," he promised.

We stayed at a motel north of the city and the next morning headed toward the skyline. Traffic choked the narrow roads leading into the city, so Ulvi took an exit and, before we knew it, we were in the middle of Harvard Square.

Even in summer, when most of the students had returned home, the streets around Harvard Square were crowded and lively. A guitarist strummed plaintively and wailed to a few people who seemed entranced by the unintelligible words of his song. A juggler threw three balls high in the air, bounced them off his forehead, his chin, then caught them and did a cartwheel. A lean black man dressed in blue, with dangling ribbons and bells, told an African folktale to a circle of enraptured listeners. A vigor I had not noticed on the campuses at Texas Tech and at Syracuse animated the faces of everyone we passed, and I couldn't help feeling buoyed amidst such energy and spirit.

When the street performers and the crowds became too much, we walked into the quiet of Harvard Yard. Students lolled on the grass, studying, smoking, chatting, making out. A group played Frisbee in front of the statue of John Harvard. A path around a long red brick building led to another huge lawn between a massive library and a white-steepled chapel. I skipped up the broad, shallow steps to the top landing of the library building. When I reached the huge wooden doors, I was stopped by a sense of déjà vu. I faced the rectangular, red brick buildings surrounding the lawn dotted with scholars, the chapel with its spire pointing to the clear blue sky.

"I belong here!" I blurted out, surprising myself.

"What did you say, Chiquita?" Ulvi called, catching up to me.

"I like it here," I amended, embarrassed at my outburst, but feeling as if I had arrived at a place I didn't know I was heading towards.

"It is beautiful place," he said, "but we have long drive to Syracuse."

We returned to the Camaro and headed west. A part of me stayed on the top step of Widener Library, looking across the lawn, repeating words I'd blurted from a part of me I had long forgotten.

"My name is Esmeralda."

The vacation in New England, meant to relax us, had the opposite effect on me. I was physically exhausted from the long days, and nights, on the vinyl seats of the Camaro. I was energized by our visit to Harvard Yard but was overcome by sadness the minute we entered our apartment high over Harrison Street.

"It is good to be back," Ulvi grinned as we walked in.

It felt like a prison. I resented the typewriter, the pages neatly stacked on the shelf next to the desk, the chair where I sat naked almost every evening typing Ulvi's papers and the first draft of his dissertation. Before he'd even put down his bag, Ulvi turned on the television news. I resisted the urge to turn around and run down the hall, into the elevator to the ground floor, out the glass doors of the lobby, into the dark streets of Syracuse. I forced myself to put away my things, then walked into the shower and let hot water wash away the grime of the road, the exhaustion, the tightness in my chest. After a while, Ulvi knocked on the door.

"Come, Chiquita, let us have some *cha*," he suggested.

I didn't want to come out of the steamy bathroom, to sip tea as he caught up with the latest developments in the vast world outside our window. I ran the water hotter, sat in the tub and let the scalding drops pound my scalp and back. It was nearly unbearably painful. My skin turned red and my heart raced, but I tightened my jaw, sucked in the steam through my teeth. Ulvi opened the door and a whoosh of cold air rippled the shower curtain.

"You did not hear me, Chiquita?" He was annoyed. "I have prepared a snack."

"I'll be right there," I spent a few more moments under a shower of cold water until I was shivering and could think of nothing but warmth.

When I returned to the hospital that Monday, I hesitated at the door to the office, expecting that while I was gone the whole department had fallen apart. A part of me hoped that was the case, but nothing was amiss. After my rocky start, the Coding Unit functioned smoothly, even without me there. The staff had adapted to my changes and to each other, and I had no more battles to fight or new systems to install. Supervising employees who knew what to do was boring. I checked in with Paula, then took my coffee break with Marie.

"How was Maine?" she asked.

"Someday I hope to travel first class and stay in suites and order room service," I said.

"I take it this was a low-budget vacation . . . "

"You could say that." I gave her the highlights without admitting we had slept in the car most of the time we were gone. "Our last day we stopped in Boston and walked around Harvard. I've always wanted to study there." Actually, the thought had not occurred to me until I said it.

"Why can't you?"

I blinked and stammered, caught in a lie. "Because . . . ah, because, it's a boy's school, isn't it? I mean they don't let girls in, do they?"

"Those men-only colleges have had to change with the times, Esmeralda. Most of them accept women now. You would probably have a great chance to get in because you're Puerto Rican."

"I'd think the opposite is true," I muttered.

"Haven't you heard of affirmative action?"

"Of course I have . . . "

"Write to Harvard and ask for an application for minority admission."

"Marie, I can't afford such an expensive college!"

"Apply for a scholarship. They set aside money for students like you."

"I've never thought of myself as a 'minority.'" I curled my fingers to put quote marks around the word.

"You don't, but other people do. Take advantage of it, all it will cost you is a stamp," she said, finishing her coffee.

Back in the office, I worked on some statistics for the head resident in pediatrics. Ruth came in with a request for time off. She was signing herself into the psychiatric ward for electroshock treatments.

"Don't panic," she said when she saw my expression. "I do this regularly and I come out better than I go in."

I wished there were some way to zap my brain, to improve its capacity somehow, to make it more efficient. As it was, my head felt full of information that I didn't want to find there, muddled impressions, dreams I'd not dared examine, ambition I had packed off to the furthest, darkest corners of my mind.

After Sunday dinner at the home of our friends Leah and Robert, Ulvi summarized human nature as a constant longing for more. "If a man is hungry and you give him bread he will ask for butter. If you give him butter, he wants jam."

"So, like the proverb says, you should not give a man a fish, but rather teach him to cast a line," Robert suggested.

"Even if you teach him to fish," Ulvi grinned, "he will blame you if he does not catch anything."

The men laughed, and Leah smiled prettily.

"What should people do then?" I wondered.

"What do you ask, Chiquita?"

"If humans can never be satisfied with what they have, should they stop wishing?"

"We can't help wishing, because the more we have, the more we want."

"I don't agree with that," I said.

"You don't agree?" Ulvi repeated as if he'd never heard me utter the words.

"In your example, the man who has bread wants butter, not more bread."

"Explain yourself, Chiquita."

"If you teach a man to fish, he will eventually grow tired of mackerel and want lobster."

"So it's a question of quality," Robert said, "not quantity."

"Exactly!"

"I can understand that," Robert sipped his wine.

"You have many opinions tonight," Ulvi murmured as he leaned over to kiss my cheek.

"It's not so much an opinion as my experience," I kissed him back.

"Your experience?" asked Leah.

Ulvi laughed. "You're not so old to have experience."

"I'm twenty-five years old. By the time she was my age, my mother already had seven kids."

"Seven children! Good heavens!" Leah said.

"I'm the eldest of eleven. Didn't I ever mention that?"

"No, Chiquita, I don't think you have," said Robert.

"You have much to say tonight," Ulvi pressed my hand.

I pressed back. "I don't know what's come over me."

Later, he paced the small rooms of our apartment and picked at his scalp. I sat at the typewriter, pretending not to notice. It was late, and one of his papers was due the following day.

"You are becoming too free, Chiquita," Ulvi finally said.

"I beg your pardon?"

"Stop typing and listen!" He pulled me out of my chair. "If you want to be with me . . . "

I released myself from his grip and put the coffee table between us. "Don't grab at me like that again or I'll walk out that door and never come back," I yelled. "I mean it!"

"What is going on with you?" he asked. "You are not the same Chiquita."

"My name is Esmeralda."

He smiled as if a spark had gone off inside his brain and walked around the coffee table, reaching for my hand. "Come, sweetheart, come, my little Esmeralda. Esmeraldita, is that how you say in Spanish?" I moved away. "You are angry at what?" He put his hands on his hips, reached up and scratched the back of his head. "I do not understand you anymore." He looked genuinely puzzled. "Have you fallen in love with another man?" he asked. "A doctor at the hospital?"

I was sure my skin glowed with rage. "Is that the only thing that could possibly ever be wrong between us? That I have a lover? Is that what you think?"

"I do not know what to think," he said. "You are changing so fast I cannot tell . . . "

"Maybe that's what's wrong. Maybe I'm changing and you're not."

"Maybe, Chiquita," he said, sadly, "you are right. But I cannot have you be a spoiled American girl."

"Aargh!" I screamed, and sat down hard on the floor, my hands over my head, curling into as tight a ball as I could make of my body.

"You are not understanding what I mean," he said, coming closer.

"Yes, I do. You don't like the American part of me and you disdain the Puerto Rican!"

His eyes opened wider. "I see, yes, I understand what bothers you. I must fix. You are good girl, Chiquita." He dropped to his knees and wrapped himself around me. We stayed like that for a long time, breathing in unison, until I had repeated the same phrase to myself over one hundred times. "My name is Esmeralda. My name is Esmeralda. Esmeralda."

The day after our argument I was so distraught at work that Marie took me to lunch. We sat at a corner booth at Pizza Delitzza.

"I can't bear to be with him anymore," I cried so bitterly and had such trouble gaining control of myself that Marie called the office and said I was not well and she was taking me home.

She put her arms around my waist and I leaned into her as we walked to her orange Volkswagen Scirocco. She settled me in with concern and care, drove slowly, asking every time she took a turn or hit a bump if I was okay.

She lived on the second floor of a Victorian house on a quiet street, in a tidy apartment with ruffled curtains in the windows and fluffy comforters on the beds. She gave me a pair of her pajamas and made me lie down in the guest room, even though it was midafternoon. I fell asleep immediately. When I woke up, it was to the sound and smells of Marie's cooking. I shuffled to the kitchen and found her dressed in jeans and T-shirt, her blazing hair, which she usually wore tied back, loose around her shoulders.

"Good morning, sleepy head," she said, stirring spaghetti sauce.

I panicked. "It's not morning yet, is it?"

"No, relax, it's just an expression. It's almost 7 p.m."

"Oh, my god, I have to call Ulvi. He must be wondering where I've gone."

"The phone is right there," she said casually, nodding toward the wall.

I picked it up and was about to dial. My knees and hands shook, my lips trembled so that I could barely make them form words. "I don't know what to tell him . . . "

Marie took the phone from my fingers, set it on the cradle, led me to a chair, pressed my shoulders down until I sat, pulled another chair closer and sat in front of me, holding my hands. "You have a decision to make," she said, her voice throaty.

"I'm so scared," I bawled.

"I know, honey," she said. "But you're not going through this alone. You decide what you want to do, and I'll help you. I'll drive you back if you're not ready to leave him and you're sure it's safe to be in the apartment with him. Or you can stay here a few days and when my husband comes back, Paula can take you in for a couple of days until you find your own place."

"You told Paula?"

"I said you might need a place to stay. She doesn't know why."

I covered my face and dropped my head to the table. "I don't know what to do."

"I have to run to the store before they close," Marie said, brushing my hair back from the tabletop. "You need a minute to think. Whatever you decide is fine, no one is going to judge you. I know what you're going through and it's not easy. If you want me to be here when you call him, wait until I come back. Okay?"

"Okay," I said without raising my head.

"I'll be back soon." She pushed off from her chair and left the room.

I heard her go into the hall, put on her jacket, jangle keys, and close the door gently. A few minutes later, the Scirocco came to life.

My head felt too heavy to lift. With my forehead on the table, my hair formed a dark curtain around my face and shoulders. All I saw was my bare feet. An inch above my right middle toe was the scar left after I dropped Mami's heavy scissors on my foot to see how much it would hurt. There had been a lot of blood, and I limped around for days afterwards. I was an active eleven-year-old then, with many cuts and scars from previous falls, accidents, and experiments like the one with the scissors. That kind of pain was familiar. The wound eventually healed, leaving behind almost invisible scars to remind me that it once hurt.

When Marie returned, I was in the same position she'd last seen me.

"How's it going?" she said, opening and closing the refrigerator.

"It wasn't as hard to leave my mother as it is to leave him, why is that?"

"Because," she handed me a paper towel to wipe the tears and snot from my face. "Your mother will always accept you as you are, no matter what you say or do."

I started sobbing again. "You shouldn't have said that!" I said, laughing and crying at the same time.

"It's the truth," she chuckled, tears in her own eyes.

"It's just that I feel as if . . . like . . . like Esmeralda is pushing through Chiquita."

"And isn't it about time, Esmeralda?" Marie asked. She was the only person at the hospital who used my name. "Isn't it about time?" she asked again.

Once I'd washed my face and cleared the hoarseness in my throat with a cup of tea with honey, I called Ulvi.

"Where are you?" he asked tenderly, concerned.

"I'm leaving you," I said. "Please don't call my office and don't embarrass both of us by coming to the hospital."

"Chiquita, do not do this."

I hung up.

The next morning I went to work as if nothing were different, except that I was wearing the same clothes as the day before. Marie drove me to the apartment when I thought Ulvi would be teaching. When we walked in, I was afraid he would have cancelled his classes and be there, waiting, but he wasn't. On the coffee table, he had left an undated note written in pencil on two yellow sheets, "Please return to your home," the first page read in large letters, "I love you & I miss you . . . Ulvi." At the bottom, there was more writing in small, tight block letters. I did not read it in front of Marie, but folded both sheets into my purse. Every time I had to get a few coins to pay for coffee, a comb, a tissue, my fingernails scraped the paper, but I did not pull it out to read what he had written. Not in front of people, not in the bathroom stall, where I was alone but worried that his message on the bottom of the sheet might upset me.

Marie took me to her house that evening. Her husband was a fireman, and he was on duty at the firehouse for a couple more days.

"Paula's kids are home with strep," she said, "but Dana has a spare bedroom." Dana was Paula's best friend, and a secretary in Administration. "I've already talked to her. You can stay there as long as you need to."

"I hate to be an inconvenience."

"You're not inconveniencing anyone. We've all been there, believe me," she said as she seasoned some steaks. "And anyway, we women have to stick together. Would you wash that head of lettuce?"

Marie was great at drawing me out, but it was harder to learn much about her other than what I already knew. Whenever something personal slipped out, she changed the subject and the trapdoor into her life banged shut.

Over dinner, we talked about work. She had a meeting to attend, and left me to myself in her apartment. The moment she was gone, I unfolded Ulvi's yellow note. His signature, double underlined and larger than the rest of the writing, sent shivers down my back. "Please return to your home." I stopped reading. Home. I had never thought of the place I lived with Ulvi as home. Home was where Mami was, where my sisters and brothers, my grandmother were. I hadn't been there in twelve years, but home was once again Puerto Rico. Home was where I was valued and respected, where I could be myself.

"I love you and I miss you . . . Ulvi."

The note below his signature was less friendly. He again reminded me that I had pushed him to make a decision, that he chose to be with me, giving up the chance of returning to Europe "or doing something else." The past four years had not been happy ones for him, either, he wrote. I had not thought about it that way before.

Ulvi had aspirations that could not be fulfilled in Lubbock, Texas, or in Syracuse, New York. The success of *Susuz Yaz*, which was about Turkish peasants fighting over water, had immersed him in a scintillating, jet-set life. He had befriended movie stars and millionaires, had lived in luxurious surroundings, had dressed in silk, had tasted caviar. He had driven across the country in a white Rolls Royce, and been the houseguest of award-winning Hollywood producers. What must it have been like for him to live in Lubbock, to give up his dreams of Hollywood, to seek a degree in industrial engineering of all things? He seemed happier when he transferred to mass communications, but he was teaching in a field that he was just learning, no more than one step ahead of his students. Did they ever challenge him? Did he doubt himself?

I had never stopped to consider that, since we'd met, Ulvi had been in crisis. He was forty-one years old. He had no money and few prospects. He had no permanent home. He was in the United States on a revocable student visa. He was financially responsible for his elderly father and young sister in Istanbul. As far as I could tell, he had only two assets, an award-winning film and an expensive watch that he seldom wore for fear he'd lose it. No, the past four years couldn't have been happy for him. I felt guilty for contributing to his misery.

The words *decision* or *decide* appeared five times in the short paragraph. "We both knew: school years wouldn't be pleasant," he continued. "Now short before the rough days are over you decide to run away! WHY?" Three letters, capitalized. Was he really expecting an answer? Did he think I would write back and list the reasons I had picked this day from all others to leave?

I considered answering his note, explaining that I felt stifled in our relationship. Could he understand that? Would he be offended to hear that I was drowning in his silence, that while we spent every moment I wasn't at work together, I was lonely? Could I admit that to him? Would that make him more talkative? Would he let me into his life? Our life was based on what was best for him. He had said, and I had believed, that what was good for him was also good for me. Would he understand that I no longer believed that, that I had dreams of my own?

I opened the second page of his note. It was a list of our debts with an estimate of his earnings for the coming year. I almost tore the sheet into a million pieces. Did he think I would return because he owed money, some of which was spent on me? I folded the pages neatly, returned them inside my purse, and kept them as a reminder of why I had left him. He might love me, as he claimed, but he had no idea, no clue whatsoever, of what was important to me.

I spent a couple of nights with Marie and toward the end of the week moved in with Dana. Ulvi did not call or come to the hospital. On Saturday, Marie picked me up and we drove to Dewitt, a nearby town. A friend of hers owned a building where a furnished studio with kitchenette was available. It was clean and bright, with a huge picture window overlooking a garden and a broad lawn shaded by elms. I took it, and that same afternoon Marie brought my things from Dana's to the new place. To celebrate, she invited me to her health club, where we weighed ourselves before and after exercising on the treadmills and stationary bikes. After sweating for about an hour, we moved to the back of the club, where there was a swimming pool, a sauna, a steam room, and a hot tub. Women of all ages went in and out of the rooms wearing nothing but swimming caps or towels wrapped around their heads.

"You're not at all intimidated," Marie marveled, as we sat on the edge of the pool, our feet dangling in the water.

"At what?"

She waved her arms to take in the vast room, the hot tub, the sauna and steam rooms, the naked women lolling in lounge chairs, swimming laps, and walking around squeezing water from their hair.

"Why should this intimidate me?"

"You're the darkest person here," she pointed out. Until she did, I hadn't noticed, but the moment she did, I was self-conscious. Everyone, it seemed, was staring at me.

"I guess you're right," I looked into the blue, blue water of the swimming pool, "but have you noticed?"

"What?"

"You're the only real redhead."

⌒

Because I couldn't drive, getting to and from the hospital from my apartment was difficult. Several of the women in Medical Records lived near enough to give me rides, and when that wasn't possible, I took the bus. I called a driving school, but lessons were expensive and I would not be able to afford them for a couple of months.

Marie drove me to the supermarket, where I loaded my cart with sweetened cereal, canned ravioli, Spam, sardines, saltines, and coffee.

"This is what you plan to eat?" she asked, horrified.

"I'm not much of a cook."

The next day she gave me recipes for meatballs, lasagna, and chicken soup.

"If you can read, you can cook," she said.

I loved coming home from work and, instead of taking a nap and typing for hours, I sat on the big, lumpy chair by the window, eating a bowl of heated Chef Boyardee meat ravioli while reading a novel until it was time to go to bed. I did not own a television, but I had bought a portable radio, where I listened to Cousin Brucie's Top 40 countdown.

I had just settled in one evening when a familiar figure passed by my window on his way to the apartments at the end of the building. He did a double take, stopped right in front of me, and grinned cheerlessly. After a moment I recognized Lenny, the psychologist hippie organizer married to Shirley, whom I had known in Lubbock. I stepped outside.

"Wow! Lenny, what are you doing here?"

"Um, I'm, er, visiting a friend," he said, shuffling his feet as if, now that I had recognized him, he was eager to keep moving. "Do you live here? Where's your old man?" He peered through the window into my room.

"Long story," I said. "Are you and Shirley in Syracuse now?"

He looked beyond me. "It's all over between Shirley and me. We're divorced."

"I'm sorry . . ."

"Yeah, well, it was a long time coming. She was too neurotic . . . "

"Len?" a woman peeked from a door down the walkway.

"Gotta go," he headed toward her. "Take care."

I returned to the now-cold meat ravioli. Lenny looked more disheveled than in Lubbock, less certain of himself, skittish. He smelled, too, as if he hadn't bathed for days and had lived on cigarettes and garlic. His hair was matted, his beard scraggly, his eyes sunken into their sockets as if hiding from what they had seen. I wondered whether he had looked and smelled like that in Lubbock, and I'd never noticed.

It was hard to picture Shirley as neurotic. She was colorful, certainly, but had seemed the most down-to-earth person I'd ever met. Maybe it was possible to be both neurotic and down-to-earth. Lenny would know, after all, he was a psychologist. I would have to be crazy, however, to entrust my deepest, darkest psyche to someone who now looked so disreputable.

Hours later, when I had shut the curtains and turned out the lights, I heard footsteps down the walkway. They shuffled right up to my door, stopped, scraped around as if turning and returning, then tried the door, found it locked, shuffled toward the window, scratched at the screen, and tried the door again. I was terrified, and had risen and quietly picked up the dull bread knife from the kitchenette counter, aware that it was probably useless against an intruder. I stood in the middle of the room, listening, and when I heard steps moving away, peeked through a slit in the curtain. At the end of the walkway, Lenny shambled into the darkness, his head bowed into his chest, looking as sad and defeated as anyone I'd ever seen. The next morning, I called the landlord and insisted he install a safety chain.

The first letter I wrote after my move to Dewitt was to the admissions office at Harvard. A week later, I received the application materials. Because I had nearly three years of academic credits from Manhattan Community College and from Texas Tech University, I planned to apply as a transfer student. Decisions on transfers were announced in early summer, after the college heard from the students invited to be part of that year's incoming freshman class. There were few slots, and I might have a better chance as a freshman, but it seemed like a waste of time, money, and energy to start over when I had enough credits to graduate in less than four years. I did not make an alternate plan should Harvard turn me down.

I had made friends with some of the doctors at the Upstate Medical Center. One of them, Omer, was a Lebanese neurology resident on his last year. Ulvi and I had met him and his wife, Marina, at one of the screenings of *Dry Summer*. Marina had finished her residency in plastic surgery and had returned to Beirut, where Omer planned to join her by the end of the year. So that she would always be close to his heart, he wore her image trapped in a locket around his neck.

Omer and I went to the movies or the theater on the nights he was off. When he was on duty, we had dinner in the hospital cafeteria, where he could hear a page over the speakers on the ceiling. He had a passion for nineteenth-century novels that we shared.

One Saturday in late October we went to the Everson Museum, steps from the apartment on Harrison Street where I had lived. As Omer parked the car, I couldn't help looking up and counting balconies to the seventeenth floor, where there was no chance I'd see Ulvi because 1704 was on the other side of the building. Omer noticed what I was doing.

"If you would like to see him, I can drop you off."

I shook my head. "Thank you, it's better if I don't."

"You miss him?"

"I miss the parts of him I love."

Omer laughed. "You are very honest."

I had refused to mourn Ulvi, but had not succeeded. I missed his gentleness, his grace, his soft voice and foreign inflections. I longed for his loving gaze, the familiarity of our nakedness together, and the warmth of his hand on mine when we walked. I missed putting my head on his knee, the way he stroked my hair as we watched football on television. I had become enamored of the Dallas Cowboys while living in Lubbock, an obsession he indulged even if he couldn't understand it.

I did not miss Ulvi's dark looks when I displeased him. I did not miss the desk and typewriter, his dissertation notes, the feeling of being trapped in our apartment. I did not miss feeling as insubstantial as his shadow.

"We are old fashioned," Omer said as we dined after the museum. "We like our women to depend on us. It makes us feel more strong, more like a man."

"I don't know how to be dependent, Omer."

"It is difficult in America because girls here are very free. It is a beautiful thing, for Americans. But it is not our way."

"I don't think of Ulvi as traditional. He hasn't lived in Turkey in years . . ."

"No matter how long he lives elsewhere, he will always be a Turk. It is more complicated for them. They think they are Europeans, but most of their country is across the Bosporus, in Asia. It is like being schizophrenic."

"I know what that's like," I said.

"Yes, I am sure you do," he chuckled. Compared to Ulvi, Omer understood that I could be both American and confused about what that meant. "He is a good man, Ez," Omer said.

"How can you say that? You've only met him a few times!"

"Are you saying he is not a good man?" Omer asked.

I remembered my interview with Agent Carson of the FBI. Then, I had said too much, and was still sorry about it. "You're trying to trick me aren't you?" I asked, coyly.

Omer shook his head. "I am trying to understand why, if you still love him, you are not with him."

"Because love means never having to say you're sorry?" I smirked.

"What does that mean?"

"Haven't you seen that movie, *Love Story?*" He gave me a blank look. "Ali McGraw? Ryan O'Neal?" He had never heard of them.

"In my experience," Omer said after a while, "love means saying you're sorry many, many times."

I dropped my gaze to the half-eaten meat loaf with mashed potatoes so that he wouldn't see the regret in my eyes. I could barely swallow the mouthful I took so I wouldn't have to speak.

"In my opinion," Omer continued, "love means forgiveness."

It was the wrong word to have rattling around my brain the next afternoon when I returned from a walk and found Ulvi casually sprawled on the lawn in front of my apartment. He scrambled up the moment he saw me.

"Surprise!" he grinned, hesitating before coming closer.

"Yes, it is," I said, trying to sound stern.

We faced each other silently under an elm that had shed most of its leaves. It was a bright late Indian summer day, the last gasp of warm weather before the implacable northern New York State winter. He was newly showered and clean shaven. His black hair still glowed wetly.

"You look good, Chiquita," he stroked my cheek.

"You do too," I said, leaning my face into his hand. I will not cry, I vowed to myself. I will not shed another tear in his presence.

He hugged me, held me tight, as if afraid I'd push away and run in the opposite direction. But I wasn't going anywhere. He kissed my hair, my eyes, and the corners of my lips. "I am sorry for grabbing you that night," he said. "Forgive me." I nodded. "Please come home," he pleaded. "We belong together, Chiquita, you know that." I nodded. "I love you very much. Only you and Ulviye are so important to me. No one will ever love you like I do." I burrowed deeper into his chest, into the warm, comforting embrace of *el hombre que yo amo.*

"Is there anything you would like to know about him?"

"You don't have to apologize to me," Marie said when I went to her office a couple of days later. "You do what's right for you."

"I wish I knew what that was."

Marie smiled.

"The truth is," I continued, "that I love him when we're not together, but within minutes of being with him, I'm wondering why."

"It's easy to love somebody who's not there," she said. "You don't keep banging against their annoying habits." Her face set, her lips tightened. When our gazes met, she blushed. "So," she shuffled papers on her desk, "now that things are back to the way they were, are you giving up your Harvard dream?"

"No way!"

"Will you go if you're accepted?" she asked casually, still rustling papers. "Even if he doesn't want you to?"

"I haven't told him about it."

She sighed as if she'd been holding her breath, then stood up to stack some files on top of a cabinet. "What if he says no?"

"He won't. He'll strut around Boston telling everyone his girlfriend goes to Harvard."

"What if he doesn't want to live in Boston? What if he wants to move to, oh, I don't know, Oregon? Will you follow him?" She turned to face me.

I had never stopped to judge whether Marie was beautiful. She was so intelligent, so earnest, so compelling, so solid, that her looks were not the first thing I noticed about her. It was her passion, the red she exuded, enhanced by her hair. Marie seemed to burn brighter than everyone around her, even through her conservative clothes, her eyeglasses, the simple hairstyle, and total disregard for a woman's prerogative to wear makeup, primp, and embellish herself. She was positively flaming crimson now, as beautiful and earthy as the goddess of fire.

"Will you give up the opportunity, Esmeralda, if . . . what's his name . . . the Turk says no?"

I spoke so softly, that I might have been speaking to myself. "If I get into Harvard, nothing . . . no one is keeping me from going."

"Will you go if it means choosing Harvard over him?"

I remembered Jacqueline, the opposite of red, assuring me that the reason we had come together was to learn from one another. I stood beside myself, certain that the answer to Marie's question was one of the lessons I was to take away from her.

I looked into her blazing eyes. "I have already chosen, Marie."

Hours after my return to the apartment high over Syracuse, I was back to the familiar pattern of my hospital job by day, and typing naked for Ulvi by night, except that now he was more loving, more attentive, more willing to "see things your way, Chiquita." He tried, anyway. When I told him I was applying to Harvard, he was surprised.

"It is a boy's school, is it not?"

"They accept women now."

"It is famous school."

"If I go there, it's going to change my life."

"I see, Chiquita." He tapped his lips with his index finger as if pushing back into his mouth what he had planned to say. "You must do what is best for you," he said, advice that was easier to hear from Marie than from him. Until recently he had vowed to take care of me if I did as he asked. Now he seemed to be pushing me out of his life.

I finished typing his dissertation soon after the Christmas holidays, and my part of his work was over. He spent the next couple of months reading and preparing for the oral exam, which he passed later that spring. His focus shifted from finishing his degree to finding a job. Mine became filing admission and financial aid forms, taking the college boards, requesting transcripts, and securing references. Whenever I was alone—in the shower, on the way to work, in the ladies room—I prayed to an unseen, unidentified, gender-neutral deity.

"Just because I've not been in touch for years doesn't mean I've discarded the possibility that you exist," I prayed. "Remember that I have not asked much from you. I've tried to handle whatever came my way without hurting anyone. This is the only thing I've ever asked for. I swear . . . I mean . . . promise not to keep asking for favors just because you answered one prayer."

I had a plan, which I wrote down in a newly acquired journal that lived inside my purse, and which I could consult whenever doubts arose. My plan required moving to Cambridge, a city where I had spent less than twenty-four hours, and getting into Harvard, a place so far from my consciousness that it had not existed until I stood in the middle of it.

My plan assumed that Harvard could not say no. I had chutzpah, Ruth had assured me. I was smart, and would follow Marie's advice to use my brain to improve my life. I was a "minority." I was disciplined. I would use these to give Harvard what they wanted and to get from them what I wanted, a chance to become the person I wanted to be.

In those last few months in Syracuse, Ulvi took pains to be supportive, encouraging, loving, and helpful. He drove me to Cambridge for interviews with admissions officers. He waited in the lobby of 500 Harrison Street when the mail was delivered every day, and brought to my office whatever correspondence bore a Cambridge address. He stood by my desk, beaming, while I read increasingly encouraging letters. When the acceptance to Harvard came, I broke into tears in front of my employees. Ulvi's eyes watered, and he took me in his arms and held me as I gripped the letter that meant freedom from him.

⌒

Ulvi was offered a position at Lehman College, in the Bronx.

"It is only three hours away, I can come to see you on weekends." He rented a studio apartment in Larchmont, which was more affordable than Manhattan but only thirty-five minutes from Grand Central by train.

Finding a place for me was harder because I refused to live in any of the affordable slums on the periphery of Harvard and could not afford the rentals in better neighborhoods. Harvard had offered me a full-tuition scholarship, and an allowance for books each semester, but my admission as a transfer student was contingent on not needing housing, which was fine with me, as the idea of living in a dorm had no appeal whatsoever. Ulvi offered to pay my rent and utilities while I was in school, but I would have to get a loan or find a part-time job to cover my other expenses.

At the end of another frustrating weekend of apartment hunting, we were driving toward Harvard Square when Ulvi swerved out of traffic and parked across the street from a red brick building on Cambridge Street with elegant writing above the entrance door: Foxcroft Manor. "Let's look there."

"Look for what?"

"An apartment for you," he started across the road. There were no signs in front of the building, nothing to indicate a vacancy. But Ulvi paid no heed when I pointed this out. "I have a good feeling about this place," he said. He went in the heavy front door and pushed the button for the superintendent. A large studio had become available, in the back of the building, overlooking the parking lot. The tenant was moving to a one-bedroom apartment next door. Ulvi wrote out a check for the security deposit, first and last months rent, and set a date for my move. It was so easy, and happened so quickly, that I was still in a daze as we drove back to Syracuse.

With his job offer in New York, Ulvi's future was secure for the first time in years. He would have a regular income, had found a reasonably priced apartment minutes from Manhattan in a pretty town with a beach. The college would be his sponsor in his quest to secure his green card and permanent residency in the United States. He would be teaching film, and would finally get the recognition he craved as an artist. He had friends in New York and looked forward to reconnecting with them. I had not seen Ulvi so optimistic in years. He even talked about bringing Ulviye to study in the United States once he settled into his job.

"Maybe she can go to Harvard!" he hoped.

It was a relief to see him so happy, making plans, charting his progress from assistant to associate to tenured professor in a few years. His unsettled status had been hard. Not knowing what would happen to him next had me on quicksand, but he no longer talked about "opportunities in Europe" or "business." He had a job with potential. He had a home, a future.

There was about our last few months in Syracuse a dwindling, as if we had both been in a river up to our necks, but the waters were receding and we saw safe shores on either side. I looked away from him more often, and his eyes were more frequently turned from mine, until the image I conjured up of our relationship was that of the Roman god Janus, his two profiles facing in opposite directions.

That summer before my move to Cambridge was the sweetest time we had spent together. After the arduous four years of graduate school, we were both relaxed and excited about the coming months. Ulvi vowed that he would drive up frequently to see me, and when he couldn't, he would send for me.

As the time drew near for us to leave, we were able to spend more time with friends. With evenings no longer consumed by his work, we could go to the movies and the theater, to parties, on long drives to romantic lakeside restaurants in the Finger Lakes. He relaxed his constant, critical gaze on me, and I gained new confidence with the acceptance to Harvard and increasing disdain for *el que dirán*, which I blamed for holding me back for years.

Toward the end of the summer, Gene Hemmle came to visit. Accompanied by a young, lean, blond, track and field NCAA champion named Brad, Gene was on a buying trip for his mother's antique shop in Lubbock. His ultimate destination was Maine, where he said he always had good luck buying china. He and Brad stayed at the same Holiday Inn where Ulvi and I had lived our first week in Syracuse. We showed them around the campus, and Ulvi made appointments for Gene to meet with some of the faculty from the music department and to tour their facilities.

"Oh, this is wonderful!" Gene was ebullient about our apartment on Harrison Street, and about our plans. He had written letters of recommendation for us, using extravagant language to praise us both. We took him for brunch at one of our favorite restaurants, The Krebs, just down the street from Skaneateles

Lake. He didn't bring Brad, who he said was "not great for conversation." We didn't ask him to elaborate.

While Ulvi was in the men's room, Gene turned to me.

"It's delightful to see you assert yourself more," he said.

"Ulvi thinks I'm too independent," I murmured, an eye on the door through which he would return.

"Oh, never mind him!" Gene waved his hand. "You are a smart girl and you're going places. You don't need him."

It shocked me that his good friend should say that. "Thank you Gene. You've always been so kind to me."

He took my hand, kissed it and lowered his voice. "Is there anything you would like to know about him?"

I was taken by surprise. "No . . . I mean . . . I don't . . . Is there anything I should know?"

"I've known him years longer than you have. He . . . "

"We should look at the beautiful gardens before we go." Ulvi was standing behind us.

"Yes, of course," Gene let go of my hand and stood up to help me out of my chair. "I certainly don't see enough gardens."

The moment passed. What he wanted to tell me was left unsaid.

A few days later, Ulvi and I were at Sibley's, a downtown Syracuse department store where he had a credit card. He wanted to buy me a watch, a gift "for all your hard work on the dissertation and getting into Harvard." Together, we chose a gold Omega with a leather band. I had never owned such a nice watch and Ulvi was delighted that I kept looking at my wrist and announcing the time. It had a square face with rounded corners and Roman numerals, but the 4 was written as IIII, like the face on the clock in the Reading Room at the New York Public Library.

As we passed the full-length mirror near the entrance to the beauty salon, I caught sight of us together. He saw me looking, stopped and adjusted us so that we stood before the mirror full frontal. We were a good-looking couple, everyone said. He was slightly taller than I was and our coloring was almost identical, down to the clothes we wore, which, because he chose them, looked as if we had coordinated outfits. We looked foreign but it was difficult to tell where we were from. I could have been Turkish, he could have been Puerto Rican.

"You are beautiful, Chiquita," he pushed my hair back from my shoulders and kissed my lips.

"I want to cut my hair," I said, breaking from him. "Maybe they'll do it here."

"Your hair is nice. Why do you want to cut?" He stroked the black strands down to my waist.

"It says Walk-Ins Welcome on that sign, maybe they'll take me now?"

"I like your hair long." He pulled it back and squeezed a ponytail around his fingers. "Beautiful."

"May I help you?" A stylist led me to her chair. "Just a trim?"

"Cut it short," I said.

"Chiquita, no! Just an inch, no more," he said to the stylist.

"I want it close to the scalp."

The stylist looked from me to Ulvi, confused. She was a middle-aged woman with a dyed, sprayed perm, blue eye shadow, and lipstick that was too pink for her skin tone. "Maybe you and your husband should talk about this first?" she suggested with a strained smile. She shifted her weight behind the salon chair.

Ulvi stood next to her, looking at my reflection from under his brows. I gathered my hair at the nape of my neck, like he had done. "If you want the ponytail," I said to Ulvi, "you can have it."

"You do whatever you like," he bit out. "I'll come back in an hour."

He stalked off and I turned to the stylist. "As short as possible," I said.

When Ulvi returned, I was sitting in the waiting area, the ponytail in a plastic bag, my hair a cap of tight curls around my skull. He stood in front of me and stared, cupped my chin, turned my face side to side. "It looks nice, Chiquita," he said. "I did not think it would, but it does. You look like little girl."

I almost threw the ponytail in his face.

My last day at work, Paula and Dana took me to lunch. When we returned, the Coding Unit was decorated for a surprise send-off from the staff. They gave me a card signed by the medical records employees and by my favorite doctors. As a parting gift, they had chipped in for a heavy clay crock that Paula had picked out.

"Thank you, I guess." I laughed, trying to lift it.

"It's empty now," Paula said, "but since you're going to Harvard, it will soon be full of sh. . . "

"It's a remembrance from Syracuse," Ruth interrupted. "We are famous for china here."

Marie dropped in to say goodbye, and handed me a wrapped present. When I opened it to find a copy of *Joy of Cooking* we both said, "If you can read, you can cook" at the same time, to the merriment of the others.

I could find no words to say goodbye to Marie, no way to thank her. She gave me a quick hug. "Don't be a stranger. Write to me." Inside the book she had written her home address.

I walked out of the hospital for the last time struggling with the heavy, empty crock, which, as Paula had suggested, would soon be full. It accompanied me through several moves over the years, until one day it broke, as if the weight of everything I'd put in it had made it burst.

～

On August 21, 1974, exactly half my life had been lived in Puerto Rico and half in the United States. I observed the day as on every year, placing an invisible mark on an invisible calendar updated every August beginning in 1961, when Mami, Edna, Raymond, and I first landed in Brooklyn. A couple of days after the thirteenth anniversary of my arrival, Ulvi drove the Camaro toward Boston, the radio tuned to analyses on the aftermath of President Nixon's resignation earlier that month.

Other than clothes and personal items, I took nothing of my life with Ulvi to Foxcroft Manor. My load was not as light as on the day I left with him to Fort Lauderdale, but it was contained in one suitcase and a couple of boxes. My clothes, toiletries, books, and the empty crock fit in the back and trunk of the Camaro. The furniture we had purchased in Syracuse was going to his apartment. He had ordered a bed for me, and I had bought flowery linens and colorful towels that he didn't approve.

"I like bright and colorful," I argued. "You're only going to see them when you visit." He relented.

While he was bringing my things up, Ulvi ran into my neighbor on the elevator and brought her to meet me. Her name was Marilyn, and it was her apartment I was moving into. She had taken the one next door, because it had a separate bedroom. She told us about the market two blocks down, and about the laundry machines in the basement.

After Marilyn left, Ulvi and I finished unloading my things. I had nothing in the refrigerator, so we walked through Harvard Yard to the Square for a late lunch. When we came out of The Grist Mill, the steamy day had clouded and the sky threatened to burst open any minute with a late summer squall. We ran back to my building and said a hurried goodbye in the parking lot. He was driving to Larchmont that afternoon, because he had to receive the movers the next morning.

As the Camaro disappeared down Felton Street, I felt a pang of dread. In the six years Ulvi and I had been together, we had parted four times with no clear idea of when or if we would see each other again. The first time was when he left me in front of the Longacre Hotel on his way to Europe, the second when he flew to Texas and I to New York after our Bahamas sojourn, the third when I left him in front of Departures on my way out of Lubbock, the fourth when I moved to Dewitt. Three of those times I had faced life without Ulvi in New York City, where my family was, where the streets of Midtown had witnessed my adolescence, where a fifteen-cent subway ride brought me to the comfort and chaos of my family.

I returned to my apartment and stood in the middle of it, surrounded by my belongings. I knew no one in Massachusetts. Other than Delsa, with whom I exchanged Christmas cards, I had lost touch with everyone in my family and had no idea where they lived. I was utterly alone. Unlike the euphoria of my first hours at the Longacre, I was terrified. In another few days, I would start college as a sophomore, eight years removed from high school and that many years older than my classmates.

It had been exactly thirteen years since I'd first arrived in the United States on a stormy night. As if to punctuate the memory, a flash of lightning tore the sky followed by deafening thunder and the patter of enormous raindrops hitting the tops of cars, the cement sidewalk, the patch of grass and shrubs behind the building. I stood at the window and smelled the wet dirt of the back garden. Two years living on a seventeenth floor had meant that the musky, warm smell of newly moistened earth never reached my nose. I stuck my hands out the window and filled them with rainwater. I splashed it on my face, my neck, my shoulders. As a child, I had bathed in the first rains of May because Mami had said they brought good luck. As a twenty-six-year-old woman, I let the August rains wash over me, remembering that wet night in August when I had first set foot in Brooklyn, bewildered by the light piercing the darkness.

"Tell me about yourself."

I spent the night unpacking as rain pounded Cambridge. Hungry and craving coffee, I left the apartment early the next morning. The city smelled newly washed and fresh. The sky was clear, as if the clouds had spent themselves over Boston before drifting out to sea. I walked through a desolate Harvard Yard, its oaks and elms whispering with dripping moisture. Harvard Square was quiet, except for the occasional jogger on her way to the river. The storefronts were shuttered. A man washing windows at The Coop grinned and wished me "*Buenos días*," his gold-trimmed upper teeth gleaming. The T rumbled under my feet. Rather than walk around Harvard Square, which I would get to know because it was my neighborhood, I decided to explore Boston, which I'd never seen.

On the Inbound Red Line platform, I consulted the transit map and planned to get off at the next hub, Park Street, on the edge of the Boston Common. The train was quieter and cleaner than New York's subways, smaller too. As we approached Central Square, I heard the throb of El Gran Combo playing full blast in spite of the hour. When the train stopped, a group of teenagers climbed on, playfully pushing each other, laughing, speaking in exuberant

Spanglish, and waving small Puerto Rican flags. A short, pudgy boy lugged the enormous boom box at which passengers sent pointed looks just as pointedly ignored. Some got up grumbling and moved to the furthest corner of the car.

The teenagers were oblivious to the racket they were making, totally engaged in their own good time. The girls looked me over, then giggled. I hunched tight into my body, wondering if they would criticize my clothes, my hair, and the way I didn't return their brazen looks if they knew I too was Puerto Rican. I wished I could introduce myself, tell them I was new in Boston, that it had been four years since I'd been in the middle of a Puerto Rican community, that I missed the camaraderie of Spanglish, its scrambled rhythms amplifying the confusion and nostalgia of a displaced nation.

When the train burst out of the tunnel and slowed over the Charles River Bridge, the group moved to the windows, crowding one another, pressing chests against backs, shoulders to shoulders, arms around waists. They oohed and aahed, pointed at the skyline, at the shimmering river, at the long narrow boat and rhythmic oars of a crew team, at the white sails puffing off from the marina.

"*¡Que lindo!* It's beautiful! Somebody take a picture!"

One of the younger girls in the group, brown as wheat, and with intense turquoise-blue eyes, beamed the most open smile I'd ever received from a stranger. I stood up and looked through my window, wanting to share that moment of beauty with her, with them.

The train bypassed the Charles Street station and plunged underground again. The boys pointed and laughed at the consternation of the people who had stepped to the edge of the platform, only to see the train speed past them.

Park Street was full of Puerto Ricans emerging from the Green Line trolleys and from the Red Line coming from the south. They were in a festive mood. I lost myself in the crowd climbing the high steps into the bright summer morning, followed them toward the modern complex of buildings I later learned was Government Center, at the far end of which floats were assembling for a parade celebrating Puerto Rican culture.

Pushcart vendors hawked Puerto Rican flags, T-shirts with pictures of *El Morro* and *La Fortaleza, coquí*-shaped balloons, cotton candy, *platanutre*. I bought a cup of coffee and an egg sandwich from a woman whose stand was powered by extension cords jerry-rigged to a street light. Pretty girls in evening gowns and tiaras were helped onto the back seat of convertibles, where they sat on the gathered canvas tops covered with cushions, their high heels digging into the seats. Boys in band uniforms blew and banged their instruments as their leaders tried to get them to line up. Another band blared a salsa version of "I Shot the Sheriff." A precision baton team practiced their moves, oblivious to the people ducking out of the way of their high kicks and twirling sticks.

Mounted police pushed the crowds to the sidewalk behind wooden barricades. Within minutes, the chaos had subsided, the middle of the street was cleared and the Grand Marshall posed for pictures in front of a Shawmut Bank banner. With a blare of trumpets, the parade began. I stood on the curb waving at the sashed beauty queens and applauding the drum corps and baton twirlers. A gaggle of *yanqui* officials sweated in summer suits while equally officious Puerto Rican men walked proud and cool in their elegant *guayaberas*.

I was so caught up in the excitement, that I didn't notice a man and woman just joining the parade in a white Cadillac convertible waving at me until a girl touched my shoulder and pointed them out.

"*¡Ven, súbete!*" the woman called, "We don't want to go empty." After some hesitation, I climbed into the back seat and sat like the beauty queens ahead of us, waving at the crowds as if I belonged in the parade.

The man turned around. "I'm Vicente, this is my wife Connie."

I introduced myself, and told them this was my first day in Boston.

"*¡Bienvenida!*" Connie shouted over the crowd.

"We always have a parade when a Puerto Rican moves to Boston!" Vicente laughed.

We passed the teenagers I had seen on the train and they squealed, pointed and clapped in my direction. "Who is she?" they asked. "*¿Quién es esa?*"

"*La Famosa Esmeralda*," Vicente shouted.

Connie leaned over and playfully punched his arm. "*Deja eso*," she scolded then turned to me. "He's always making jokes."

The parade wound through neighborhoods that became more rundown the further we were from the city's center. The signage changed from English to almost exclusively Spanish—bodega, *botánica, Se Vende, Se Alquila, Alianza Hispana, Productos Tropicales*. I had no idea where I was, but kept waving at the residents of the three-deckers and brownstones, who appeared at their windows or on their stoops at the first drums and horns of the bands, some of them seemingly surprised that a parade was going through their neighborhood.

The procession ended at a park, where families had set up feasts around picnic tables. Men roasted chicken drumsticks, hotdogs, and hamburgers over the blue smoke of hibachis and portable grills. Young girls ran after kids as women set out bowls of macaroni salad, *arroz con gandule*s, and *guineitos verdes* smothered with onions. Vicente and Connie led me to their family group. They had a good laugh over Vicente picking a stranger in the crowd to ride in his car.

"You should have seen it," he crowed. "Everyone thought she was a *vedette* or something."

"There was no way he wasn't going to show off his new car in that parade," Connie laughed.

I ate until I could barely breathe. It had been years since I'd had Puerto Rican food, and Vicente's family had outdone themselves.

Everyone, it seemed, had a boom box blaring salsa, merengue, and, in the younger groups, funk and soul. I couldn't stop smiling, thrilled to be jumping easily from Spanish to English, dancing barefoot on the grass, sharing a Sunday afternoon with these total strangers who had welcomed me so warmly and memorably to Boston. At the end of the day, Connie packed food for me to take home, and then she and Vicente drove me to Cambridge. When I reached my apartment I realized we had not exchanged phone numbers and I had no idea what their last names were, where they lived, or if we'd ever see each other again.

The first few days at Harvard were a blur of orientation meetings, welcoming receptions, interviews with advisors, and hours poring over the thick course catalogue, trying to figure out which classes would fulfill the requirements of the core curriculum. I had enough credits to be a junior, but the college didn't accept them all. I came in as a sophomore hoping to concentrate in Visual and Environmental Studies, Harvard's studio arts department. Because of inadequate facilities, admission to the media arts at VES was limited to a handful of students. Besides a formal application, students had to be recommended by a member of the VES faculty following an interview, which in my case was with photographer Barbara Norfleet.

She was a slender, elegant woman with a gentle manner and restless brown eyes that seemed not just to see but also to study me. As a teenager I had modeled for a portrait painter who had that concentrated gaze, more focused and directed than that of other people.

Ms. Norfleet's studio-office was on the top floor of Sever Hall. Huge windows looked out over the oaks toward Quincy Street into the brick façade of the Fogg Art Museum and the curved concrete of the Carpenter Center. Her office was as warm and cozy as a living room, with worn Orientals on the floor, a comfortable old couch, and easy chairs. She prepared us tea then sat across from me, her feet curled under her.

"Tell me about yourself," she said, tilting her head as if to catch a different angle of my face.

Not sure what she wanted to hear, I gave her the short version. "I was born in Puerto Rico and came to the United States when I was thirteen. I'm the eldest of eleven children. I graduated from Performing Arts High School eight years ago but have studied part-time ever since."

"Why didn't you go right to college after high school?"

"The summer after graduation I worked as an extra in a movie, maybe you've heard of it, *Up the Down Staircase*. And soon after that, I auditioned for a children's theater company and was hired as the female lead in their Broadway production."

"So you wanted to be a star . . . "

"I liked being on stage."

"Did you make any more movies?"

"I auditioned for a few things, but was never called back . . . "

"I've always wondered how actors manage to stay confident when they face so much rejection . . . "

"I became a dancer," I said, and it didn't sound funny until it left my lips. We both laughed. She asked what kind of dancing I did and I told her about Indian classical dance, feeling as if the purpose of the interview was getting away from me. I searched for a way to return to the subject of my application to VES.

"My boyfriend won the Golden Bear at the Berlin International Film Festival."

"Uhm," she said, sipping her tea. "Eleven children . . . what was that like?"

I had already forgotten that part of the conversation but told her how much fun it was, how lively our parties, how charming my little sisters and brothers could be.

She listened attentively, sipped her tea, picked up threads I had deliberately dropped. "What do your parents do?"

"They, ah, my father is a carpenter and, uh, my mother is a seamstress."

"It must be hard to raise such a large family on their income."

None of your business, I wanted to say. "They work hard."

"Where in the United States do they live?"

What does this have to do with my application to VES, I wondered. "They were in New York, but they're back in Puerto Rico."

"You must miss them."

"Yes." I rummaged inside my purse. "I brought you the transcripts from the communications courses I've taken . . . "

"I can look at those later. I'm more interested in you. Did you speak English when you came to the United States?"

"No." Somewhere inside me, a barrier began to crumble. It felt like warmth radiating from my chest, a flush on my skin, tightness in my throat, a tickling around my lashes. Ms. Norfleet's intense eyes never left mine. Her head alternated encouraging nods with barely perceptible shakes of disbelief or sympathy as my real story spilled forth. I spoke more openly and vulnerably than I ever had to Shirley in Lubbock, who had understood my "deal" with Ulvi, to Marie in Syracuse, who had not cared what the deal was so long as I knew it wasn't binding for the rest of my life. Ms. Norfleet asked so gently, and I was so full of answers no one had ever wanted to hear, that our meeting overran the allotted period and expected formality of an interview for admission into VES. By the time it was over, we were both weeping, neither of us quite sure what had just happened.

"Believe me," she sniffled, "I've not had an interview like this before."

I was so exhausted that I walked the two blocks to my apartment and fell into bed fully dressed, my shoes still on. I didn't wake until 11 p.m., to the shrill sound of the phone and, when I answered, Ulvi's voice asking me how things were going.

A couple of weeks later, I was accepted to VES.

⟿

In Cambridge I had to set up a household on my own. Ulvi wasn't there to observe, evaluate, or criticize. He could no longer choose my clothes, the decorations in my apartment, the friends I made. It both excited and scared me.

I spent hours in the Harvard Coop's basement, baffled by the array of kitchenware necessary to prepare a meal. In our rented apartments, Ulvi and I had functioned with the battered pots and mismatched dishes left by previous tenants. At home, the most important pot was the heavy-bottomed *caldero* where the daily rice was prepared. Nothing like it could be found among the copper-bottomed Revere and imported French pans dangling from hooks against the walls of the Harvard Coop. I had to consult *Joy of Cooking*, which never mentioned a *caldero* but did recommend a heavy-bottomed pan for cooking rice. The white Corningware pots with blue fleurs-de-lis on the side seemed heavy enough, but I once again had to check the cookbook because I'd never learned to make the most basic item in a Puerto Rican diet.

At Dickson's Hardware on Brattle Street, I bought curtain rods and a tool kit with hammer, screwdriver, and measuring tape. As a child I had helped Papi when he worked around the house and he had taught me how to swing a hammer, how to begin and maintain the rhythm for sawing wood evenly, how to properly tap in nails and drive in screws. They were skills that had gone untested for years, and I derived such pleasure from reconnecting with that part of me, that I became a regular at the store crammed with plumbing supplies, light fixtures, nails, screws, giant staples. I admired the latest power tools, tested the most secure dead-bolt locks, wondered why anyone would put adhesive-backed one-foot-square cork tiles on their walls. I built my own bookshelves, somewhat crooked and not at all an example of fine woodworking, but it was one of the most satisfying things I'd ever done.

Unlike the Longacre Hotel, there was no maid service at Foxcroft Manor and Ulvi was not around to keep my studio neat. The task of picking up after myself filled me with anxiety, especially when Ulvi was coming to visit. I ran around in a panic then, dusting, mopping, scrubbing, and washing bedclothes. He once stroked his fingers across the top of the doorjamb, to see how well I'd cleaned. He was not impressed. From then on the doorjambs and sills were the first things I dusted during the weekly cleanup.

Without his constant gaze, the "elegant" style Ulvi had imposed on me soon gave way to the costumey flowing skirts and colorful fabrics I had favored in New York. Ulvi had not liked it when I wore makeup or jewelry, but I loved bright lipsticks, dangly earrings, and the intricately crafted necklaces, bracelets and rings of Asian cultures. Most of all, I liked choosing my wardrobe, deciding for myself when I wanted to be "elegant," when "exotic," when "groovy." The first few weeks in Cambridge, I spent more time gazing into the mirror than I had my entire life, trying to see myself through my own eyes, quieting the critical voice that had judged my every action over the last six years.

Alterity

I joined a group of off-campus students who went ballroom dancing on weekends. At the Revere Ballroom, or at Moseley's on the
Charles, in Dedham—the two remaining live-band ballrooms in
the Boston area—we were usually the youngest dancers. "The kids
are here," the elders would say happily when we entered, as if we
belonged to them. They were thrilled to teach us variations on the
fox-trot and tango. The men were courtly, smelled of spicy after-
shave, and glided across the floor in white patent leather shoes.
The platinum-haired ladies wore beaded gowns. Their eyes were
shadowed in iridescent blue, their earlobes and fingers heavy with
jewels.

I tried out for and won a leading role in a production of An-
tonin Artaud's *The Cenci*, a depressing play I might have thought
brilliant when I was an existentialist. The concept of Theater of
Cruelty espoused by Artaud, not entirely convincingly portrayed
in our production, was as inscrutable as my friend Ralph's writings
in his *Destructivism: A Manifesto*. As always when confronted with
highly intellectual theories, I felt insufficiently sophisticated to
understand them.

I loved being on stage again, however, and went around calling everyone "Dahling!" as if I were an old theatrical diva. Ellen, another student, was so annoyed by this affectation that she told me "If you call me darling one more time, I'm going to punch you in the mouth." She meant it too. I stopped.

At one of the many orientation and welcoming events that Harvard hosted for transfer and first-year students, I met Lupe, a community organizer from Albuquerque; Anna, a grandmother from Athol; and Doris, a secretary from the District of Columbia. They had started college later than I had. As we talked about the joys and challenges of being older than our classmates, we decided to meet to discuss some of those issues at greater length. We formed Older Women Students, and added our posters to the hundreds defacing lampposts and utility boxes around Harvard Square. A few more women joined us to complain, get advice, and exchange stories but mostly, to act as one another's cheerleaders.

We OWS had "been around the block a few times," as Ruth used to say. Lupe had daughters the same ages as our classmates, and Anna's were in graduate school. At twenty-six I was closer in age to our classmates than to most of the OWS, but the distance between us was not so much a generation gap as an experiential divide. I loved being around women who already had full lives, for whom a college education was another phase, not something they had to do between high school and "the real world."

Lectures, tutorials, long reading lists, and deadlines for what were expected to be erudite papers guided my days. I had spoken English for thirteen years, had taken numerous courses, and was an avid reader, but I still needed a dictionary to keep up with my professors' vocabulary. My notebooks were filled with circled words that I had to look up: *reified*, proposed Mr. Guzetti in the photography survey course, *alterity*, offered Ms. Felice in sociology, *nisus*, suggested Dr. Loeb, my VES advisor.

Academically, I was well prepared by Performing Arts, Manhattan Community College, and Texas Tech. As a scholarship student,

I felt pressure to do well so that the college would continue to waive my tuition. I was so grateful for the opportunity to study at Harvard that I wanted to excel, not just pass with the minimum acceptable grades. I had no doubts I could do that. More challenging, however, was my nonacademic education.

Days after I moved to Foxcroft Manor, there was a knock on my door. I opened it to a woman slightly taller than me, zaftig, with short-cropped salt-and-pepper hair and aviator-style eyeglasses.

"Hi, I'm Liz," she said, "I live down the hall. You shouldn't have opened the door without first asking who it was."

"I'm sorry," I said. " Would you like to come in?"

"I can't," she continued in a thick Boston accent, "but I wanted to tell you that there was a rape in this neighborhood a week ago. There have been several rapes around here in the past year and the police haven't caught the guy. Don't let anyone you don't know into the building, even if they claim to be tenants who forgot their keys."

"I won't."

"I don't mean to scare you, but you should be careful. If you come home alone late at night, walk in the middle of the street and look around before you enter the building. Carry your keys like this." Through the space between each finger of her fisted hand protruded the sharp end of a key. "If a man jumps you, use them. Go for his eyes."

"Okay," I said.

"I work in the Women's Center in Inman Square," Liz handed me a purple flyer. "We offer health and birth control counseling, support and discussion groups. It's free."

"Thank you."

"Welcome to the neighborhood," she said. "See you around."

I went to meetings at the Center led by women who were passionate about changing patriarchal culture and by men committed to equality between the sexes. It was a different education from the one I was getting at Harvard. Putting what I was learning into practice was tough, however, because feminist theory didn't address the emotional costs of equality. On paper what needed to change was clear, but when Ulvi came to see me in Cambridge, or when I went to him in Larchmont, it all became murky and hard to sort out. I felt like a hypocrite, spouting feminist theory while I continued to be Ulvi's Chiquita.

I had the impression, those first few weeks at Harvard, that the people I met didn't know what to make of me, and there were times when I didn't know what to make of myself. I had spent the last five years isolated from both my Puerto Rican culture and my generation. I could no longer identify the latest Puerto Rican celebrities or musical trends, didn't know which party was in power on the island, or who was governor.

I did not identify with any "movements," had never been drunk or high on drugs, and was just beginning to read feminist theory. I was not well informed about *estadounidense* or world events except for what inevitably seeped into my brain through the barrage of television news and stacks of newspapers and magazines that Ulvi was addicted to. At a dinner in Dudley House, I was placed at the same table with the governor of Massachusetts, whose name I didn't learn until we were introduced.

I did know a lot about medical records, broadcast communications, and how satellite technology could be used to further economic development in poor countries, hardly what my Harvard classmates expected or were interested in. My leisure reading was eclectic. I was as likely to carry in my purse George Eliot's *Daniel Deronda* as Steven King's *Carrie* or the latest issue of the *National Enquirer*. My friend David pointedly asked if I worried I was a dilettante, and I was not offended until after I looked up the word.

David taught and managed the audiovisual equipment at the Carpenter Center. He introduced me to Edgar, a Puerto Rican political science student who was working on a documentary about the violence following court-ordered school desegregation in Boston. Edgar had political ambitions, but was torn between his conviction that Puerto Rico should be an independent nation and his certainty that it would never happen.

"We have become accustomed to the status quo," he said. "The United States has scared us into thinking that Puerto Rico will become another Cuba if we're independent."

"Won't it?" I asked.

"Becoming another Cuba would not be such a terrible fate," he said sadly. "They, at least, have preserved their culture."

"But they're communists!"

"Communists don't eat babies, Esmeralda, don't look so scared!"

Conversations about the political status of Puerto Rico did scare me. I had told Edgar about my uncle, Vidal Santiago Díaz, who had been the barber and look-alike of Puerto Rican nationalist patriot Don Pedro Albizu Campos. Tío Vidal was in a three-hour standoff in his barbershop in Santurce that ended in a shootout with the Puerto Rican police. When I was a child, he showed me the scars. The most frightening was a hole on his forehead from a bullet that, miraculously, didn't kill him. Following that experience, Tío Vidal's nationalist zeal was redirected toward born-again Christianity.

Skeptical of organized religion, I mistrusted political fervor even more because it was always centered on a charismatic, flawed man. Edgar himself was intelligent, charming, and magnetic. I could envision him as the leader of an independent Puerto Rico, if he ever decided to make public his conviction rather than follow the path of least resistance. He would never support statehood, he said, but would work with the Commonwealth party as the lesser of the two evils.

"How are we ever going to become independent if leaders like you are more focused on winning elections than on changing minds?" I asked.

"You can't change the status quo without the votes," he said.

I understood the complexity of the problem, but had no suggestions for how to solve it. The question didn't go away, however. Almost everyone I met at Harvard asked me "the status question" as soon as they learned I was Puerto Rican. I stumbled through answers as unsatisfying to me as they must have been to them. I became defensive.

"Not every Puerto Rican has an opinion on status," I complained to Edgar.

"Every Puerto Rican should," he said.

He gave me books and pamphlets, and over coffee, talked about the politics of the island. Like the discussions about feminism at the Women's Center, Edgar's informal lectures were a supplementary education to that offered by my Harvard professors.

A few days after Edgar finished the research for his documentary, he was ready to start filming, and asked me to help. I couldn't because Ulvi was coming that weekend.

"I can help you next week," I offered. He couldn't postpone the shoot in Dorchester. I felt bad about it, but felt even worse when, the following Monday I saw him at Sever Hall. His face was bruised.

"What happened to you?"

"I was mugged," he said. "They took everything."

Edgar explained that he had finished the interviews and the student who was recording sound went back to Cambridge, leaving the equipment with Edgar, who was to return it. Edgar decided to film some street scenes before the light faded. A gang jumped him, beat him up, and ran off with the Carpenter Center's 16mm camera and sound recorder.

"They think I stole it," Edgar said, looking resentfully toward the equipment room.

When I saw David later that day, I asked him about Edgar's mugging.

"It's suspicious," David said. "He was alone in a high-crime neighborhood with expensive equipment and it didn't occur to him he'd be mugged?"

"That doesn't mean he stole it, David! It just means he wasn't careful."

"We don't buy it. They didn't take his wallet and he didn't file a police report."

Edgar was sure that he was under suspicion because he was Puerto Rican. "If this had happened to a *blanquito*," he said, "they would have believed him."

"Why didn't you file a police report?"

"Whose side are you on?"

I explained that it was common sense to report a mugging to the police. He thought I should accept his story without questions. I thought he was acting guilty, but didn't accuse him. We parted in the worst possible way two friends can part, each of us mistrustful of the other.

Some days later David told me that Edgar had withdrawn from college. I felt guilty that, by not sticking up for him, I had added to the suspicion that he had made up the mugging story and had stolen the equipment. I also felt complicit in a crime I wasn't sure had taken place, just because we were both Puerto Rican.

At the next Older Women Students meeting, I talked about it. I hoped the group, but especially Lupe, who was Chicana, would help me sort out my feelings. They listened for a few minutes, but said nothing. Then Lupe took off her glasses and wiped them on the hem of her T-shirt.

"*Mi'ja*, you've bought into the Anglo notion that all Puerto Ricans are criminals."

"No, Lupe, that's not it. I've fought that stereotype all my life. I'm a model Puerto Rican."

"Listen to yourself, *pues!* Why do you have to be 'a model Puerto Rican'? To set yourself apart from the other Puerto Ricans, the ones who, unlike you, steal?"

"No!"

The women in the group averted their eyes. Doris, who was black, seemed particularly uncomfortable.

Lupe continued. "I've worked in the community a long time, and I've seen how prejudice and racism get under our skins. If we are successful in Anglo terms, we start to see our friends and neighbors through the eyes of the oppressor, making ourselves the exception, of course, because we're different. The proof is in the fact that we're functioning in Anglo culture and they're not. Do you understand?"

"I think so . . . "

"I'm not accusing you, *mi'ja*. I'm speaking about myself, too. I'm sure Doris knows what I'm talking about."

Doris concurred, but so did Anna, who was white Anglo Saxon protestant.

"It's the same with sexism," Anna said.

Lupe looked at her, and for a moment I thought she was about to disagree, but she turned to me again. "It's hard to block out those negative messages, but racism," she glanced at Anna, "and sexism too, do the most damage when we absorb their principles without even realizing we're perpetuating them."

"I hadn't thought of myself as 'oppressed' . . . "

"It's a strong word, I know. But you have to name things before you can understand their psychological impact. The civil rights movement taught us that."

The other women agreed and the meeting moved on to a discussion of whether you could be a feminist and a racist. Anna said no. Doris said yes.

Walking home, I thought about what Lupe had said. It made sense, but it didn't make me feel better, rather the opposite. I had failed Edgar by not accepting his story without doubts or questions. But on the other hand, he had behaved suspiciously. Or was I projecting the suspicions onto him? I could not convince myself one way or the other. Lupe's challenge that I had bought into the negative Anglo view of Puerto Ricans did not relieve the guilt for Edgar's actions nor for my reaction to them. I hated the idea that I was "oppressed." It made me feel like a victim, powerless and outnumbered, weaker than I would acknowledge, crushed under the weight of processes I did not want to name and refused to admit applied to me.

"You are the last person
I expected to see in Boston."

A poster in the Science Center announced the opening of Adonna's Belly Dance Studio, near Porter Square. Remembering the joy of dancing with my Middle Eastern friends in Lubbock, I signed up, and was soon structuring my days around Adonna's classes. No matter how overwhelmed or lonely I felt during the day, the minute I entered her studio my mood changed. The class always ended with improvisations that built on what had just been taught. Those five minutes of free dancing were like meeting my real self, wrapped in veils and clinking *zills*, moving as a woman should.

Several weeks after I started belly dancing, I saw a notice for a beginner's Indian classical dance class being offered in the Back Bay. On one of the first frosty nights of the Cambridge winter, I joined a group of teenagers in a school gym at a private school. The teacher was Dulal, a dark, short, rotund man with beautiful thick black hair, delicate features, and small, graceful hands.

He told us that he began training as a child in his native Bangladesh, where he became famous for his Kathak interpretations. He gave a class in Bharata Natyam, however, the oldest of the classical dance styles of India, associated with the southern part of that country. The class was too challenging for most of the beginners there, and Dulal was annoyed when they couldn't perform the steps he thought they should master. Indian dance gurus take their students' development personally because the dancer's abilities reflect the guru's knowledge not only of the traditional choreography, but also of the guru's evaluation of the student's talent.

I had not had a Bharata Natyam class in four years, but dancers rely on muscular memory, the concept that the body never forgets what it has learned. As Dulal went through the movements for the traditional beginner's dance, *Alaripu,* my limbs knew what to do at the first notes of the music. I had practiced that dance hundreds of times, beginning to end. I no longer had the precision or stamina necessary to perform with artistry, especially as the steps became more complex and the rhythm faster. But the euphoria of its pure dance sequences returned the minute I began to move. As in Adonna's studio, I felt most myself in the expression of music, in my body as an instrument as rich and articulate as the sitar and the tabla.

After a few weeks of group classes, I asked Dulal if he would teach me privately. We set a date for the following Tuesday in his apartment, where he would test me and decide if he would take me as a student.

The last thing I needed was more to do, especially because Dulal lived in a part of Allston accessible only after a long bus ride. I also did not need another expense. My savings and what was left of a student loan were going fast and I had begun to look for a job with no sense of where I would find the time to work.

I sketched out an hour-by-hour schedule of my days. It allowed me to sleep from midnight to 6 a.m. every single night during the semester, except for the weekends I went to see Ulvi. He soon realized that what I looked forward to most when I came to visit him was sleeping.

When Dulal agreed to teach me, he did so only if I promised to practice at least an hour and a half a day on my own, in addition to two private lessons a week. I came after supper, and we worked in the kitchen, fragrant of spices and roasted chilies. His wife and two daughters went into the next room, divided from the kitchen by green plastic beads, where the girls did their homework under their mother's supervision.

How they could concentrate with the noise Dulal and I were making was a mystery. Dulal insisted that I wear the traditional *ghunghrus*, brass ankle bells, which I had to buy from him because I had left mine in New York and they had disappeared with my family's move to Puerto Rico.

He did not teach me with recorded music. He sat on a cushion on the flowered linoleum and called out *talas*, rhythm combinations I was supposed to perform as he drummed them on the tabla. This allowed him to increase the speed at will, and also made it possible for him to sing out the *talas* in random order, which meant I had to learn the steps until there was no thinking involved, only muscle memory.

While my training had been in Bharata Natyam, I was learning Kathak from Dulal because that was his specialty and, he insisted, more appropriate for my body type and personality. After the first lesson I agreed with him.

Kathak means storyteller, and it is the ultimate goal of a Kathak to use body movements and rhythmic expression to move the audience through the artful suggestion of human emotions and actions—a maiden's first sigh of love for example—or animal characteristics, such as the strut of a peacock. Indian audiences are familiar with the story-dances taken from holy texts, the choreography passed down through generations. Every performance also includes pure dance sequences, however, to show off the dancers' and musicians' virtuosity.

A pure-dance Kathak performance at its most sublime is an improvised competition between the dancer and the accompanists. It is an exchange of sung syllables representing movements, which are then played on the tabla and, finally, performed by the dancer and drummer at increasingly fast speeds that require not only virtuosity but also trancelike concentration.

Rather than giving me choreography for specific story-dances, Dulal began by teaching me *talas* and urging me to practice them until I could perform each step sequence with speed and accuracy. He was furious when I came for a private class after insufficient practice. He could tell because I kept stumbling over the stylized walks called *chals*, or fell over when I should have been doing quick turns on my heels.

Kathak was added to a full schedule of courses, hours of study, term papers, and creating projects for a conceptual art class that might reveal why a truckload of ice left to melt in the garden of the Museum of Modern Art was, in fact, art.

I practiced my *talas* in the mid-afternoon, before the other tenants in the building came home from work, so as not to disturb them with my foot slapping and ankle bells jangling. One day I found a note under my door:

> What are the sounds I hear coming from your apartment at this time every day?
> Marilyn (your next door neighbor)

I knocked on her door and began an apology, but she was not annoyed, just curious.

Marilyn was a musician, as I had figured out from hearing the sweet sound of her flute coming from her side of the wall that divided our apartments. Her job, however, was as a junior high school English teacher in a suburb of Boston, which is why she was home earlier than our other neighbors. We hit it off right away. She had lived in Boston for years and had many friends not affiliated with Harvard whom I came to know.

Marilyn invited me to classical concerts in churches and chapels, where the echoing music filled me with joy as solid as my limbs.

When I was feeling low, I could count on her for an empathetic ear and willingness to join me at the Orson Welles Café, where we exchanged confidences only possible over quiche, red wine, and chocolate mousse. Of all my friends in Cambridge, she was the only one privy to my angst and doubts over my relationship with Ulvi, whom she had met the day I moved in. I tried to be as good a friend to her as she struggled with a job she didn't like and the possibility of changing careers more suitable to her serious, quiet temperament.

The furious pace of my days, the friends I was making, the hours of study and paper writing, did not erase the throbbing question of my relationship with Ulvi. The longer we lived apart, the sweeter he became, the more he insisted that Ulviye and I were the most important people in his life. As in previous separations, he asked me to "be good girl," to be patient, to trust that we would be to-gether again. He assumed that's what I wanted, but I wasn't so sure.

On the other hand, I was not ready to give him up, not when he was paying my rent and was a quick escape from the stresses of school. Not when he had convinced me that no one would ever love me like he did. Not when he loved me more than I loved him, which Ruth had said was the best kind of relationship.

I wasn't so sure about that either. How could it be, when it was lopsided? I was tending toward the feminist ideal of a relationship based on mutual respect and collaboration, of shared goals and open communication. I was certain, however, that Ulvi wasn't ready for that kind of commitment because he had too many secrets.

With my doubts about Ulvi, and with too much to do and too little time, I thought that romance would be the furthest thing from my mind. But a college campus is not just a place of learning and growth. It is, as my OWS friend Doris described it, "a whirlpool of pheromones." Flirtations and seductions were as much a part of the atmosphere as the weighty ghosts of the distinguished Harvard graduates of previous generations.

As a twenty-six-year-old, I was the same age as some of the teaching assistants and junior faculty. But it was my classmates I found most appealing. I had lived with a man seventeen years my senior for five years. Although he was healthy and youthful at forty-three, Ulvi could not compete with the young athletes and artists who wooed me in between lectures on the history of Latin America or the increasingly preposterous experiments in conceptual art.

Their bodies were in constant motion, their eyes brazen. They slumped on the orange plastic chairs of the Carpenter Center knees apart, jeans bulging. They shambled into early morning lectures with the smell of sleep still on them, hair uncombed, stubbly cheeks creased by pillows. When we stopped to talk in Sever Hall or the Yard, they shuffled their enormous feet inside their shabby sneakers as if unsure whether to go or not, impatient for a signal. They thought they were men and I, who had been with a man for so long, saw them as the boys they were by comparison. They were as irresistible as candy, and, while they mostly left me as unnourished as a bag of M&Ms, I derived the same short-lived pleasure from our flirtations.

I was not in love with Phillip, didn't envision a future with Charles, didn't want to hear Julian's theories on who really wrote Shakespeare's plays. I wanted to touch them. But when I thought about "my boyfriend," it was Ulvi I referred to, Ulvi whose phone calls I ran home to answer not a minute later than eleven every night.

⤳

A few days before the Thanksgiving break I was walking across the Square when I heard a familiar voice behind me. I turned around and there was Shirley, my friend from Lubbock. She looked enormous, wrapped in a billowing, hooded, full-length wool cape. Her hair peeked out in curly, graying wisps around her face. In spite of the snowy slush on the sidewalks, she wore battered suede Birkenstocks with striped wool socks.

"You are the last person I expected to see in Boston," she laughed, hugging me warmly after looking around to make sure I was alone. "What are you doing here? Where's your old man?"

We walked to Elsie's, and, over an egg salad sandwich and coffee, I brought her up to date. Her size, I learned as soon as she removed her cape, was due to the imminent arrival of twins. "I really shouldn't have come to this conference," she said, "but I signed up over a year ago and can't afford to forfeit the deposit." She combed her fingers through her hair. "Look at me! Pregnancy has turned me prematurely gray!" She tousled my short do. "And you look about twelve years old!"

There was such sparkle in Shirley, that I skipped Professor Womack's lecture and sat with her for a couple of hours.

"Lenny and I divorced, you know."

"Yes, he told me."

"You saw him!" She was so shocked, and spoke so loud, that diners turned to look at us. "When? Where?"

"Uh . . . let me think, about a year ago, in Syracuse."

"Wow," she whispered, and shuddered, as if a draft of cold air had just hit her. When she looked up, she was subdued. "It must have been right after that they found him."

"Found him?"

"Those last few months in Lubbock were terrible, horrible for him, for us. He got into some bad shit, I mean really bad." She made a gesture as if injecting herself. "I couldn't stand it any more, you know? I wanted a family, and a normal life. Well, not normal, but you know what I mean."

"Yeah."

"After our divorce he disappeared. I had no idea he'd end up in Syracuse. They found him in Albany."

"Found him?" I repeated, my heart galloping.

"Overdose."

"Oh, God! I'm so sorry." I told her about the last time I'd seen him, and about how Lenny tried to break into my apartment. Shirley's eyes misted.

"That's awful. I'm sorry he put you through that. He was fucking brilliant. I just don't know what happened, to tell you the truth. One day he was organizing cowboys to march against the war and the next he was stealing my jewelry to pay for heroin. It's such a fucking waste."

"But you're happy, Shirley, aren't you? Things are going well for you?"

She was living in Brooklyn, working at a mental health clinic that sounded exactly like the one she had volunteered for in Lubbock. Her husband, also a psychologist, was its director.

"And can you believe it? He's black. My parents almost died. But he's the best thing that ever happened to me."

"I'm so happy for you," I squeezed her hands, just like she had squeezed mine years ago.

"Life couldn't be better. Will you call me when you come to the city?"

We exchanged phone numbers and addresses, hugged as we parted in front of the T station. Our short visit felt like punctuation to a story begun years earlier. I never called her nor wrote, and she never called me either.

When I went down to Larchmont for the long weekend, Ulvi had just received a note from Laila, another of our Lubbock friends, asking us to meet her for tea at the Algonquin. She looked different, still thin but less delicate, older. Deep circles shadowed her light brown eyes and her lips were scored with tiny wrinkles. The first thing we wanted to know, of course, was how Günter was.

"He's dead," she said flatly, her musical Swedish accent gone.

After Lubbock they had returned to his hometown in Germany. He didn't want to be there. He couldn't hold down a job. He didn't like their apartment. "He returned from the United States not liking his life anymore," she said.

One day he called her at work to tell her he was going to kill himself. By the time she reached the apartment, he had shot himself in the mouth.

It was Thanksgiving, my favorite holiday, a time when I wanted to feel grateful for the changes in my life, for the good things that were happening. But within a couple of days I had heard about two men I knew whose lives were squandered. I was pierced with grief that Ulvi didn't know how to soothe. I didn't understand it myself. Lenny had been little more than an acquaintance and Günter more Ulvi's friend than mine. But I couldn't stop mourning and feeling as if the good things in my life owed something to their suffering.

⌒

"Chiquita, would you like to spend Christmas in Puerto Rico?"

I couldn't believe my ears. Ulvi thought we both needed a vacation, but that was the last place I'd ever expect him to suggest. He explained that because he had applied for permanent residency in the United States, he could not travel outside the country, but Puerto Rico, being an American territory, would not be a problem. A good friend of his, a Turkish businessman based in Germany, was vacationing there around the same time.

"We cannot stay at fancy hotel," Ulvi said, "but it will be at least warm and sunny."

Two more beautiful words did not exist in the English language than warm and sunny. Northeastern winters had tested my mental health from the first one I experienced in Brooklyn. It was the darkness that I couldn't bear, the dusk that fell earlier every day beginning in early fall, shadowing the world, subduing the meager light of the migrating sun. Friends insisted that if I took up a sport like skiing or ice-skating, I would love winter, but the last thing I wanted to do was strap two slippery narrow boards to my feet and hurtle down a mountain. The idea of gliding over frozen water, however gracefully, was even less appealing.

"I want to see my family if we're going to Puerto Rico." Even to me it sounded as if I were asking permission.

"Yes, of course you can see," Ulvi said, "but do not include me."

With those words, *el hombre que yo amo* confirmed that there was no future for us as a couple. How could there be when he refused to acknowledge my family? With those words, every vow I had made to be patient, to "be good girl," to trust that we would be together, evaporated. With those words I saw Ulvi for what he was, a stop along the journey. And as I had already discovered, another train would come.

"You used to be prettier."

The first thing I saw as the plane turned and dipped toward the runway in Isla Verde was a billboard for Mercedes Benz. Next to it was another for Burger King. The third was the first one in Spanish, for *es de Velasco*, which I later learned was a department store in Plaza las Américas, the biggest shopping mall in the Caribbean. It was not the Puerto Rico I remembered.

I had come a few days ahead of Ulvi, and was glad not to have his gaze on me as I tried to make sense of what I saw compared to what I had expected. I had not expected Puerto Rico to have changed. The island, my sun-filled days on it, were shaped in memory like the figures I used to sculpt from Macún's orange clay. I had not counted on time being like that clay that dried and crumbled into dust, to be reshaped again.

As the plane touched land, the passengers clapped and cheered. We were home, *¡Llegamos! ¡Gracias a Dios!* I was just as excited, and finally understood the meaning of the phrase "butterflies in my stomach." I tingled inside and out with anticipation fed by absence.

A blast of hot, humid air embraced me as I stepped down the metal staircase from the plane to the tarmac. I wanted to recognize the terminal from thirteen years earlier, but it, too, was different, bigger. The observation roof from where Papi had waved goodbye until he was a dot on the landscape was not there any more.

Because Mami moved around, I had lost track of her, but had stayed in sporadic touch with Papi and wrote to let him know I was coming for a few days. He lived in Caguas with his wife, Fela, and, he wrote back, Mami now lived in Campanilla with the six kids still at home. Norma and Alicia were married and had their own households and children.

Papi was standing near some bushes, a jaunty straw hat shading his features. Next to him was a woman I assumed to be Fela. Next to her was Mami, wearing huge pink-framed rhinestone-studded eyeglasses. I hugged one after the other, letting my mother and father bless me and hold on to me for as long as they wanted. Papi introduced Fela, who kissed my cheek. Mami put her hands on my shoulders, studied me for a second.

"*¡Ay, si tu antes eras mas linda!*" was her assessment. She laughed and hugged me again. Maybe I was prettier five years earlier, when we last saw each other, but so was she. I said nothing, however.

A skinny, huge-eyed, big-haired little girl tugged on my dress. It was Cibi, seven years old. I was moved by how much time had passed since I'd held her in my arms. Behind her were my brothers Charlie, now eight and Ciro, six. They hung back shyly, kissed me dutifully when Mami pushed them forward.

"*¿No se acuerdan de Negi?*" They did remember me, and took charge of my suitcase as we walked to Papi's car.

Cibi leaned her head on my shoulder, her arm wrapped around mine. Her light-brown, tightly curled hair felt like a soft, furry creature against my skin.

As soon as we left the airport road, we were in the middle of a traffic jam.

"*Bienvenida a los tapones de Puerto Rico,*" Papi laughed.

I had forgotten that my father was always cheerful. Even when complaining about traffic, he seemed to be conveying good news. Fela smiled. Mami's eyes scanned the peddlers swarming around the stopped cars to offer geegaws, *platanutre*, bagged oranges, bunches of bananas, candy.

"*Cierren esa ventana*," she ordered the kids, who were practically dangling out the window, coveting. We were stuck in front of a dilapidated urban renewal project, the balconies overhung with laundry. "*Esta área es peligrosa*," Mami explained. Even without her telling me, I sensed it was a dangerous barrio by the expression of hopelessness and frustration in the eyes of the men and women loitering in its sidewalks.

The vendors ducking between cars stuck in the *tapón* did not like it when they approached and the people inside their vehicles did what we were doing—closed their windows, locked their doors and fixed their gaze ahead, pretending not to see the aggressively proffered goods. The more assertive vendors banged on the hood, or pressed their faces against the glass on the driver's side and cursed everyone inside, their breath forming an angry ring of vapor. We breathed easier when the traffic cleared enough for Papi to take a side street out of the area.

"*Me haces recordar*," she said, "*el primer día que llegamos a Nueva York, ¿te acuerdas?*" I too was remembering our first time in New York, but in my memory it was night. She said what made her think of it was my eyes, taking everything in as if it were the last time I'd see it. "*Se te quieren salir los ojos*," she said and the kids stared at me, hoping my eyes would really pop out of my skull.

I was still smarting from Mami's comment that I used to be prettier, and everything she said felt like a criticism, a barb to see how I would react.

"*¿Y tu marido?*" asked Fela, whom I'd just met, whose business it wasn't where my "husband" might be.

"*Él viene pasado mañana, pero nos vamos a quedar en un hotel.*" I didn't say why Ulvi and I would be staying in a hotel, and no one pursued it.

Ulvi was coming in two days. I planned to join him in the Condado, where we would stay for two weeks. After he left, I was to visit the Harvard swim team, which was training and competing in St. Croix after the holidays, and would fly back to Boston with Steve, a classmate and champion swimmer whose solar plexus I found enchanting.

Right now, however, in the car on the way to Alicia's house, where I would be staying until I joined Ulvi, I wanted nothing more than to get outside, into the fresh air, to shake the overpowering feeling that in the five years we hadn't seen nor spoken to one another Mami had not forgiven my insults *echándole todo en cara* in Fort Lauderdale.

I never asked her forgiveness, had not thought about that day, my accusations, the person I was then until the moment I saw Mami standing next to Papi, the pink rhinestones in her eyeglasses winking in the sun. Maybe it was the remorse she saw on my face that made me look less pretty, the shame that heated my cheeks and caused me to lower my gaze before her and refuse to meet her eyes.

Alicia lived in a neat cinderblock house on a quiet, narrow street in Toa Alta. The rest of the family had gathered there to greet me, except for Tata, who lived too far away. What surprised me most upon seeing Alicia was how much she looked like Mami. They had the same coloring, the same high cheekbones and hourglass figures. She was married to Felix, a graceful carob-colored man with a gentle manner and ready smile. Jeanette, their eldest daughter, was a cherubic rosy-cheeked five-year-old with jet-black Shirley Temple curls. They also had a six-month-old son, Papito, whom Felix carried around as if afraid the baby would get up and run away.

Norma, too, had a young family. Raquel was also five, and Hectitor was a toddler. I walked into a house full of children, my sisters now women, their men proud and possessive, affectionate with the kids who kept running in and out of the house, or resting between games in a father or uncle's arms.

My mother and sisters didn't ask many questions. I volunteered the minimum. There was no need to say much. They knew me better than anyone. They knew the best part of me.

When she saw me cuddling Papito, Fela wondered why I didn't have children.

"She travels too much," Mami answered before I could. Yes, I agreed, I travel too much. My sisters and I, Mami and I, exchanged looks that said it was nobody's business why I didn't have children. The old rules still applied. We "in the family" stuck together. Fela, an adjunct, was left out. I understood it. She must have too, because she stopped prying.

After everyone left, I lay in bed listening to the night sounds of Puerto Rico. The *coquí* trilled its nostalgic song. Cars lacking mufflers roared down the narrow street toward the *autopista*. Distant radios chattered incomprehensibly, competing with the babble from television sets. Papito woke up crying and Alicia soothed him with murmurs and kisses. Laughter and music came from a party a few blocks away. A breeze rustled the leaves of the breadfruit tree in the next yard, dogs barked, a rooster crowed at midnight. A coconut palm whispered its welcome.

Mami picked me up at Alicia's house the next day, and we drove to Macún. We passed the school where I had drawn my first letters under the stern eyes of Miss Maysonet and Miss Jimenez. It was much bigger now, built from cinder blocks, not wood. Its yard was narrower because the added buildings had encroached on the play space. *El comedor* was in the same spot, and seeing it brought back an image of myself, small as a bird, hunched over the long table, staring suspiciously at the too-yellow reconstituted powdered eggs on a blue enameled tin plate. The memory made me gag.

Papi's brother, Tío Cándido, still lived in the same house, still tended the same *pomarrosa* tree I had climbed as a child to pick the sweet, juicy, rose-scented fruits. The tree was not as tall as I remembered. Nothing was as I remembered.

We visited with Tío Cándido for a few minutes. Their daughter, Jenny, had moved to New York's Lower East Side. Mami blinked rapidly and looked out the window. New York Puerto Ricans had definite opinions about the other Puerto Rican enclaves of the city. We were Brooklyn Puerto Ricans, and rarely ventured to the Lower East Side, El Barrio or the Bronx, being as wary of those neighborhoods as *estadounidenses* were.

I was eager to see the spot where our house had been.

"*La casa la tumbaron,*" Mami warned as we walked down the road, which was now paved but full of potholes. Our house, and that of our neighbors Doña Lola and Doña Ana, was torn down to make way for the highway that would bring tourists to a gated community and golf resort in what was once a sugar plantation.

"*Era allí,*" Mami pointed to a mound in the middle of an overgrown lot. A rusty barbed wire fence sagged on rotting posts that contained what was left of what used to be our land. A woman approached us from up the road and Mami greeted her with alacrity.

"*¿Te acuerdas Negi? Es Doña Zena.*" I had played jacks with Doña Zena's daughters on their cement porch festooned with bougainvillea. We hugged, and she and Mami began one of those catching-up conversations that all children, regardless of age, dread because it goes on longer than it should and has nothing to do with you. I walked away and tested the barbed wire fence. It gave, but the barbs were still pointy sharp.

"Where are you going?" Mami called nervously from the safety of the road.

"I want to stand on our land again." I climbed over the fence.

"*Está loca,*" she said to Doña Zena, and they laughed.

Birds flitted and chirped in the overgrown hibiscus hedge near where we once grew eggplants. Lizards slithered into the weeds and around the annatto bushes under which I used to hide, near the oregano shrubs, still fragrant. I stepped up to the mound in the center of the land, testing it first to make sure it would hold my weight. To my right, traffic roared toward what I assumed were the gates to the golf resort.

"Does she have children?" Doña Zena asked Mami.

"No," Mami answered casually, "she and her husband travel too much."

I closed my eyes and listened to the soughing leaves, the flapping wings, the chirruping, tweeting, trilling life around me. I stood immobile, listening, discarding the throb of cars and trucks, the thunder of a plane overhead.

"*Vámonos, Negi, que se nos hace tarde,*" Mami called nervously.

When I opened my eyes Doña Zena was walking up the road toward her house. My shadow painted the downslope of the mound where I stood at 11 o'clock, an elongated human shape that I confirmed was me by raising my arms to form a steeple over my head. I turned clockwise, until I returned to my shadow in the *cohitre*, the *morivivi*, the tiny red flowers of Don Diego, and the fine leaved grass. At my feet I saw blue. I squatted and brushed away the clumps of orange dirt. It was the bluest tile I'd ever seen, but I had no memory of it being on our floor. I looked up at Mami, who had not moved an inch from where I'd last seen her. Even through her glasses I saw the sorrow in her eyes.

⟿

Two days later I joined Ulvi in the Condado. The third-floor room was small, damp, and faced the ceaseless traffic on Ashford Avenue. The hotel was under renovation, which is why Ulvi was able to get a good rate right in the center of San Juan's oldest strip of hotels, casinos, restaurants, and shops. He rented a car with the intention of driving around the island, but we didn't go far. His first goal was to toast in the sun and swim in the ocean, and there was a beach right behind the hotel. He alternated sunbathing with long swims in the crashing Atlantic surf. I sat under a beach umbrella reading Gabriel García Márquez's *Cien Años de Soledad*, which I had bought when Alicia and Felix took me to Plaza las Américas.

At night, we went to the casinos. I had never been inside one, and found the lights, the noise, the excitement of the players and watchers at the blackjack, craps, and roulette tables endlessly entertaining. Ulvi played a few games of craps, asking me to blow on his dice for good luck. He won a couple of hundred dollars and shared the winnings with me.

His friend, Adnan, called from the Caribe Hilton and we joined him for dinner. Adnan was about thirty, tall and long legged, darkly handsome and haughty. His business was the manufacture of fine hand-painted china. He greeted me with a supercilious nod and eyes that skimmed over me and decided they'd seen enough. During dinner, the two men spoke in Turkish or German, which left me out of the conversation. Afterwards, we took a turn around the casino, where Adnan blew several hundred dollars at the craps table and tried to get the attention of every tall, busty blonde who passed him.

The next morning Ulvi announced that we were moving to the Caribe Hilton.

"I thought we couldn't afford to stay at a nice hotel."

"It's okay, Chiquita, Adnan and I have to discuss business and it is better if we are in same place."

During the day, Adnan and Ulvi talked in sotto voce Turkish as we sat around the pool. We went to dinner at a different restaurant every night, took in variety shows at the hotels, or spent hours in the casinos. I didn't know where the money was coming from for the fun we were having.

We went dancing in the late hours, when the clubs were most crowded and the live music scorching. Ulvi was a wonderful dancer, who caught the Latin rhythms as if he had been hearing them his entire life. I loved dancing with him, the effortlessness of our bodies moving in time, the sensual motions of hips against hips, his warm breath against my ear. Whatever happened between us, the arguments, the inability to trust one another, the truths we refused to speak, and the secrets we carried into every moment of our lives together disappeared when we touched. Had I believed in reincarnation, I would have said we had traveled through the ages, coming together just like this, our bodies melting into one.

We drove to Luquillo Beach, where we feasted on *lechón* and *frituras* sold by cheerful women along the side of the road. We visited El Morro, the ancient fort I had last seen on a field trip in elementary school. We walked around Old San Juan, and both Ulvi and Adnan said it reminded them of parts of Istanbul. But mostly, we stayed at the Caribe Hilton. Around its pools, in its restaurants and casino, surrounded by other tourists, speaking English almost the entire day, we could have been in any resort on any sunny coast in the United States.

Our room faced the immensity of the Atlantic Ocean, so that, when I stood on its narrow balcony, my back was to Puerto Rico. If I turned around, however, it would be Ulvi I would face, sitting on the wicker chair laughing at something Irmchen had said into the phone across the miles from Germany. He always looked happy when he talked to her, even when it was problems he was sharing. I wondered what his expression was every night at eleven o'clock when he called me from Larchmont, whether his hand, as it was now doing, migrated across his chest, down his belly, into his groin as he exhorted me to be good girl.

High above the ground, within the air-conditioned rooms of the Caribe Hilton I was Ulvi's Chiquita, whose past held no interest for him. But it was getting harder to maintain the act. We fought constantly those two weeks because he thought I was "too free" when I thought I was being myself. I derived perverse pleasure from testing him, from deliberately doing what I knew would upset him or challenge his sense of propriety.

One afternoon he walked off with Adnan for an indoor meeting I wasn't invited to. When he returned poolside, I was laughing and joking with Ricky, a Puerto Rican man, and Ulises, his Dominican boyfriend, who had set up camp in the lounge chairs next to mine. They were both dancers in a show at the hotel, and wore bikini swimsuits smaller than the Speedos worn by my friends on the Harvard swim team, which left nothing to the imagination. I saw Ulvi coming, waved at him, but continued my conversation with the guys. Ulvi dove into the pool and did a few laps, stopping at the shallow end each time to look around, always ending with a frown in my direction. Months earlier, I would have shrunk into myself and done whatever it took to stop having a good time he didn't approve of. Now I ignored his stern lips and squinting eyes. The men and I were speaking Spanish, and even though they both also spoke English, I made no effort to switch so that Ulvi could hear that they were telling me about life as chorus dancers.

"Okay, Chiquita, let's go," Ulvi said, drying off and looking everywhere but at the two young men, who also pretended not to see him.

"Where are we going?"

"We must get ready to go out," he said.

"It's early," I shaded my eyes with my hand so I could see his face. He was chewing his lip. "You go ahead. I'll be there in a minute."

"Very well then." He stalked off.

"*¡Diantre! Ese está que no hay quien le beba el caldo,*" said Ricky, shaking his hand until his fingers snapped. I laughed at the image of Ulvi being hotter than boiling broth.

"*Que jodienda son los hombres celosos, ¿verdad?*" laughed Ulises, winking at Ricky, presumably because he, unlike Ulvi, was not a jealous man.

"If you need a place to stay tonight," offered Ricky, "look for us after the last show."

"We mean it," said Ulises.

"He'll get over it," I said, trying to convince myself.

Half an hour later, I took the elevator up, wondering just how angry Ulvi was and how he would express it. He was lying on the bed naked, watching television. I took as long a shower as I could. When I came out, he was still in the same position.

"Come here, Chiquita," he said.

His voice was quiet, inviting, and I prepared for a lecture instead of an argument. He didn't say a word, but made love to me as if we hadn't been together in months. Afterwards, when we had showered again and were getting ready to go out, he asked:

"Who were those two men you were talking to?"

"They're dancers in the hotel," I said.

"Do you often talk to strange men, Chiquita?"

"They're homosexual," I said to stave off the accusations rumbling toward me.

"You are a cheap whore," he spit out, and left me in the room, half dressed for a night on the town.

Months earlier I would have sobbed into the pillow until my chest ached, until my lids swelled my eyes shut. Now, I continued dressing as if nothing had taken place, as if his insult had not been uttered. It was the worst thing I'd ever been called in my life, worse than spick, worse than sellout, token, *blanquita*. The only thing that kept running through my brain though was the nursery rhyme: "Sticks and stones may break my bones, but names will never hurt me." I pushed my true feelings as far from my consciousness as possible, soothing the hurt with rhyme and singsong.

I stepped onto the balcony to clear my head. My instinct was to pack my bags and call Alicia to come get me. Before I made the call, however, I wanted to come up with a reason why I had left the hotel sooner than planned.

Ulvi must have expected me to be crumpled on the bed, as on other occasions when he had walked out in a huff, because he returned fifteen minutes later to find me standing on the balcony, looking out to sea.

"What are you doing, Chiquita," he asked nervously.

"Don't worry, I'm not about to jump," I said coolly, even though I was burning with rage. "I'm not stupid enough to kill myself over you."

He winced. "I am sorry, Chiquita." He stood next to me, but made no effort to touch me. "Sometimes you make me so angry, I do not know what to do. You are changing so much since you went to college."

"Some people would think that's a good thing," I snapped.

"It is maybe a good thing for you, but not for my girlfriend."

"Are you saying you don't want me anymore?"

"I did not say that. I have told you a thousand times, Chiquita, that you are most important person next to Ulviye."

My resolve to leave started to melt. "I can't help it if I'm changing. I'm supposed to be changing. It's called growth, maturity, development, evolution. It happens to people as they get older. It will happen to Ulviye, too."

"You do not need to be sarcastic."

"You expect me to be the same girl you saw on Fifth Avenue and Thirty-ninth Street. I'm almost twenty-seven years old. That innocent girl you met has been through a lot in six years. She's gone, Ulvi."

"No, no, no, Chiquita, that is not true." This time he did take me in his arms, kissed my hair, my eyes, my lips. "You will always be my Chiquita, no matter how many years pass, you know that. No one will ever love you as much I love you."

The effort to hold on to my rage made me tremble. To be with Ulvi, I had to be Chiquita, who was nothing. Perched on that wind-swept balcony high above the Atlantic Ocean I believed that he did love me, but could not help adding the phrase "in his own way." Except that his way and my way were going in opposite directions. I couldn't help gazing back to see how much distance there was between us, however. When I saw how far he was, I panicked, and ran back to the comfort of something that never existed, but that I kept wishing would.

The rest of the time we spent at the Caribe Hilton, I remained suspended in time, Chiquita with no past and a future that belonged to Esmeralda. I enjoyed what could be enjoyed, ignored what couldn't be changed. We fought, we made love, we fought again. I tried to receive each moment with the same equanimity as the one before it. The less engaged I was, the less I had to pretend. When Ulvi left, I returned to Alicia's house.

"Why didn't you bring your husband to see us?" Alicia asked.

"He's not my husband, he's my lover."

Alicia blushed.

"I'm not introducing any men to the family unless I plan to marry them," I said.

"Damn!" she laughed, "how many candidates are there?"

"Right now, none," I laughed with her. "I'm beginning to like the idea of remaining *jamona*."

"Marriage is good," she said, serious again. "If you find the right man."

I rattled a toy in front of Papito's face. The baby smiled happily and my heart almost broke to imagine him a grown man, mired in the traps of love.

Papi and Fela had asked me to have Sunday dinner with them. They lived in a bright yellow house on a corner lot surrounded by *gandules* bushes. When we drove up, Fela was picking the ripe pods and dropping them into a coffee can that she kept upended on a fence post for that purpose. Her children, whom Papi had stepfathered, were grown and lived in nearby towns. Pictures of them studded the walls of the hallway between the living room and the rooms in back of the house.

I was jealous of the progression of these total strangers from childhood to adolescence to graduations to church weddings and baptisms for their children. Those should have been pictures of me and my sisters and brothers. That bright house with its *gandules* bushes along the side, its neat rooms, the crocheted doilies on the side tables and furniture should have been so prettily maintained by Mami. The house should have been the one where I grew up, where Mami and Papi had raised their children.

Soon after we arrived, we sat to eat the elaborate meal that Fela had prepared. I did not want to like her, did not want to give up the feeling that because of Fela Papi had not come to get us in New York and bring us back to Puerto Rico, as I had hoped he would. She was a humble countrywoman who was delighted to have me in her home, admiring her things, enjoying her cooking. She treated Papi with a deference that would have been impossible for Mami, even if she thought he deserved it. She cooked my favorite dishes, and watched for my reaction at every bite with such expectation, that even though I didn't want to, I did like her. I could also see that she was a better match for Papi than Mami was. The difference between Fela and Mami, as I saw it, was that Fela lacked Mami's nervous energy and ambition. For a man of Papi's romantic, easygoing temperament, that must have been a relief.

Later, Papi read me some of his poems. He had a gift for rhyme and for the traditional *décima* rhythm. Some of his poems were funny, dependent on wordplay and puns. The political ones, and the ones dealing with his religious life, I either didn't understand or found too sentimental, but still admired their careful structure and original language.

After he read, he showed me a folder of the letters he had received from me over the years. There weren't many, but he had saved them all. He also had pictures of me that I didn't even remember sending. In one I was dressed in the theatrical version of a Hindu princess and in another as a Japanese lady, both for productions in the children's theater company. In another I was standing in front of Cinderella's Castle the year Ulvi and I drove to Disneyworld from Lubbock. In a picture from Syracuse, I was dwarfed by 500 Harrison Street, and had drawn an arrow pointing to the balcony of our apartment. In every photograph, I was alone.

The night before my return to Boston, I was awakened from a deep sleep by the scratching of *güiros*, the rattle of maracas, singing and clapping. It was an *asalto*, the Puerto Rican Christmas tradition of surprising householders with a serenade in the middle of the night. I thought the *asalto* was for the house next door but when I looked out, there was Mami surrounded by my sisters and brothers, singing and making enough noise to wake up the neighborhood.

Alicia and Felix let them in, and the party started. Within minutes the women were cooking an *asopao* and neighbors straggled in, bringing more food and drink, instruments, and good will. We sang *aguinaldos* and danced *plena y bomba* until dawn. Before she left,

Mami gave me two bottles of her homemade *coquito* to bring to Cambridge. She had thought up the idea of an *asalto* for me, she said, so that I would never forget how joyful the Christmas season was in Puerto Rico.

That afternoon, I returned to Boston. A few days earlier, when I had stood on the high balcony at the Caribe Hilton, refusing to cry within the arms of *el hombre que me ama*, I silently said goodbye to Ulvi. Had I paper and pen in hand, I might have written a letter to the man who loved me, just as I had done to Mami. But I didn't have the words, and all the days after, the words did not rise to where I could form them even to myself. *El hombre que me ama* would just have to wait until they did.

"We have to talk."

During our vacation, and in spite of his lavish spending trying to keep up with Adnan, Ulvi revealed that his contract at Lehman College would not be renewed. In a couple of months he'd be out of a job and unable to help with my expenses. I had supported him for four years as he pursued three graduate degrees, but when reminded he was offended.

"You were not the only one working, Chiquita," he said. "I did too. I gave up many possibilities to be with you."

I found a part time job as a bilingual secretary a few blocks from Harvard Square. My hours were flexible, and some of the work could be done at home and on weekends.

The daily exposure to Spanish and the time spent with my family over the holidays left me hungry for more contact with Puerto Ricans. I had met students from the island at Harvard, but they were in different departments and I seldom saw them. Feeling lonely and nostalgic one sleety Sunday afternoon, I scanned the phone book for Puerto Ricans, wishing one of them would call me. Alvarez, Bonilla, Cruz, I read. Diaz, Escalera, Figueroa. There was at least one Spanish name in every letter section of the Boston white pages. Torres, Urbina, Velazquez.

"If my finger lands on a Spanish name," I said to myself, "I'll call." I opened the book to a random page. My finger landed on Agudelo. I wasn't sure if that was Spanish. I tried again, McCarthy. A third time, Sullivan. The fourth try yielded O'Neill. The Spanish names had vanished.

I remembered the only Turkish words I'd learned from Ulvi, *Inshallah*—if Allah wills it—and *kismet*, which meant destiny or fate. When I first heard *Inshallah* I had a light-bulb moment. It sounded like one of my favorite Spanish words, *ojalá*, which Papi had said came from the Arabic for *si Dios quiere*, if God wants it. I felt more comfortable saying *ojalá* than *si Dios quiere*, unaware that I was invoking the Muslim God. *Kismet* I imagined as a bare-armed goddess in a toga that enhanced her full breasts, her flowing hair tamed by a diadem, and long, slender fingers pointing the way.

My own stubby index finger hovering over the dense print of the Boston white pages, I was more specific about what *kismet* should reveal.

"If it lands on a Spanish name," I said, "I'll call them. *Inshallah!*" Collazo in Dorchester.

"Hi, Mr. Collazo. My name is Esmeralda Santiago and I'm a Puerto Rican student at Harvard," I began, "*¿habla español?*"

I could not reassure Mr. Collazo that I wasn't selling anything, and he hung up on me.

"No, Mrs. Rivera," I explained to the confused woman in Jamaica Plains who answered my call. "I'm not a Harvard employee, I'm a student. No, I don't know if they own your building. No, I don't know if you have to move."

I was not her son's guidance counselor, I told Mrs. Sanchez of Charlestown. After the fourth call, to P. Martino in Watertown, who turned out to be Italian, I addressed *kismet* directly. What I was trying to do by calling total strangers on a sleety Sunday after-

noon was to make an instant, friendly connection with a Puerto
Rican family in Cambridge who would adopt me. *Inshallah!* On the
fifth try, I reached A. Colon.

"Hi, my name is Esmeralda Santiago and I'm a Puerto Rican
student at Harvard," I said, "*¿habla español?*"

Antonia and Antonio Colón, known as Toñita and Toño, lived
near Inman Square with their six children, four-year-old twins Talia
and Dalia, six-year-old Henry, ten-year-old Tere, twelve-year-old
Lily, and fourteen-year-old Junior. When Toñita answered, I knew
by the sound of her voice that I had found the family *kismet* meant
for me. Toñita was cheerful, warm, and thrilled that she had picked
up the phone when I called. Once we established that I lived less
than a mile from them, she told me to come right over. She had just
started an *asopao*, the perfect meal for such a cold day, *¿verdad que sí?*
She hoped I liked *tostones* because she had found the most beautiful
plantains in the market the day before and if she didn't fry them up
today they'd be *amarillos* by Tuesday and anyway she thought *tostones*
went really well with *asopao*, don't you agree?

Their apartment was on the top floor of a three-decker on Columbia Street. As I climbed the steep wooden stairs, the familiar
scent of *sofrito* made my mouth water. Latin music thumped behind each door as I rose. No sooner had I reached the top step of
their floor than the Colón's door opened and the moist air of their
apartment embraced me. They hugged and kissed me as if I were a
long-lost relative. I wished I'd brought presents.

Walking into their living room was like stepping into the apartments in Brooklyn where my family had lived. The floor was covered in shiny, immaculately clean linoleum, a different pattern in
every room. The sofa and two easy chairs were encased in plastic.
Flowered curtains divided the apartment into living and sleeping
areas with bunk beds. The side tables were laden with figurines and
on the wall, Jesus hovered over portraits of Martin Luther King
and John F. Kennedy. A huge television set that was never off the

entire six months I knew the Colón family dominated a corner of the living room. Atop it was poised an enormous ceramic tiger about to devour a blonde doll wearing a ruffled pink-and-white crocheted gown and hat.

Toño was a lab technician at Massachusetts General Hospital, where Toñita was a nurse. They were from Manatí, and had lived in Cambridge for five years. They remembered the parade.

"We were there!" said Tere.

When I told them about Vicente and Connie inviting me to ride in the back of their convertible, Lily stared in awe.

After we ate Toñita's delicious *asopao* and crispy fried plantains, Tere and Lily showed me their Menudo clippings from newspapers and magazines. I followed them into their room and listened to an entire Menudo album, as the girls, Talia and Dalia included, lip-synched and demonstrated the steps that went with each song.

Junior and Henry were wild about baseball, and could name every player on the Red Sox roster, their positions and stats. As the eldest, Junior was too cool to agree with anything his little brother said until it came to Luis Tiant, the Cuban pitcher whose 1974 season he had memorized.

"He pitched seven shutouts. Seven!" Junior held up four fingers on the right and three on the left hand, as if merely saying the number were not enough to convey the magnitude of Tiant's accomplishment. "With Luis pitching, the Red Sox will definitely win the World Series this year." I loved that he referred to the player by his first name, as if he were a brother.

"We also have Jim Rice," Henry couldn't leave out his favorite player, and ran into the bedroom. Junior's cool carapace dissolved when Henry returned with two shoeboxes bursting with baseball cards. He fingered them with reverence, turning each one over to read the information aloud, even though he knew most of it by heart.

Watching Henry and Junior handling the baseball cards, Toño no more than ten feet away, I imagined he too was their hero. He was dignified and solid, with a quiet authority that left no doubt about who was the enforcer when the children misbehaved. Toñita adored him, and as I played with the kids, she perched on the arm of his easy chair, leaned against him and caressed his hair. Without taking his eyes off the TV screen, he put his arm around her waist and the two of them stayed like that for a few minutes, their eyes glued to a movie, while in the bedroom the girls danced to Menudo and on the floor Henry and Junior argued over whether Carlton Fisk was a better catcher than the Yankees' Thurman Munson.

I visited the Colón family almost every Sunday after that. I helped the children with their homework, and over several weeks watched as Junior prepared for the beginning of baseball season at Rindge High School, where he was a freshman. In May, Toño and Toñita told me that as soon as the school year ended, they were moving to Hartford, Connecticut. There was a shortage of trained lab technicians and nurses in the United States, they told me, and they had both been recruited and offered an increase in salary and benefits. They could finally afford a house with a yard for the kids. I was thrilled for them, sad for myself. But I thanked *kismet* for pointing the way to this family who every Sunday reminded me of how much I missed my own.

Over the summer, I couldn't visit Ulvi as much as he wanted because I took a job at a hospital in addition to a full load of courses so that I would begin the next semester as a junior and graduate the following June, instead of a year later.

At the end of August, Ulvi suggested that we go to Cape Cod for a few days. Being in the Camaro with him on a long ride brought back memories of the silent miles we had traversed inside its vinyl turquoise-blue interior. As on previous holidays, we alternated staying in motels with sleeping in the car. We spent a few days in Provincetown, much of it on a nude beach where there were few women. I felt too conspicuous to take off my swimsuit.

"Chiquita, we have to talk about our plans," Ulvi said one afternoon as we sat on a dock waiting for our lobsters-in-the-rough to be cooked.

I did not know we had plans, and dreaded hearing that phrase, "we have to talk." The conversations that followed were never, in my experience, pleasant ones.

Ulvi had not found a job and thought that, to save money, we should live together again. Because it was easier for me to get work, he suggested I take a leave from college.

"No."

"I thought you wanted to help, Chiquita," he pouted.

"I'm not quitting school, even though next year is going to be hard. My scholarship only covers tuition, so now that you can't pay my rent and expenses, I'll have to work full-time. It's not fair to expect me to support you, too."

"That is not what I'm asking," he growled. "I will look for jobs in Boston."

I sought the gray horizon of Nantucket Sound, "I don't think I can live with you again. I like having my own space, my own friends, my own life."

"Is that so, Chiquita?"

"Why does that surprise you?"

"It doesn't. You have become independent. It is good for you."

"Yes, it is," I stood up because our number had been called in the cookhouse.

The silences in the car, on the beach, in the places where we parked to sleep grew longer. When we did speak, it was about his future. Once I said no to quitting college and living with him, he admitted that he had some "opportunities" for "business" that he had to "look into."

"I might return to Europe," he said, watching my reaction.

"It's worked for you before," I said, remembering his calls to Irmchen.

"If I go, I might not be able to return to the United States because I don't have a green card."

We were sitting on a beach in Chatham. I did not like the beach. Not this beach, any beach. I did not like baking in the sun for hours. I hated the grains of scratchy sand in the seams of my bikini, in my navel, between my toes, behind my ears.

"It might be easier," Ulvi continued when I didn't answer, "to get my green card if we marry . . . "

I felt a thrill in spite of myself. "Is that a proposal?"

"It would be the last resort, for us to marry," he hedged.

I was torn between wanting to run screaming into the ocean and plunking him on the head with the beach umbrella under which I sat. "You're right, that would be the worst possible way to start a marriage."

"Why you get so insulted?"

"You say you love me, but for years refused to marry me. Now it's a possibility, but only if you're forced into it. Why wouldn't that be offensive?"

"You are not understanding me, Chiquita. I cannot explain more, but it is the same as always was. I cannot marry you unless it is the only way . . . "

"I don't want to marry you if it is 'the only way'" I screamed. He looked away, both of us embarrassed by my outburst. When I had regained control, I spoke softly. "It would be better if you find another alternative."

Back in Cambridge, I contemplated how much our relationship had changed. It was the end of August, almost a year since he had left me standing under an imminent thunderstorm in the parking lot of Foxcroft Manor. My chest hurt from the sadness of what was happening to us, the way we were coming apart as slowly as pulled taffy, prolonging the inevitable. I didn't know how to make the process faster, how to make a clean cut that would hurt intensely for hours, days, weeks, even months, but would eventually heal, like childhood wounds. I felt sorry for him, for us.

He attributed the constant failure to achieve his goals on bad luck. I didn't believe in luck, and blamed failure on personal flaws, in myself and in others. The minute I tried to analyze Ulvi's short-comings, however, I had to stop. The list maker in me knew that every one of his corresponded to one of mine. Our relationship was a web of matched neuroses and it was up to me to untangle them if I ever wanted to be free.

Reify

Dr. Arthur Loeb, my advisor, wrote asking me to make an appointment to discuss my senior thesis. As a VES student, it seemed logical that I should make a film or a photographic essay. But I had no ideas for either that compelled me enough to want to devote almost a year to it.

The night before my appointment, I woke up in the middle of the night with the words "the song of songs" on my lips. I wrote them down on a scrap of paper, but forgot them until later that morning, in Dr. Loeb's office.

I had met Dr. Loeb at Dudley House. He and his wife, Lotje, were Dutch, and both spoke a formal, slightly accented and precise English. They organized the waltz evenings in the Dudley House dining hall and they sometimes joined our ballroom dancing group at the Top of the Hub, a restaurant with live music atop the Prudential Building in Copley Square. The Loebs were musicians in an early music group that performed in period costumes around the Boston area. He was also a writer, a painter, and a scientist.

I was thrilled to have Dr. Loeb as my advisor because he was so accomplished and accessible. I could bring the craziest ideas to him, for final projects or to fulfill coursework, and he encouraged me to continue thinking creatively, even if what I envisioned had not been done, or involved rattling the university bureaucracy.

After explaining that I had decided against a film as my honors thesis, he suggested that we brainstorm to see what else might appeal to me.

"You are a dancer, Esmeralda. Have you considered doing something with dance?"

It hadn't occurred to me.

"Maybe I can write a thesis about the use of Indian classical dance in the films of Satyajit Ray. That would be fun."

"Yes, but you might consider something closer to your own heritage. The traditional dances of Puerto Rico, maybe."

"I like the idea of researching and writing about *bomba y plena*. I grew up with that music."

"Why don't you think about it and draft a proposal? We can discuss it next week."

As I was leaving his office, I remembered my dream. "Maybe you can help me figure this out," I said. "I woke up from a dream last night saying 'the song of songs' aloud. I'm guessing it's the title of a book, or a piece of music. Have you ever heard of either?"

"The Song of Songs is one of the most famous books in the Old Testament," he said. "I'm sure at least parts of it have been set to music, but you might first consult the original text."

I blushed from head to toe. "I didn't know it was from the Bible."

"It's been attributed to King David himself. He was a poet, you know. You might wish to read several translations because they will vary. Check the Divinity School Library."

Hunched over dusty old Bibles, I read every version of the Song of Songs I could find in English, Spanish, and French. With each line my heart expanded, my skin tingled and I was filled with immense happiness. The language was exquisite. Even the words I couldn't understand moved me to a joy so deep that I didn't want to stop reading, didn't want to return to a life where there were no shepherds and no Daughters of Jerusalem, no mountains of myrrh or hills of frankincense, no comforting with apples.

I ran back to the Carpenter Center and caught Dr. Loeb as he was leaving.

"I've decided what my thesis should be," I was breathless. "A dance interpretation of the Song of Songs."

We went back to his office and he talked me through how I might approach such a project. It was as if the idea had been stewing for years, and had just then become manifest.

"I don't want music," I said. "I'll dance to the words, spoken live. Three . . . no, four voices, two women for the Daughters of Jerusalem. They'll be like a chorus, and always speak together. The female voice for the beloved should be sweet and expressive, like a flute. One male voice can play Solomon and the shepherd. I'll choreograph and dance every part. I'll do a blessing of the stage at the beginning, like in the Indian tradition. And at the end a pure dance sequence, improvised. I'll need music for that, Middle Eastern maybe, not Indian."

As I spoke, Dr. Loeb took notes. He was as excited as I was and set about listing what I would need. As the list grew, I became nervous about what a huge enterprise it was.

"You will still have to write a thesis," Dr. Loeb added. "You can write about your creative process. It doesn't need to be a scholarly paper on the meaning of the Song of Songs or anything of the kind."

The minute I left his office, my knees turned to jelly. I'd just outlined an ambitious project that would require weeks of research, writing, choreography, rehearsal, design, and performance. I'd have to arrange progress evaluations with a committee far in advance, and stick to the dates. I'd need a place to rehearse. I'd have to audition music for the beginning and end sequences. The longer the list grew, the more alarmed I became. It was October. The final evaluation would have to be no later than the end of April of the next year. I had six months.

I redrew my daily schedule and figured that the only way I could work forty hours a week, carry a full load of honors courses, study, write papers, dance three hours a day, choreograph and rehearse a performance, and have a social life, was to sleep from one-thirty to five-thirty in the morning.

Ulvi had postponed a return to Europe, but was depressed about his prospects. He didn't want to leave the United States, but he worried that he had no alternative. Every once in a while he mentioned the "last resort" of us marrying, but he was not that desperate. Whenever it came up, I clamped my lips together and bit my tongue.

I went down to Larchmont for the Thanksgiving holiday. In a corner of his living room there was a strange-looking machine with a keyboard.

"What's that?"

"It's a telex," Ulvi said.

"What does it do?"

"It sends and receives messages. It's less expensive than telegrams."

The telex hummed and clicked in the corner, like an expectant robot waiting to receive an order to come to life.

After dinner, we lay on his couch and talked. He was more depressed than I had ever seen him. His habit of pulling his hair when he was nervous had left bald patches and scabs on his scalp and he was beginning to tear at the hair on his chest. He looked worn, with deep, dark rings under his eyes and a constant downturn to his lips that made him look like the Tragedy theatrical mask.

It saddened me to see him this way, but nothing I said helped. He had never asked for nor trusted my advice. If I expressed an opinion, he looked at me skeptically, as if asking, "What would *you* know about this?"

One night he dropped his face into my bosom and sobbed. This was only the second time I had seen Ulvi cry. The first time I hadn't been much comfort, and he'd had to call Irmchen. I wondered why all of a sudden I had become a confidante, whether Irmchen too had abandoned him. But if I asked too many questions he would clam up, so I listened.

The reason things never worked out for him, he said, was that he had a terrible childhood. I had wondered whether Ulvi came from a wealthy Turkish family that had fallen on hard times. Other than his father, stepmother, and sister, he had never mentioned any relatives and until he told me about Ulviye I had assumed he was an only child.

Now he revealed that his father, Hassan, was born in a remote village in Anatolia. When Hassan was a boy his family was killed and their homes burned during one of the pogroms against Armenians by Turkish soldiers.

"He hid in the woods near a river," Ulvi said. "When he came out in the morning, the river was flowing with blood and there were bodies everywhere he looked."

Hassan walked from Anatolia to Istanbul, where he married and where Ulvi was born. Ulvi grew up in the streets of Istanbul and when he was old enough, he immigrated to Germany.

"It was not easy, Chiquita," he said. "I could not speak the language. Everywhere I went the Germans hated me. They are very impatient people."

I was grateful to him for even this sketchy information about his life. He didn't, and didn't need to, elaborate on the story of Hassan walking from Anatolia to Istanbul. I filled in the gaps, imagining a barefoot boy dressed in rags, an orphan spurned everywhere he went, scrapping his way across a continent. What did he expect was waiting for him in Istanbul?

"Does this mean," I asked, "that you're Armenian?"

"No, Chiquita, I'm Turkish," he said with such hauteur that he forgot his troubles. He got up, went to the bathroom to wash his face and the revelations were over.

We were awakened in the middle of the night by the rattling of the telex. Ulvi jumped out of bed and sat in front of the machine as the pale yellow paper rolled over the platens with a message from Saudi Arabia about their need for concrete. Ulvi was ecstatic. Because I typed faster than he did, he dictated a reply involving his proposal to ship tons of concrete to Riyadh at what he said was a reasonable price, in the hundreds of thousands of dollars.

"You don't own a cement factory. Where is the concrete coming from?"

"I will buy it, Chiquita, then sell it to them."

"Where will you get the money to buy the concrete?"

"It is business, Chiquita. Do not concern yourself."

I never knew whether or not he ever shipped concrete to Saudi Arabia. The telex machine was gone by the end of the year.

"I have other opportunities," he said when I wondered about it.

In his efforts to find work and a sponsor that would help him obtain his green card, he had reconnected with an executive at Dupont whom he had known when he worked as a textile engineer in Germany. Mr. Tower had retired, and subsequently had an incapacitating stroke, but Mrs. Tower received Ulvi as if he were her long-lost son. The Towers lived in a sprawling apartment overlooking the East River, and when I next came to New York, Ulvi took me over there for dinner. Mrs. Tower, Ulvi, and I sat in the formally set dining room, while from the back of the apartment came the sounds of frequent coughing and the tender assurances of a Jamaican nurse.

He took Mrs. Tower and me to a couple of glamorous parties. One of them was at the United Nations, hosted by the United Arab Emirates, which I had never heard of but turned out to be seven Middle Eastern countries where Ulvi was hoping to sell products he had to buy from somebody else. The most memorable part of that party was that I met one of my heroes. Men in caftans and women in evening gowns surrounded him, but I managed to walk right up to Muhammad Ali, introduce myself and shake his enormous hand. He looked me straight in the eye, which I appreciated, and asked me where I was from.

"Oh, yes, I've been there," he said in his surprisingly soft and gentle voice.

The circle around him closed as if by previous arrangement just as Ulvi located me in the throng of rustling silks and clinking glasses. Everywhere he went now he was Dr. Dogan, but he still introduced me as Chiquita. Muhammad Ali, however, met Esmeralda.

Dr. Loeb asked me to perform in a Christmas celebration he was organizing at the Carpenter Center. He suggested I do an Indian classical dance but I was more interested in testing my idea to dance the Song of Songs to words rather than to music.

"I'd rather find a poem," I said to him, "that I can choreograph."

He suggested "How the Hibernators Came to Bethlehem" by Norma Farber. It was a charming fable about how the animals found the manger on Christmas night. The imagery was vivid, and it gave me a chance to create characters and to perform the various *chals*, stylized walks suggesting animals that I had learned from Dulal in a different context.

My studio apartment was big enough that I could put my bed, desk, and shelves against the wall and free up the middle for dancing. Peter, a Jesuit priest who was a graduate student at the Divinity

School, volunteered to be my reader. He had an expressive voice, and a flair for characterization that enhanced my interpretation.

Ulvi could not come to the performance. He was spending a long weekend with Mrs. Tower and her friend, whom Ulvi referred to as Horsewoman, because she owned a farm of thoroughbreds in Virginia.

I couldn't afford to get a costume made, but found scarves and ribbons at Oona's, a used clothing store where I bought vintage gowns for ballroom dancing. I tied red ribbons to my hair and around my wrists, and wore my *ghunghrus*, their rich brass jingle particularly appropriate in the Christmas season.

The Carpenter Center lobby was packed with people seated around a makeshift raised stage for the musicians and standing on the steps to the second floor. When my turn came, the audience was asked to move back because many who couldn't find chairs had settled on cushions on the floor in front of the stage. Peter's voice echoed against the cement walls and granite floor. It was cold, and the stone was hard under my bare feet, but I hardly noticed. I entered a zone of inspired concentration and danced with the artistry I had always dreamed of but had never fully achieved. Toward the end of the performance, a little boy jumped from his father's lap and wandered into the circle where I was dancing the adoration of Baby Jesus by the animals. He couldn't have timed it better. His big eyes followed me as with my hands, my face, the jingles, and *chals*, I suggested a badger, a bear, a tortoise, a bat, a brilliant star. The little boy became the object of the poem, and I its expression. At the end, there was a moment of silence, and then the audience broke into such loud and appreciative applause that the child burst into tears. His father turned out to be Mr. Guzetti, the photographer who had enriched my vocabulary with reify.

Nisus

By the beginning of my last semester, I had not choreographed a step of the Song of Songs, but had done most of the research. I read every version I could find. Hundreds of scholarly articles interpreted the text, explored historical documentation for its author, or analyzed its structure using the literary conventions of the period in which the paper was written. Early in the process, I fixed on it as a love story between the shepherd and his bride, a captive in Solomon's harem. The ecstatic religious experience, I thought, would emerge in the rapture of the dance moment, the synergy between words and motion, the expression of higher meaning through movement.

Each version I read had a different rhythm and use of language, but none in its entirety had the music I heard in my head. I combined the versions into one script, which meant taking verses or phrases from one translation, attaching them to another, and simplifying or enhancing some of the language.

"You're the first student," Dr. Loeb chuckled, "to propose to rewrite the most beautiful words in the Old Testament."

A married couple Ulvi and I had befriended in Syracuse had recently settled in Cambridge. Don had been a graduate student in communications and now worked for the media division of Houghton Mifflin Publishers. His wife, Betsy, was a gifted seamstress, and it was to her that I appealed to make the costumes. It was an expensive undertaking because there were five costumes altogether. Mine was the most elaborate, but I also had to dress four readers. I was already working forty hours a week transcribing dictation at a hospital near my apartment, but managed to pay for the fabric and Betsy's time by typing for other students and performing at children's birthday parties.

In late winter, the hospital could no longer allow the flexibility I needed to work nights and weekends. Don introduced me to his boss at Houghton Mifflin. Paul hired me as a part-time consultant for a documentary his department was planning about Latin American family structure.

Since he had lost his teaching job Ulvi had stopped paying my rent, but seeing how hard I was working, he sent a check now and then. In mid-January he called to say that he was traveling to Saudi Arabia to pursue some business. He didn't know how long he'd be gone. We spent a poignant weekend together, his hand never far from mine, his assurances more passionate than ever that his sister and I were the most important people in his world.

"I am doing this for you and for Ulviye," he said. "It is not easy to start again."

I did not know what he was starting, or why it had to begin in Saudi Arabia. I had visions of lines of barges filled with bags of cement floating one after the other into the Red Sea, received by men in flowing caftans like the ones worn by the diplomats at the party for the United Arab Emirates.

〜

Once satisfied with my script for the Song of Songs and with no objections from the evaluation committee to the liberties I took combining and altering translations, I began the choreography. Dulal grudgingly helped me develop *chals* for each of the characters. He did not approve of what I was doing. Not only was I using his teachings in an unorthodox way, I was preparing for a solo performance after less than two years of training without having consulted him first. It is the guru who determines when the student is ready to perform in public, he said, not the student. When he heard that I was combining Kathak with belly dance he nearly had a conniption right in the middle of his kitchen. He accused me of disrespecting the tradition and him as my teacher. I had to assure him that I would continue studying for my Kathak debut and that I would not call the Song of Songs an Indian dance performance so that, if it wasn't any good, it wouldn't reflect on him.

It took me weeks to choreograph the program. I worked on it constantly. Sitting in a lecture hall, I took notes with my right hand as my left practiced mudras. While waiting for the bus that brought me to and from Dulal's, I ran through *talas* on the icy sidewalk, my *ghunghrus* jingling in the dance bag slung over one shoulder. Sitting next to Marilyn at a concert celebrating Mozart's birthday, I mentally went through the progression of the opening dance, which I planned to perform on a dark stage with lit candles in my hands. I frequently woke up in the middle of the night, my arms and feet moving in a combination I hadn't been able to work out during the day.

Once I had drafted the choreography, two professional actors, Chris and Constance, and two of my best friends from VES, Julia and Phoebe, became my readers. I had auditioned the actors, but had begged Julia and Phoebe to work with me because of their lovely voices. They were excited about the project and wanted to be a part of it, even when it meant taking time from their own work and rehearsing at weird hours. The professional actors were more temperamental. Hassles surfaced within days, but I didn't have the time or energy to stroke egos. When Chris resisted my direction, I replaced him with Jonathan, also a professional actor, with a better attitude.

With Ulvi in Saudi Arabia, I had more time to be social because I didn't have to be in my apartment by eleven o'clock every night. It also freed up my weekends. I preferred going to him in Larchmont so that my life in Cambridge was not available for him to criticize.

It annoyed me that Ulvi could not believe that a man and a woman could have a relationship that didn't involve sex. We argued over it, and he was offended when I suggested that the reason he thought this way was because *he* couldn't imagine a relationship with a woman that wasn't sexual.

"I have many women friends," he said. "It is different for a grown man."

"Why then, can't I have men friends?"

"You do not understand, Chiquita. Young men only want one thing."

I could not walk through Harvard Square without running into a man I knew from classes, from work, or from activities at Dudley House and around campus.

Tom was the eldest son in a huge Italian-American family. We were in the ballroom dancing group along with William, who was active in the Harvard Gay Students Organization. I spent nearly every Sunday evening with Pepe, a Mexican political science major, and his best friend Roberto Alejandro, a Spanish-Chinese art student who had grown up in the Philippines. The three of us enjoyed hanging out in my apartment drinking red wine, eating crusty bread with sharp cheese, and speaking Spanish. Eric, the animation professor with whom I had studied over the summer, had moved to San Francisco, but we corresponded and he called occasionally.

Before he went to Saudi Arabia, Ulvi was visiting one weekend when he saw a photograph of me with Richard, another of my ballroom dancing partners, taken at a costume party whose theme was the 1930s and '40s. I wore a white crepe sequined gown and

Richard his tweed hunting jacket and cap. We thought we looked spectacular together. When the disc jockey had played enough disco to exhaust even the most devoted fans of the Hustle, he turned to vintage music. With the first strains of a tango, Richard took my hand and someone snapped a Polaroid. I took it home and forgot about it until I noticed that Ulvi kept walking past my desk and staring at something. He didn't ask, didn't pick it up and examine it and it wasn't until he went into the bathroom that I saw the snapshot and put it away. When he next passed my desk he noticed that it was gone and glowered, but I ignored him and he never mentioned it. Still, I knew what he was thinking.

I had grown close to another VES student, Keith, a gifted cinematographer with a sweet, quirky style. In a short film about his grandmother, he had conveyed insight into her personality through a long, loving exploration of a philodendron she had pinned and trailed up her wall and into the rafters of her house.

Keith had a girlfriend and knew I had a boyfriend in Larchmont. He was in love with Karen, but their relationship seemed as troubled as mine with Ulvi. They broke up, came together, split up again in a painful dance for Keith, who seemed as unhappy with her as without her. We didn't talk about Ulvi and Karen to one another except in the most general terms, but there was no need to be specific. We might both have been confused when it came to them, but wordlessly and unabashedly, we understood each other.

Two months after he left, Ulvi called to let me know when he would be back from Saudi Arabia, and asked me to be at his apartment. He sounded upbeat.

"It was the right decision to come here," he said. "I will tell you about it."

My thesis evaluation was in a month and taking a weekend off was both a relief and added pressure. I had been working so hard that a couple of days with no jobs, no rehearsals, no dance lessons, no lectures or tutorials seemed like a great idea. On the other hand, a weekend away would set me that much farther behind. I couldn't, however, tell Ulvi that it wasn't convenient to see him, not when he had been gone two months, not when he sounded so optimistic and wanted to share it with me.

Our reunion was romantic and tender. It reminded me of why I couldn't simply break up with him and go my own way. Even though he was jet-lagged, he understood I needed taking care of and made sure I had enough sleep. He took me to dinner at restaurants where I could linger over a meal and savor the food rather than gulp whatever was handy while rushing to work, a dance class, or a rehearsal. I knew his rhythms and didn't press him to tell me about his trip until he was ready.

On a sunny, windless day in late March, we went for a walk in Manor Park overlooking Long Island Sound. I could tell something was on his mind because he picked at his scalp constantly and sighed deeply following what I imagined were distressing internal dialogues.

"I have taken a job in Saudi Arabia," he finally said. I didn't have time to recover from the surprise before he continued. "Will you come with me?"

"Yes!" I said without hesitation. "After graduation."

"Of course," he agreed.

It would be hard, he added, to live in the Middle East.

"Will I have to wear a veil?"

He smiled. "No, Chiquita, Western women do not wear veils unless they want to. But you will have to cover up more, out of respect. They are strict Muslims."

"Are you a Muslim?"

"All these years you live with me and you don't know this?"

I blushed.

"Don't worry," he put his arm around me and kissed the top of my head. "I am not Muslim like they are Muslim."

"Do you believe there are seventy virgins waiting for you in Paradise?"

He laughed. "Good Muslims are lucky men."

"Do good Muslim women get seventy men when they get to Paradise?"

"Do not joke about that, Chiquita."

I never did find out, and returned to Cambridge to finish the semester and fantasize about a trip to Riyadh. At the same time I was certain that, like Ulvi's other schemes, this one was doomed. All he had in Saudi Arabia was the *possibility* of a job, he clarified a week later during one of our nightly phone calls, and insisted he'd never said he had taken a job, which is what I heard.

He drove up to see me more frequently now, but if I had any obligations related to my thesis, he went to the movies or disappeared into the streets of Cambridge until I was free. One early afternoon he called from Harvard Square when I wasn't expecting him. I was in the middle of a full cast rehearsal in my apartment.

"Come over," I said. "We're almost done."

"No," he said, "I do not want to be involved with those people."

Those people were my friends and collaborators. "Come at eleven then," I said, not explaining why "almost done" had suddenly become nearly ten hours. When he did, he skulked around the apartment as if looking for evidence of a crime. We spent the next two days bickering about how I never had any time for him after he had given up so many possibilities to be with me.

"We will spend a lot of time together when we move to Saudi Arabia," I said.

I was so sarcastic at times that I was sure he would slap me, like he did in Lubbock, but he controlled himself. Our fights were more pointed now, targeted at the other's weaknesses and insecurities. We knew each other well enough to know what hurt the most.

"The trouble is," I told Marilyn over quiche at the Orson Welles Café, "that I feel sorry for him because he loves me. I'm pretty sure I don't love him anymore, but I want to go to Riyadh."

"You can go there without him," she suggested.

"Yeah, but I want to see it with him. I want to meet those princes he says he knows, and stay at the hotel with the gold fixtures that he wrote about."

"Do you think he's lying about that?"

I waved at the waitress and ordered chocolate mousse. "The only thing I know he's not lying about is that he loves me—in his own way. And I wonder if my way to love him is to be this ambivalent."

"You don't seem ambivalent. You date other men . . . Keith for instance . . . "

I squirmed. "My relationship with Keith is an affair, not a life commitment. He was bummed out over his love life and I was there when he and Karen broke up for the umpteenth time. He's in love with her and will probably end up marrying her. We're just having a good time until she comes to her senses."

"I hope you don't end up feeling sorry for him, too," she warned.

As the date for my performance neared and I grew more hysterical with the pressures and expectations, Keith offered to help.

"You need a producer," he said.

He took over a part of the program I had been worrying about but hadn't had time to coordinate. He recruited his friends and roommates to paint the backdrop for the stage. He took the picture for the poster announcing the show, and on the days of the performance, organized crews to turn the Lehman Hall cafeteria into a theater. He stage-managed the performance, and afterwards, offered to clean up and help me carry props and the rented lights and audio equipment back to my apartment. I couldn't have asked for a more supportive partner, and I appreciated that he didn't seem threatened by my "fucked-up relationship with that old guy."

The Song of Songs would be performed three times over a weekend, timed to coincide with its traditional place in the Jewish liturgy during Passover. Once the audience was seated, the lights would go down and a slow *ciftetelli* rhythm would begin softly, then rise as I appeared from the back of the house, carrying a candle in each hand. The candle dance was a reference to the Raks al Shamadan, an Egyptian dance traditionally performed at weddings in which the dancer wears an ornate lit candelabrum on her head.

For five minutes I would perform in the dark, making patterns with the flame and slapping my feet to punctuate the music and jingle my ankle bells. It was a complicated sequence requiring total concentration, especially because I was wearing flammable fabrics. My costume covered my arms to the wrists, my lower torso to the ankles. To prevent setting my hair on fire I would wear it inside a turban wrapped with ribbons. The only parts of my body that would be visible were my hands, my feet, my neck, and my face.

When the music ended I would blow out the candles, leaving the audience and the stage again in total darkness. When the lights came up, I would be posing in front of the backdrop, and the readers, who were in the balcony above the audience, would begin to recite:

> Let him kiss me with the kisses of his mouth:
> for his love is better than wine.

The final dance in the performance was Rampi Rampi, a Karsilama rhythm, which is fast. I would put on finger cymbals and perform what I called Middle Eastern folk dance because every time people heard I belly danced they asked if I wore a jewel on my navel. At the end of Rampi Rampi, the cast joined me to take our bows.

The complexity of the production was not my biggest concern as I prepared for the three performances. I had confidence in my readers. I knew that Keith would manage the technical aspects with care and competence. But the Song of Songs was more than my thesis. It was how I explored and conflated my interests, skills, worries, and concerns. I researched, interpreted, wrote, designed, directed, choreographed, and performed one of the most beloved and well-known poems ever written. Each performance explored and expressed themes of race ("I am black but comely, ye daughters of Jerusalem . . . look not upon me because I am black"); love, passion ("Thou hast ravished my heart, my sister, my spouse; thou hast ravished my heart with one look from thine eyes, with one chain of thy neck"); loneliness, longing ("By night on my bed I sought him whom my soul loveth: I sought him, but I found him not"); nostalgia, power and powerlessness ("The watchmen that went about the city found me, they smote me, they wounded me; the keepers of the walls took away my veil from me"); and alienation from culture, family and lover. It was as close to a biography as I could come.

On the days leading to the performances, I rehearsed to exhaustion. Minute gestures were revisited and perfected in dreams, until I was certain that my body could express what the poem meant to me. I also retreated into an emotional cocoon, saving myself for the dance.

In performance, from the moment I lit the flames that danced upon my fingers until the last note of Rampi Rampi and the final clink of my *zills*, I was as vulnerable as an exposed heart. When the Shulamite cried for her bridegroom, tears came to my eyes. When the shepherd raced over the fields seeking his beloved, I was desperate to reach the gates of Solomon's palace. I grew taller with the King's power and glorious presence, emanating rays of gold and scent of myrrh. I floated over the tiles like the Daughters of Jerusalem, envious of the possibility of true love beyond the walls of the seraglio. Each word of the Song of Songs, each mudra, each step, each jingle of my ankle bells was a bit of Esmeralda, emerging. The tiles of Lehman Hall, cold beneath my feet, received the shadow me, lit by the flames in my hands. The rich bronze tinkle of my *zills* sang with freedom and joy. After the last note of the last performance, I was a different person.

Dr. and Mrs. Loeb attended every performance, smiling encouragement and pleasure. The other members of the evaluation committee came on different nights, bearing tulips and compliments. Dulal sat in the front row with his wife and daughters, and afterwards made sure to tell everyone he was my guru. Ulvi came the last night. At the end he gave me a bunch of flowers and kissed my cheek.

"This dance suits you." He backed away to watch people congratulate me.

Throughout that evening, Ulvi's presence had felt like a giant mollusk from within whose shell I was emerging. He believed I was his creation, but I had created myself under his protection, not in his image. Seeing him standing in Lehman Hall among my friends and teachers, I felt the philosophical distance that separated us. He sought to pretend in order to become. I sought to be and leave pretense behind.

On the stage, Keith took down the backdrop and organized the crew to clean up and return the Lehman Hall cafeteria to its original function. I went over to thank him. He kept a respectful distance, aware of Ulvi's eyes on us.

"Don't worry about me," he sounded annoyed.

"I do worry about you."

"You don't have to. I'm a big boy."

"Okay, then you're right, I shouldn't worry about you . . ."

I couldn't stop laughing over the next few weeks. I was ecstatic and everything around me was delightful. It was spring and the trees budded bright green, the sky was clear, the sun brilliant. My friends were the best people in the world. The goat cheese Roberto Alejandro brought was sharp and the wine Pepe brought was mellow. Tom and I danced the fox-trot at the Top of the Hub on a night when we could see clear down to the South Shore. My thesis committee gave me an A. In a couple of weeks I would be graduating from Harvard *magna cum laude*. I was so proud of myself, I wanted to crow.

A few days before graduation, Keith invited me to a party on a boat cruising Boston Harbor. I had only seen the harbor from a dock in the North End the previous February, while Ulvi was in Saudi Arabia. Pepe, Roberto Alejandro, my friend Sonya, and I had vowed to stay awake the entire weekend to celebrate her birthday. On Sunday morning, the sun was just coming up when Roberto Alejandro decided he needed to change clothes. I went with him to his loft in a converted factory in the North End. When we walked in I was surprised to see, in a corner of the area that served as his office, a telex machine with several messages on the continuous roll of yellow paper that had collected on the floor. After he showered and dressed, he scanned them and spent a few moments replying. The fact that he was a college student had not freed him from working for the family business in shipping, he said. We drove to a commercial pier nearby where an enormous ship was docked. It belonged to him, he said.

Now nearly four months later, on a balmy evening in June, the Boston Cruises boat motored past commercial piers and I wondered if any of the rusty battered ships docked there belonged to Roberto Alejandro. As I tried to remember the name of the one he had shown me, Keith came up from the bar area carrying plastic cups filled with pink punch.

"Thanks," I said, touching mine to his.

"We have to talk," he said.

The cruise was filled with Harvard students. A group of his close friends, some of whom had crewed on my thesis, had gathered not far from where Keith and I stood. A seagull came out of nowhere and plunked into the water, then flew off empty beaked.

Everyone who saw it laughed, because the gull seemed dazed by its failure to catch a fish.

"We have to talk," Keith repeated, annoyed.

"Here?"

"Where else?"

His friends kept sending looks in our direction, and I knew that they knew what he wanted to talk about.

"Okay." I had trouble swallowing the sweet spiked punch Keith had given me and spilled it over the side.

As Keith stood next to me, building up courage, I watched Boston Harbor recede and was seized by my fear of drowning. It was still daylight and I mentally measured the distance between the boat's deck and the cobblestoned streets of the Haymarket.

"Can we talk later?" I asked.

"No, now is good for me." He shuffled his feet, looked down at the water, sipped his sweet punch. He took a deep breath. "I think we should break up."

I was so relieved that I burst out laughing.

His face scrunched into an expression that wanted to be angry but showed hurt. "Why is that funny?"

"I'm sorry, it's *not*. It was a nervous reaction. Why do you want us to break up?" I laughed again. "I'm so sorry."

"You laugh too much." He stared at the skyline. "It's not right. You have your old man, I have Karen. If there's to be a future with her I shouldn't be playing around with you."

"That's probably a good idea," I said.

"I had fun though!" he grinned.

"I did too," I grinned back. We hugged.

It was the first official breakup I'd ever had. Until then, my romances had simply fizzled out when one of us left town or graduated. The words had never been spoken. It seemed so easy.

"Leave me out of your plans."

I spent the weeks before graduation preparing for life after college. Earlier in the year, I had applied to the Fletcher School of Law and Diplomacy at Tufts and was accepted to the graduate program in international relations. My interests were in the artistic and cultural legacies of developing countries. I dreamed of living in Puerto Rico someday, and sought expertise I could bring to its artistic heritage.

I applied for a grant to make a documentary film about Puerto Rican artisans. Since my Christmas vacation with Ulvi almost two years earlier, I had planned to return to the island for an extended visit. But I didn't want to come as a tourist or to be a leisured guest in Mami's or my sisters' homes for a couple of weeks. I wanted a reason to be there other than nostalgia for home and family.

When the grant came through, my friend David suggested that I locate a cameraman and sound technician with documentary experience in Puerto Rico.

"Competent technical people can save your neck," he said.

I wrote to Papi and asked him to find technicians for me, but he didn't know where to begin looking for someone with that experience. On my next conversation with Ulvi I asked him to help.

"No, Chiquita," he said. "Please leave me out of your plans." He did offer to pay my rent and utilities while I was gone.

I explained my situation to Keith, who again volunteered. If I arranged for the equipment and a place to stay, Keith said he would shoot the movie. His friend Geno agreed to join us as the sound recordist. They both wanted to be away from Boston during the Bicentennial celebrations that already clogged the streets of the city with tourists.

Since Keith and I had "broken up," I insisted that our relationship in Puerto Rico be a professional one.

"No hanky-panky," I said, and he agreed with a grin and a wink.

My twenty-year-old sister Edna had moved into her own apartment and said I could stay with her. Papi offered a casita his sister owned so that the guys would have their own place from where they could come and go independent of my plans. I was grateful for my family's help and assurances, for the way the summer was coming together. I was excited about the work Keith, Geno, and I planned to do on the island, and looked forward to introducing them to my culture. It seemed right that I should go to Puerto Rico right after graduation. It felt as if I were closing a gap in a circle. I never asked myself what my family would think when I showed up with two young, handsome gringos in tow and Ulvi nowhere in sight.

Two weeks before Commencement, everything was in place. Ulvi had deferred his trip to Saudi Arabia—so that he could attend my graduation he said. While I was filming in Puerto Rico, he would be in Riyadh. I did not tell him that Keith and Geno were coming with me. We would set the date for me to join him when I finished the film. His changing circumstances, however, made it impossible for him to pay the expenses he had committed to paying for me just a few days earlier. I didn't argue or press him. I had stopped counting on him even when he had the best intentions. I worked as many hours as possible at several jobs to pay my rent and for spending money while I was making my documentary.

Marilyn was confused about what seemed like conflicting plans. "If you go to Saudi Arabia," she asked, "does that mean you're not going to graduate school?"

"No, I'm going to Fletcher . . . "

"But if you go with him . . . "

"This is what will happen," I counted the steps on my fingers. "Ulvi will say he's going to Saudi Arabia but a few days later I'll get a letter from Germany or Ceylon or who knows who cares where. He'll keep dangling the carrot of my joining him but will postpone it with each letter and phone call. He'll keep telling me to 'be good girl' and to wait for him, because, to quote the immortal Diana Ross," I sang, "Someday, we'll be together." I felt like crying. "Do I sound bitter?"

Marilyn's face softened. "Why don't you break up with him?"

"I don't know, Marilyn. I don't know why it's as hard to leave Ulvi as it was to leave my mother." I wiped my eyes. "I wish that he'd go wherever it is he's going and stay there."

Because Ulvi would be at my graduation, I did not invite my family. I would have drowned in Ulvi's silent condescension and in their scorn for him. I still tensed at the memory of the night he sat on Mami's sofa lying to Papi, Don Carlos, and Don Julio, promising to marry me when he returned from Europe. To him, they were nothing. To them, he was *el hombre que le hizo el daño a Negi.* They had no idea how much damage had been done, and there was no way I would let them see me as his Chiquita.

"You have many
men friends, Chiquita."

In the days before Commencement, Harvard Yard and Square were
festive, decorated with crimson flags and seals. President Bok
would graduate us as a class on the lawn in front of Widener Library, and diplomas would be handed out in the Houses afterwards. In the days preceding, there were dinners, speeches, Class
Day activities, alumni seminars, picnics, and reunions.

Ulvi came up on the Tuesday before graduation. We walked
around the Square hand in hand, enjoying the balmy weather, the
proud families, the young people laughing, horsing around, captur-
ing the last hours as students before they started their "real" lives.
As we ambled along the streets of Harvard Square we ran into a
score of classmates and former faculty. Every few minutes I stopped
to hug someone I knew who was returning home, or exchanged addresses with a classmate I hadn't been able to catch up with until
we ran into each other in front of Massachusetts Hall, The Coop,
or the Science Center.

"You know many people," Ulvi said, seemingly surprised.

"Yes, aren't they great?"

He stood aside as I talked to, laughed with, hugged, made plans to visit, and exchanged goodbyes with a quirky international collection of artists, medical students, future sociologists, political scientists, librarians, divinity students, dancers, future economists, and athletes.

The day before graduation I was exhilarated, filled with a joy so complete that it imbued every thought, every encounter, every moment awake, every dream. Ulvi seemed bemused by my good humor, and laughed frequently at how silly I could be, dancing along the raised planters in Holyoke Center, eating an ice cream cone from Brigham's as if it were the first and last one I'd ever tasted. There was a dinner in Lehman Hall the night before graduation, followed by dancing. Ulvi came with me, dressed in a dapper blue suit, gray shirt, and silk paisley tie. He saw me in the arms of men with whom I was comfortable and familiar because we had danced together almost every week since I'd arrived in Cambridge. I introduced Ulvi as "my friend," but everyone knew he was more than that.

On the way back to my apartment we walked through Harvard Yard under a sky so full of stars that we leaned back on our elbows on the steps of Widener and admired them, neither of us knowledgeable enough about the constellations to be able to name them, but still enjoying the brilliant twinkling light across the purple summer sky.

The phone was ringing when we reached my apartment. It was after midnight, and the only person who ever called that late was Ulvi. On the other end of the line was Eric, my former animation teacher and friend, calling from San Francisco.

"Congratulations!" he said. "I know how hard you worked and you deserve every success that comes your way."

I sat cross-legged on the floor and answered his questions about how I'd done in classes. "I made magna! Can you believe it?"

"Of course I can believe it. Listen, I'm coming to Cambridge for a visit later this summer and want to see you."

"Sounds great. Let's talk about it when you have dates. I have to go now though, it's late and my friend is here."

"He's there, is he? Will you be making love tonight?"

I giggled. "Yes."

"I'm jealous."

"I really have to go," I said, "thanks for the call."

"No, you can't go. I'm not done telling you how great you are."

Ulvi paced around the apartment, annoyed when I didn't hang up after a few seconds. But it wasn't often that someone called from the other end of the continent to stack one compliment on top of the other.

"Whoa, stop!" I laughed. "My head is getting so big I can barely fit in my apartment. Save the flattery for another time!" I hung up with a smile on my face. "That was so great," I hugged myself.

Ulvi settled on the edge of my bed, his hands clasped in the air between his knees. "Who was that, Chiquita?"

"One of my professors from last year. He's moved to San Francisco and wanted to congratulate me. He waited until it was officially graduation day. That's why he called so late. Wasn't that sweet?"

"It is a man?" His voice was getting tighter by the second, his features darkening.

"I'm sorry we talked so long, but he wanted to know about my grades."

"You have many men friends, Chiquita."

I felt my spine straighten, and a chill rise up to my scalp. "Yes, I do. Many."

"Are they your lovers, too?"

I sighed and rolled my eyes. "No, they are not. In the last two years I've made many friends here, women as well as men. There is nothing wrong with that, Ulvi. Not all men only want one thing."

"Is that so?"

"Yes, it is so. Didn't you see how happy I was that Eric called? He's proud of me. He wanted to remind me how hard I've worked. He wanted me to know that he's happy I made it. It's great to have supportive friends. He cares about me and I care about him."

"It is not good, Chiquita." He stood up and paced, tearing at his hair. He was enraged, but didn't know what to do with his anger. I remained cross-legged on the floor and watched him stride from side to side as if seeing him through a telescope. His elegant lightweight blue gabardine suit fit him perfectly, every French seam carefully crafted, every button tight but not strangling the fabric. There were no wear patterns on the elbows, knees, or seat. The shirt beneath his jacket was a fine Egyptian cotton, almost transparent, soft as baby hair. He wore his expensive watch. "You have become too free. You want too much independence. I cannot allow it."

"I am not giving up my friends because you don't like them," I said.

He stopped pacing for a moment and glared at me. I didn't take my eyes from his. This was it and I knew it. He headed for the door. "Very well then." He turned, his hand on the doorknob, his features contorted in disdain. "Forget my name, forget my address, forget my phone number."

"I will," I said, my gaze steady, no tears, no tremor in my voice. "As soon as you walk out that door."

He stalked out. His suitcase was by my bed. I picked it up and ran. He was already by the elevator. "You forgot something." I set it in the middle of the hall, returned to my apartment, and pressed my back against the door.

I heard him come up the corridor, pick up the soft leather overnight bag, and walk in the opposite direction. The elevator doors opened, closed, the machinery rumbled and creaked as the cage brought him down. A few seconds later there were footsteps around the back of the building. I turned off the lights and ran to the window. He threw his case into the passenger seat of the Camaro and climbed in. Four years in New York and he still had Texas license plates. He didn't turn the ignition right away and I was afraid he had changed his mind and was about to return. He didn't. The headlights reddened the parking area and I pulled away from the window. When I next looked, the taillights of the Camaro were turning down Felton Street.

I waited one, two, three seconds then wailed. I threw myself on the bed and punched the pillow. Seven years, I kept repeating, seven years and all I had to say was that someone else cared about me. That's all it took, someone else who loved me. I cried so uncontrollably that I scared myself. I didn't want to be alone with my rage, my heartache.

"Marilyn?" I whispered into the handset when she answered, scared to be awakened in the middle of the night by a ringing phone. "I can't be alone right now. Can I come over?"

"Yes, of course, come." I walked the few yards that separated our doors and fell into her arms.

"What happened?"

"Ulvi just left, forever I think."

She led me by the hand into her bright, neat kitchen. I was still wearing my party dress. While she put the kettle on, I went into the bathroom and washed my face. My eyes and lips were swollen and there were deep rings under my lids. "I look like hell," I said when I returned.

"How did it happen?" Marilyn handed me a cup of chamomile tea with honey. I told her about Eric's call, about sitting on the floor listening to someone say nothing but nice things about me into my ear.

"I never thought that Ulvi would object to someone congratulating me on such an important day. I mean, I'm graduating from Harvard in . . ." I looked up at her kitchen clock, "less than seven hours." Tears sprung to my eyes again. Marilyn jumped up and found a box of tissues. "I don't know why I'm crying, to tell you the truth."

"You were with him a long time. It will take a while to believe it's over."

"Oh, it's over!" She rubbed my shoulders as I indulged in one last jag of tears. I shuddered. "Alright, that's it." I blew my nose. "I've cried enough. Time to move on."

"Give yourself a couple of hours," she laughed.

A ringing phone pierced the night. We listened, looking everywhere but at each other because the sound was coming from my apartment.

"If you'd rather stay here tonight, I can offer you the couch." She found me a pair of her pajamas, flannel sheets, a comforter. "Is there anything else you need?" she asked.

"No, this is great. Thanks." She headed for her bedroom. "You know something?" I asked. Marilyn came back. "If I had known it would be as easy as telling him other people loved me, I would have done it a long time ago."

She tucked the blanket around my shoulders. "Well, you had to believe it first," she said.

"A pen makes
a lovely graduation gift."

Dawn rose gentle and bright, the scent of spring still in the air, even though it was late June. I woke up disoriented and stiff from the awkward position on Marilyn's couch. The moment my eyes opened, I closed them again, trying to dive back into the dreamless sleep from which I had awakened. Ulvi was gone. The pillow was damp under my cheek, as was the edge of the blanket. My lids felt heavy. I pushed myself off the couch, stared at the delicate flower print on Marilyn's pajamas. Ulvi was gone. I folded the bedclothes, left them on the couch, grabbed my party dress, high-heel shoes, keys, and walked the few yards to my apartment. There was the spot where I had set his black leather case. I looked for something dropped, an indentation on the vinyl tiles that marked the spot, but it was immutable.

Ulvi did not have a key to my apartment, but I pressed my ear to the door and held my breath, listening for his. Downstairs, the elevator rattled to life, and I didn't want to be seen in the hallway in Marilyn's pajamas, my hair disheveled, my face creased with sorrow. I went in. The shades were up and light streamed into the room, which was neat, as always when Ulvi came to visit. Books were on shelves, not on stacks on the floor or furniture. Dance costumes were folded inside a basket by my closet. No tights, leotards, or underwear hung over the shower rod. No shoes were scattered where I took them off. No dirty dishes were stacked inside the kitchen sink. But Ulvi was gone.

I showered. There was not a spot on my body he had not touched. He had kissed the inside of my knees, the bump behind my right ear, the scar on my left thigh. He had tongued my little toe, the bend in my elbow, the ridge on my hips, the warm hollows. I didn't cry.

Inside my closet were his graduation gifts. Wrapped in tissue was a turquoise and lilac silk scarf with a paisley design in gold embroidery. It was as light as a breath. Folded into a square inside a white box there was a black silk chiffon veil with tiny silver baguettes along the edges. It was as heavy as a sigh. Both were perfumed in a spicy scent that rose from the sheer fabrics and seemed to bring ghosts into the room.

"This belonged to a Saudi princess," Ulvi had said, and I didn't ask then, but wondered now how he managed to get the scarf and veil of a Saudi princess. I pushed them to the back of the closet.

I put on a long white cotton dress, white leather sandals, my cap and gown. The afternoon before I had pressed the gown, and Ulvi made me wear it so he could see me in it. On the cap's tassel there was a golden "76."

"It looks good, Chiquita," he said.

I didn't cry. This was supposed to be a happy day, my Harvard graduation.

It was a glorious morning in June, not a cloud stained the sky, a perfect day for a Harvard Commencement in the Tercentenary Theater, created on the lawn between Memorial Chapel and Widener Library. Fathers and mothers, sisters and brothers, grandparents, stepparents, aunts and uncles, cousins and spouses hovered around their graduates, beaming. I was alone in the crowd. There was no one there for me, no one to take my picture in my Harvard cap and gown, no one to see me line up with the other magna cum laude graduates. Mami should have been here, my sisters and brothers, Papi. I didn't cry.

Led by the oldest alumni, former graduates solemnly proceeded into the Tercentenary Theater. When the Class of 1976 was spotted, heads turned, eyes flashed. Smiles grew on the faces of my classmates as they found their loved ones in the audience. A man gave the thumbs up. A woman wiped the corners of her eyes with a lace-edged handkerchief. Another man sat stoic, facing the stage where the faculty and honorees stood in their finery. I wanted to cry.

There were speeches, honors bestowed, music, dumb jokes that sent surprised chuckles rippling up and down the aisles. We were exhorted to take our place in the future. We were encouraged to contribute to society. We were advised to take care of ourselves and of our loved ones. We were warned of the pitfalls ahead, the hard work, and the disappointments. But, we were told, it would all be worth it. We would someday look back on this day, this Commencement, and see it for what it was—a beginning.

President Bok declared us graduated and congratulated the Harvard Class of 1976. We waved our caps in the air and turned toward the loved ones behind us, looking for pride in our mothers' eyes, for pleasure in those of our fathers. I turned along with my classmates and looked into the faces of several thousand men and women, not one of them there for me. I cried then.

After the ceremony, there was a break before the awarding of diplomas in the Houses. I wandered around Harvard Square in my pretty new dress, envious of the family groups gathering under the trees, on the sidewalk cafes along Brattle Street. In contrast to the day before when, with Ulvi beside me I had seen almost everyone I knew, there was not a single familiar face in the hundreds of people I passed in my aimless ramble.

I found myself standing before a display at The Coop, where there were Harvard souvenirs for sale. A case held tie clips, pins, bracelets, and rings with the Harvard seal. None of the rings were like the class rings, with 1976 along the sides. These were generic Harvard rings. I wished I'd been able to afford the class ring. I'd wear it proudly. A lump came to my throat, but I swallowed it back.

"May I help you?" The salesclerk was a willowy young black woman with Asian features. She wore a tight green top, and her hair was puffed into a startling yellow Afro around her round face. She looked like a sunflower.

"Just looking, thank you."

"We have some nice pens here," she offered. "Special graduation sale. Did someone you know graduate today?"

"Yes."

"A pen makes a lovely graduation gift."

"Does it?"

She slid the glass door of the display case and brought out a black fountain and ballpoint pen set inside a satin-lined box. "These are popular. We can engrave them with your graduate's name."

Next to where the set had been there was a sterling silver Parker pen scored in a tiny checkerboard pattern. "How much is that one?"

"Let me see. With the 30 percent discount it will be $60." She handed it to me.

It belonged in my hand, solid and real, warm. With use, the patina would become richer; the nib would flow across a page with familiar authority and weight. But $60 was exactly half of one month's rent. The salesclerk saw me coveting.

"Do you have a Coop card?" she asked. I nodded. "I can put it on your Coop card and you won't feel it until next month."

It was the most expensive thing I'd ever bought for myself. I still have it. Whenever I take it in hand to write a note, to sign my name, to make an entry in my journal, I remember the loneliness of that day, and the salesclerk's incongruously yellow hair around her smiling black-Asian features.

"It takes a long time
to get over a breakup."

Every time the phone rang, I expected it to be Ulvi. For days, I turned the key on the outside lock of Foxcroft Manor peering into the lobby, expecting to find him waiting in one of the overstuffed, seldom-used chairs. I remembered him on the leaf-strewn lawn in front of my apartment in Dewitt, our reunion as sweet and senti-mental as a movie scene. He might send a special-delivery letter or a telegram like the ones he sent when I ran to Mami's house on Fulton Street. I waited in vain for a call at the usual time, or in the middle of the night, testing if I was there, or at dawn, like he often did, with a cheerful, "Time to wake up!"

Each time I'd left him it had taken him longer to come after me. In Syracuse, he had waited a month. In a few days I was leaving for Puerto Rico, and he had no way to reach me. I had not given him Papi's phone number. I didn't think he even knew my parents' names. I cried some more over the next few days, usually at night, after a full day of organizing my trip to Puerto Rico and saying goodbye to the friends still around. It hurt that, after seven years, our love affair had ended in anger. I wished our breakup had been as civil as the one with Keith, acknowledging that, while it didn't work for us, we did sometimes have fun.

I wrote Ulvi a letter, thanking him for having been in my life, begging him to remember the good times, to forget the hurts we had inflicted on one another. I went so far as to slide the three-page letter into an envelope and address it to Chatsworth Avenue, Larchmont. But I never sent it. Every time I picked it up, my good intentions dissolved into fury at his possessiveness, his philandering, his use of me to get what he wanted, his misuse of my trust and naïveté. The next moment I blamed myself for having held on to him for so long. I kept asking myself why I had been unable to walk out of his life as easily as he walked out of mine, but could not come up with an answer.

I went through the papers I'd saved from our correspondence. There were letters dating back to the Longacre Hotel, telegrams, photographs, a red leatherette folder with Inter-Continental Hotels embossed in gold letters and, inside, fine ivory-colored paper and envelopes from the hotel in Riyadh. I cringed at the sight of his loose, flowing script, "Dearest Chiquita." No one would ever call me that again. I stuffed everything inside a box, sealed it, and pushed it onto the high shelf in my closet, next to my journals and ramblings.

As the day for my trip to Puerto Rico neared, I focused on the packing and preparations. I paid July's rent and utilities in advance and gave Marilyn a key so she could water my plants.

Over the following days Ulvi, and the hold he'd had on me, became a dull, achy pressure on my chest whenever something reminded me of him. I froze when the phone rang, or when a hand-addressed envelope showed up in my mailbox. I lingered before his gifts, remembering the occasion or the way he had presented them. Whenever I looked at my wrist, the Omega watch reminded me of the day I'd had my hair cut because he loved it long. The television set he'd given me was off except when he was there, but I now turned it on, seeking comfort in the tri-tones as the NBC peacock unfurled its colorful tail. In Larchmont Ulvi would be watching David Brinkley. I envisioned him leaning back on the couch, his left hand behind his head, his right fingers drumming his flat abdomen as necktied men read nothing but bad news.

"I don't recognize myself," I said to Marilyn, whose motherly attentions I looked forward to every day when she came home from work. "I just want to forget him and be done with it."

"Give it time . . . "

"I'd never cried as much my entire life as I have since I met him." I thrust the spoon into the Orson Welles Café's deep bowl of chocolate mousse slathered with whipped cream. "I didn't expect it would hurt this much to be rid of him."

"You're still grieving, Esmeralda. It takes a long time to get over a breakup."

"The relationship was over long ago. Why can't I just move on?"

"Because it's only been five days!" She fanned her fingers. "Five days is not nearly long enough to 'move on.' It might take you weeks, months, maybe even years."

"Please don't say that! I've already given him the best years of my life."

She laughed. "You're twenty-eight! You still have a few good years ahead of you."

"I had a friend in New York who believed people come together to be one another's teachers."

"I believe that."

"Ulvi always said he would teach me everything, that's what he liked about me."

Marilyn nodded. "Did he?"

"He taught me a lot," I pressed my eyes to push back tears. "But neither of us counted on what I had to learn being different from what he wanted to teach."

"Alábate pollo . . . "

Exactly one week after graduation, I stood on line at Boston Logan airport, waiting for my boarding pass to San Juan. I remembered the day seven years earlier when, frightened but determined, I had left Mami's house in Brooklyn to begin my travels with Ulvi. It seemed appropriate that our relationship should end just as I was going back to Puerto Rico. I was returning to my family free of a man who disdained my people and me. I was returning having exceeded even the most optimistic expectations for a poor girl from a huge family raised by a single mother under the most challenging conditions in a hostile culture and environment. I was returning to Puerto Rico with a funded project that would draw attention to part of our artistic and cultural heritage. I was so proud of myself, I strutted toward the Departures gates. I had forgotten the Puerto Rican saying that Tata muttered in our direction whenever we boasted about something we had done: *Alábate pollo, que mañana te guisan.* Boast now, chicken, tomorrow you'll be stew.

Acknowledgments

For me, it would be impossible to write memoir without thanking every person who has ever crossed my path as friend or foe, because each contact, however brief, has brought me here. Whether you passed me briefly, walked alongside me a few steps or a few miles, or lingered a moment at the crossroads before we parted ways, I am grateful to you for being in my life.

Every night before I fall asleep I give thanks for the daily joys and challenges that ask me to measure myself against who I was yesterday, and whom I hope to be tomorrow. Whether in good will or ill, each encounter adds to a life so full it often feels as if I will burst from happiness or sorrow.

Writing memoir, however, involves making painful choices about what to reveal, what to leave out. I have been blessed to know men and women whose love, advice, comfort, dancing ability, cooking skills, and willingness to talk for hours, have sustained me. If you do not see yourself in these pages, you have not been forgotten. Our lives are inexorably linked.

Some names have been changed, some at your request, others because they were the same as members of my family, or because someone with the same name entered my life earlier. You know who you are and I know who you are. Thank you.

I am grateful to my writers group. Terry Bazes, Kate Buford, Ben Cheever, and Marilyn Johnson listened to portions of this book as it was being written and sent me home feeling like the little engine that could. Marilyn, I am especially indebted to you for taking the time in the midst of your own writing to read the last draft of the manuscript. Your read was invaluable in helping me shape the final version of this book.

Joie Davidow stole time from her novel to read a draft, and asked questions that made the last chapters better. ¡Gracias, comadre!

Dr. Nina Torres Vidal, my friend and translator, read a longer draft and understood the reasons why *The Turkish Lover* had to end where it did. Yes, Nina, I plan to write the story of what happened in Puerto Rico that Bicentennial summer.

Molly Friedrich, your intelligence and passion are an inspiration. Thank you for your solid advice and friendship.

I am proud of my now decade-long work with my magnificent editor Merloyd Lawrence. It was your idea that I write memoir, and you set me on a path I never imagined for a jíbara from Puerto Rico who somehow, miraculously, ended up at Harvard. Thank you, Merloyd, for seeing the writer in me and for guiding me through the mazes of memory.

To my beloved mother, Ramona Santiago, my father, Pablo Santiago, my sisters and brothers, Delsa, Norma, Héctor, Alicia, Edna, Raymond, Francisco, Carlos, Carmen, and Rafael, I owe more than thanks. You have encouraged and supported this difficult work and have walked alongside me with grace and dignity. Even when you disagree with my version of events you have given me the freedom to speak my truth, and that is the greatest gift anyone can receive.

Thank you Ulvi Dogan. Our lives intersected at a crossroads and we walked a rocky path together, but when we parted, we were each richer for having shared the way.

Marie Celeste Scully, how can I ever thank you for coming into my life when I most needed a friend? Thank you for having been there then, and for the miracle of finding one another again after thirty years.

You held my hand, Frank Cantor, when we first met, and you haven't let go, even when I have pulled in the opposite direction. Thank you for giving me the room and rooms to write. Thank you for being a loving and devoted husband and father to our talented, beautiful children, Lucas and Ila. I could not be who I am if not for the unconditional love all three of you have given me.

About the Author

Esmeralda Santiago is the author of two other memoirs, *When I Was Puerto Rican* and *Almost a Woman*, which was made into a Peabody Award winning film for Masterpiece Theatre. She is married to filmmaker Frank Cantor and is the mother of two adult children, jazz guitarists Lucas and Ila.